Holy Hitchhiking Foreign Highways

VERNON G. ELGIN

To a colleague in ministry
Beverley Shrumm —

Vernon G. Elgin

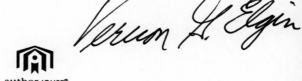
authorHOUSE®

AuthorHouse™
1663 Liberty Drive
Bloomington, IN 47403
www.authorhouse.com
Phone: 1-800-839-8640

First published by AuthorHouse   4/9/2010

ISBN: 978-1-4490-9874-2 (e)
ISBN: 978-1-4490-9873-5 (sc)
ISBN: 978-1-4490-9872-8 (hc)

Library of Congress Control Number: 2010903403

Printed in the United States of America
Bloomington, Indiana

This book is printed on acid-free paper.

Table of Contents

Dedication

I express gratitude
To one who is Seminary Educated,
A practical theologian, and my wife of fifty-six years
Who gave hours critically reading the text
And helping me edit and improve the material:
Marjorie C. Elgin.

I express gratitude
To a professional reader who began the journey with me
But died mysteriously in our cold December snow,
Apparently attempting to obtain help when the power failed at her house
And was found dead at her car. She had the handicap of a lower leg
amputation:
Mary Savella.

I express gratitude
To all those angels who stopped in response to my raised thumb or
waving arms
And gave me rides in their comfortable cars, and in some not-so comfortable
vehicles,
And who entered into holy conversation with me:
Mostly unknown and unremembered except by God.

I express gratitude
To the God of Jesus Christ who loved me and gave himself for me,
And for the world;
And who gave me the gifts and experiences that inform the book,
My Creator and my Redeemer.

I express gratitude
To all those who have encouraged me in the writing of the book,
Our sons and their families;
And numerous interested and supportive friends:
God's prods.

Acknowledgments and Permissions

Books

Calvin, John; *Institutes of the Christian Religion;* *"Translated from the Latin and Collated with the Author's Last Edition in French by John Allen; Seventh American Edition, Revisions and Introductions by Benjamin B. Warfield, D.D., LL.D. and an Account of the American Editions by Thomas C. Pears, Jr., L.H.D.; In two Volumes.* Philadelphia, Presbyterian Board of Christian Education. (Date not printed on opening pages.)

Coronation of Her Majesty Queen Elizabeth II, 2 June 1953; The; Approved Souvenir Programme; King George's Jubilee Trust; Printed in England.

Davis, John D, Ph.D., D.D., Ll. D. and *(Revised and Rewritten),* Gehman, Henry Snyder, Ph.D., S.T.D; *The Westminster Dictionary of the Bible*; The Westminster Press; Philadelphia, 1944.

2009 Mission Yearbook for Prayer & Study, Witherspoon Press, Louisville, Kentucky; Editor, Billie Healy; Produced by Mission Interpretation Team, General Assembly Council, Presbyterian Church (U.S.A.).

Steinbeck, John, *The Grapes of Wrath;* First Published in the United States of America by The Viking Press, Inc. 1939; Published in Penguin Books 1976, (Quoted) Edition with an introduction by Robert DeMott published in Penguin Books 1992; Copyright John Steinbeck, 1939, Copyright renewed John Steinbeck, 1967; Introduction copyright @Viking Penguin, a Division of Penguin Books USA, Inc., 1992.

SCRIPTURE QUOTATIONS

Scripture Quotations Copied from the New Revised Standard Version of the Bible, copyright 1989, by the Division of Christian Education of the National Council of the Churches of Christ in the U.S.A. "Used by permission. All rights reserved." All Biblical Text comes from <u>THE NEW INTERPRETERS' BIBLE, NEW REVISED STANDARD VERSION WITH THE APOCRYPHA,</u> Copyright @2003 by Abingdon Press, 201 Eighth Avenue South, Nashville, TN 37202. (Certain quotes are from memory.)

PERIODICALS

Newsweek, Inc.; Chief Executive Officer: Tom Ascheim; Editor. John Meacham; The Washington Post Company; 201 Varick Street, New York, NY 10014.

Foreword

HOLY HITCHHIKING FOREIGN HIGHWAYS is not my first published book. Besides my Ph. D. dissertation (1953-9), typed without the benefits of a Computer or an Electric Typewriter, I wrote and had published, *OBITUARY THEOLOGY: Reformed Doctrine of Dying and Death, Re.: Obituaries.* (2009).

OBITUARY and *HITCHHIKING* have themes in common. Both relate spiritual experience and both include theological scholarship. Religion served an interpretive role in *OBITUARY*, an ancillary one in *HITCHHIKING*. *OBITUARY* targets Theology Professors and Students, and the Funeral Industry. It also appeals to the populace, and it is both analytic and pragmatic. *HITCHHIKING* targets the general reader, but it can also educate Professors, students, and Funeral Directors.

Why did I write *HITCHHIKING?* For some of the same reasons I published *OBITUARY*. One of the main goals is to preserve for my family and myself some of the most adventurous epochs of my life. In both my professional preparation and practice as well as in my professional retirement, I have had the privilege not only of studying in Scotland but also of traveling in Europe, North and South Africa, and the Middle East. Those experiences—for both economic reasons and because of a lack of public transportation—frequently necessitated hitchhiking. I also did it for adventure. I frequently attempted to engage my host drivers in religious talk.

In the opening Chapter—the only one of the eight with a domestic setting—I write about my first days of "thumbing rides." I had to hitch rides to work, and to college. My foreign hitchhiking happened while I was studying "abroad," and living or serving as a missionary globally, doing at least the first two of the major services that characterized Jesus' ministry: preaching and teaching and (to a lesser extent) healing. In many situations either transportation was unavailable or inconvenient; or as in Chapter 8, a vehicle breakdown necessitated my taking a thumbing stance at the side of the highway. Much of the time I hitchhiked for adventure or to save money.

My earliest hitchhiking coincided with my spiritual awakening. As a virgin evangelist, I felt that my time alone with a driver—as happened in most of my rides, and most of the time with males—afforded me an opportunity to talk religion, or otherwise to make the time together holy. "Salvation of souls" did not feature as primary in my motivation. I am a "frozen-chosen Presbyterian," a baptized and saved-for-life, but personally and consciously related to Christ Christian. I was interested in comparative holy experience. As I matured chronologically I also developed spiritually. I exercised little hesitation to talk about God, Jesus, Church, prayer, and other religious subjects. To my delight I became increasingly amazed about how non-Bible-Belt persons proved more eager to talk about religion than I had anticipated. On occasion my hosts expressed disinterest in things holy. At those times the conversation ended short. However, I found hitchhiking more enjoyable when I could have both driver and rider on a holy track.

I was raised religious. My parents had me baptized in the United Presbyterian Church of North America when I was three months old. At the age of eleven I made a commitment to faith in Jesus Christ and to membership in his Church. I was a good boy in high school, and attended the Presbyterian Church in Blacksburg, Virginia when I was an Air Corps enlistee and reservist participating at the Virginia Polytechnic Institute Army Specialized Reserve Training Program. After induction into the Air Corps as an Active Duty soldier, I faithfully attended Base Chapel services. I maintained an active church involvement through my College-University years. During my Senior Year I made the decision to enroll in the Pittsburgh (in 1949 the Pittsburgh-Xenia United Presbyterian) Theological Seminary. I hitchhiked occasionally during my Seminary Career, and even more frequently when I went to study in Scotland for my Ph. D. degree. I became more skilled at introducing religion during hitchhiking rides, and I determined that if I listened impartially and non-judgmentally I had many religious lessons to learn, even from people who did not appear religious.

I engaged seriously and frequently in hitchhiking while in residence in Scotland. Back in the United States I did it only in an emergency. I resumed it when I returned to Edinburgh with my family three years later. In the subsequent years of parish ministry I hitchhiked scarcely. However, in retirement, and volunteer and part-time-paid global ministry my practice of it resumed. It intruded again as a necessity in 2005 in Africa when the van a friend and I were driving on the way to the Lilongwe, Malawi airport—from which I would fly back to the United States—malfunctioned.

Holy hitchhiking, whether domestic or foreign, has afforded me transportation, satisfaction, inspiration, education and evangelistic expression. The novelty, romance, and evangelism of my experience has encouraged me to share it. Recalling, revisiting, and recording it have provided me the privilege of reliving it. With the current financial crisis in the U.S.A., I may be compelled to return to it.

May *HOLY HITCHHIKING FOREIGN HIGHWAYS* take your mind off your troubles, relieve your anxieties, excite your imagination, make you more considerate, educate your judgment, encourage you to go greener, and refresh your holy spirit. Writing it has performed all those benefits for me. It has also increased my appreciation for persons who have shared their cars, and less judgmental of those who for some reason refused or chose not to. Perhaps God had a hand in the turndown. I am convinced that by engaging drivers in holy talk, I have contributed to transforming the inside of an occasional automobile into a holy sanctuary, and I have possibly challenged a driver to think about life more meaningfully. I myself have been enlightened and challenged by the more faithful and intelligent drivers. I am pleased that seldom has any of them expressed the unfortunate position one of my best and longest-term, one-time Presbyterian, friends related till his dying day: "When I die it's the end." As a life-long Presbyterian I am convinced of the truth of the start-over that Jesus told Peter would initiate hundred-fold blessings for disciples: "the renewal of all things, when the Son of man is seated on the throne of his glory." (Matthew 19:28.)

Vernon G. Elgin

Chapter I

Kicks on U.S. Route 66

*"I am the Lord your God; sanctify yourselves therefore,
and be holy, for I am holy." (Leviticus 11:44.)
"Jesus prayed, 'Holy Father, protect them in your name that you
have given me, so that they may be as we are one.' (John 17:11.)
"...at the Mount of Olives, Jesus sent two disciples, saying to them,
'Go into the village ahead of you, and immediately you will find a
donkey tied, and a colt with her; untie them and bring them to me.
If anyone says anything to you, just say this, "The Lord needs them."
And he will send them immediately.'" (Matthew 21:1b-4.)*

Hitchhiking has doubtless ever saved a soul. Few hitchhikers probably
do not involve their drivers in religious talk. When I first started hitchhiking
I practiced it sparsely. I was timid. If I were lucky enough as a kid to receive
a ride, I usually ended up with a mutual acquaintance. Presbyterians show
reluctance about talking religion with family, neighbors, or close friends.

Hitchhiking started for me before I was religiously articulate, at
thirteen or fourteen years of age. However, I was on the path of religious
commitment. I was a church boy from birth, particularly from the time of
my baptism at three months of age. As a teenager I started becoming both
more restless and more religious. I needed something to do and someone
other than my parents or my pastor to talk religion. I was so devoutly
thankful, therefore, one Sabbath after Church when one of our elders,
Calvin Frye, offered me one dollar per day if I would come to the farm

and help him during hay-cutting and wheat-threshing seasons. I took the job. The problem I faced was transportation. The Frye farm was located two miles away on a dirt road, one-and-one-half miles off a blacktop. I was determined that I would either hitch a ride to work, or walk. I hadn't given much thought to doing holy conversation with the drivers, partly because I usually knew my benefactors. I feared that they may ask, "What business is my faith to you?"

I had no trouble getting rides from the first day I worked for Mr. Frye. I customarily started tackling the hike walking. I was usually at the farm on time; time was flexible. The job turned out to be more sweaty and gross than I had anticipated. Getting a ride to Frye's was simple and easy by comparison. Being a town—very small town—kid, I was not accustomed to swinging a pitchfork. Not only did I have to master the fork, I also had to take on other chores like cleaning out the horses' stalls in the evening and scattering fresh straw in them. By the time I arrived at the farm, Cal—at the time he was "Mr. Frye" to me—was usually finishing reigning the horses and attaching them to a wagon. Then we took off for the field, Cal driving the horses while I bumped along in the back of the wagon.

Days on the Frye farm proved long and boring. I carried a sack lunch to work and usually stayed with Frye's for a bountiful supper. After eating I headed to the barn to complete my smelly duties, then headed out toward the "blacktop." I usually succeeded in receiving a ride. I looked forward to Friday or Saturday, and Mr. Frye's handing me five or six dollars. He reminded me to tithe it. Working with Calvin Frye eased when I received employment mowing graves at the local cemetery, picking pickles at a farm to which I had to hike a distance about equal to the Frye's, maintaining lawns in town, washing windows, and caring for young children.

At the age of sixteen my hitchhiking expanded when my employment elevated to a more sophisticated activity. I found work—the job will be described in more detail later—that required traveling fifteen miles from my hometown, Elderton, to Indiana, on Pennsylvania Route 422. Eventually I graduated to hitchhiking U.S. Route 40, and finally and occasionally, to the trans-national Route 66. Covering the longer-distance introduced me to more worldly pleasures, as guaranteed in the lyrics of the 1940's popular Hit Parade Song, "You Can Get Your Kicks on Route Sixty-Six." The hit had become one of my favorite tunes on the "Lucky Strike Hit Parade."

Concurrence with my more far-reaching hitchhiking experience happened in my teenage interest in things spiritual. In the early 1940's my church involvement increased, and I was simultaneously developing a taste for higher levels of highway conversation beyond, "Where are you going…where are you from…how do you like the weather…what does your father do… do you have children?" Sometimes neither driver nor rider talked at all; the driver was more interested in listening to KDKA-Radio from Pittsburgh, or enjoying silence. My enterprise benefited from a World War II influence on consumer products. Fewer cars were on the road at the same time more hitchhikers showed up.

HOLY HITCHHIKING FOREIGN HIGHWAYS relates my interfacing—sometimes intentionally, sometimes coincidentally, and sometimes accidentally—of hitchhiking and a holy calling. Taking God and Church more seriously was taking place at the same time I was more frequently seeking free travel. At first it met my need of a frequent escape from my village in Elderton, Pennsylvania, to the faster life in either Kittanning or Indiana, twelve to fifteen miles away, in opposite directions. Making a dollar or two a day, I had the quarter for occasionally going to a picture show, frequenting the five-and-ten cent stores, sometimes just walking the streets and gawking at the traffic and pedestrians or decorated store windows, and on one occasion shop-lifting. I was so scared and felt so guilty that I ended up with only a ninety-eight cent pair of socks from Kresge's. My Mother discovered my theft and immediately drove me back to the store and made me return the item. Later in the day Dad's punishment was inflicted. Little did I dream at the time of being able, having the opportunity, or facing the need to travel sometime in foreign places other than unfamiliar roads in the U.S.A., like Canada, Europe, the Middle East, Asia, New Zealand, and finally, Africa.

Holy conversation intruded into my hitchhiking in part because of my innate curiosity about everything. My Mother often commented that my favorite word, next to "No" was "Why?" I attribute my holy hitchhiking to encouraging and clarifying my eventual commitment to ordained church ministry. I felt more comfortable and judged myself increasingly successful in engaging drivers in talk about God, Church, Jesus and the Bible. I wanted to know what people, other than the people connected with our local United Presbyterian Church, thought about these subjects, and how their knowledge was making changes in their lives. Sometimes I found myself in deep water. I needed to be smarter, wiser, and holier.

At the ages of seventeen to twenty-two I would have been ecstatic to have had the experience, with perhaps a little less fervor, that my wife and I experienced in public on a 1987 visit to Korea. Among other conveyances, we traveled on the new subway system designed for efficient movement of people in the upcoming Olympics. We were visiting Presbyterian missionary friends and Institutions; they spoke the local language. Our conversation and skin color—and usually our height—identified us as foreign. Never in our lives have so many Presbyterians on the street or in the subway or on buses asked us, frequently in English, "Are you saved?" I quickly developed several scripts for the question, many of them out of the English vocabulary range of the questioners. Our hosts would assist with translations.

Statistics on the popularity and practice of religion today could discourage a hitchhiker from attempting holy conversation, or expecting a positive response to it. It is not unusual to run into an unwillingness to enter into conversation about spiritual matters with a stranger. A smaller segment of the population shows interest in or has knowledge of God and the Bible and theology, especially religion with an institutional twist. Many religious or church folk have a low theological IQ, and in the Pacific Northwest's social diversity the Christian Faith has lapsed into a minority status. Fewer American families here "go to Church," or preface lunch or dinner with prayer. Korean Christians in the Seattle area, along with many African American churches, evidence more holy profession and action than Caucasians. The leadership of most mainline churches look with envy and sometimes confusion, and even suspicion, at the growth of Evangelical, Pentecostal, and Fundamental religious bodies. Lutheran, Presbyterian, Episcopal, United Methodist, and even Roman Catholic and Southern Baptist constituencies are increasingly graying and not growing. In spite of, or perhaps because of, this malaise, and the crisis in the American economy, secular culture could find a new mission field in holy hitchhiking. Time spent in cars in religious conversation could redeem the travel time. It could prove equally valuable if it takes place in the environment covered in this book, in a foreign car, on an airplane or boat. It has both given me satisfaction and confronted me with a challenge to engage my foreign hitchhiking hosts in clean talk.

The practice also offers the advantage of making the miles speed by faster. At no time in my hitchhiking has a driver stopped when approached with a holy topic and told me to get out of his/her car. More often thanks have been extended for the engagement. On occasion a stranger has made a commitment to explore religious activity further; or, as a young Parisian female said when I engaged her in spiritual conversation while crossing the North Sea on a ferry from England to France, "I will think about the Church when I get older." I may be cynical, but I am not much encouraged that she did.

My increasing skills in making a hitched ride holy grew in proportion to my attempts at the practice. By the time I entered the fifth grade, I had become aware, but had only a rudimentary understanding, of the American cherished right to the pursuit of both holiness and happiness. Our small school had a downstairs for the first through fourth grades, and an upstairs for the others. Both downstairs and upstairs school days began—in winter, if the pot-bellied stove had heated the room comfortably—with Teachers Virg and Stan (Mrs. Woods and Mr. Schall to the students) complying with Pennsylvania law, long since repealed, by reading ten verses from the Bible, and leading us in "saying" the Lord's Prayer. Mr. Schall on occasion followed the religious exercise by having the classes repeat patriotic sentences he had written on the chalkboard. One that caught my attention was from the Declaration of Independence. The Document, we recited, guarantees every American citizen the right to "Life, liberty and the pursuit of happiness."

As written earlier, I was being raised in a good Christian (Presbyterian) home, but not strictly fundamentalist. As I merged into puberty, most of the time I liked both church and school. I did well in my classes. In fact, until I entered the eighth grade, when I heard the upper grades recite from the front-row desks, I put aside my own assignments and challenged myself to learn the tougher stuff the upper classes were studying. Hearing Mr. Schall say repeatedly that education is the way to prosperity and to some extent, happiness, I believed that I would be hotter on the pursuit of the two if my family had more money. I had visions of becoming rich myself, and I would make my money as a movie star. Jimmie Stewart and Bette Davis were my idols, along with Clark Gable and Carole Lombard. Jimmie inched higher in my estimation because, as noted earlier, he was from Indiana, not more than fifteen miles from my hometown of Elderton. His father and I would eventually become acquaintances.

Although I became frequently bored, I finally accepted the fact that life at our home was not all that restrictive or poor. Dad seemed to have recovered from the effects of the great depression of 1929 without too much debt. We always had a comfortable late-model car, big enough for us four siblings in the back seat. (And we knew the consequences of "acting up" or misbehaving. "Mum" had made it clear: "...the next time you will stay home." That announcement worked as discipline, but was never carried out.)

Home life for me in childhood was not all that bad. In fact, as far as I could determine, it was good. My younger brother commented two years before he died, "We had the best dad there ever was." He and our

Father entered into a lot more activities of mutual interest than Dad and I ever did, like working together on cars, hunting deer and wild turkeys and other outdoor activities. (The only hunting I ever did with Dad was autumn coon hunting at night with our coon dogs, and I never shot a gun.) We had a nice big radio in our living room, but no TV yet of course; the time was still in the early 1940's. Our town had no organized sports except high school basketball and baseball; no movie theater, no roller skating rink, no bowling alley, no casinos, no races; just churches and church organizations and activities, school sessions nine months of the year, an Elks Lodge, and in my young manhood, an American Legion Organization, which I joined after my discharge from the U.S. Army Air Corps. Our house had a party-line hand-rung telephone, one camera with black and white film, one wheelbarrow, one wagon, and one bicycle for us four children. Summers, nevertheless, went too quickly, and winters too slowly. Dad took me on an occasional summer trip to watch the Pittsburgh Pirates play baseball. Almost every summer we drove to a park in the area to attend the Gibson family reunion. We took an occasional weekend drive up to "Camp," in the Elk County Mountains. A group of Elderton men owned a hunting lodge, and Dad belonged. More frequently, we went to a picture show in Indiana when the family had enough money to buy the tickets at twenty-five cents for children and fifty for adults. The one Elderton restaurant was open occasionally, but it had a beer license, so not many local residents patronized it; its owners lived "upstairs." One of my seventh-grade girlfriends lived next door, and one day she took me in to see the place and meet the wife of the owner. I knew her; she went to the other Presbyterian Church in town, and in my Mother's estimation, she was not a very good Christian because she sold beer and served it to the few persons who patronized the "establishment." I had never eaten at a restaurant or bought "fast food" before I was seventeen.

In October, high school activities included practicing basketball—both boys and girls. By November intramural games were being played. I was not a very tall or quick player, but I developed an interest in officiating girls' basketball games. At that time the playing team was made up of six girls, with the centerline as a dividing line between the defensive and offensive sides. In my junior year, the school became a beneficiary of a gift from the previous senior class: a record player. We began occasional dances after basketball games, and in 1943—I was a junior—we had our first Junior-Senior Prom: music supplied by records. We also put on plays in the spring and the fall, and since I was interested in drama, I was often chosen for the male lead. If a guy did not hunt or trap or fish, his life was limited to creating his own recreation, hanging out with pals or cousins, sled-riding, playing pick-up softball or baseball, and other homespun activities. On summertime Saturday nights the biggest crowd could be found on the steps and the front porch of William's Grocery Store. Folk from the country came to the village for their shopping and took advantage of the gathering to catch up on news and to gossip. In the wintertime the storeowner took the benches inside for "loafing" and visiting. Both town and country teenagers paraded the streets like hens and roosters on Saturday nights. (I hesitate to say, "Like chicks and cocks!") Town kids looked down on the country kids—until they were together in high school. In spite of all the wholesome and occasional changes in life in Elderton, Pennsylvania, it was too quiet for me; I wanted to live in a city.

Sundays—we United Presbyterians called it "Sabbath"—of course were holy days for the Methodists and the two Presbyterian Churches. Solemn worship services—and for us "UP's" evening services—broke the routine. We United Presbyterians regarded ourselves slightly more devout than other affiliated believers, since we practiced the Fourth Commandment more literally. Our attitude toward and practice of Sabbath observance could probably be more realistically described as threshold hypocrisy. The two grocery stores (both owned by United Presbyterians) were closed, as were the Bank and the Post office. The Hardware Store (also owned by a United Presbyterian) was closed. The two Service Stations (one owned by my Grandfather and Father, and the other operated by a Presbyterian, and across the street—Highway 422 until the 1940's) also shut down. On summer "Sabbath" afternoons Dad would spend two or three hours at the garage, "pumping gas." I would occasionally join him. When a car from Ohio stopped for a purchase, I wished I could have hidden in the trunk of their car and left Elderton with them. The "heathen" Restaurant-Tavern stayed open, but I never saw any cars parked out in front or any evidence of patrons. Our church had Sabbath evening worship every second week, and our family attended. Traffic on our main street (it had no official name then and it still hasn't except that it is locally referred to as "Main Street") along Route 422 was sparse, and hitchhiking was invisible.

My predominantly Protestant town's subsistence depended on agriculture and a small coal-mining operation. The lack of recreational and entertainment enterprises created a tedium syndrome in youth and tempted some of us with grandeur visions to take to the road. (Some older youth were escaping by joining the military services.) I was becoming increasingly desirous of making money. Although Elderton's egalitarian milieu satisfied many of my contemporaries, I wanted to reach farther and stretch higher. I never had the ambition to be a car mechanic, like my father. I wanted a higher education—although he and my mother had both graduated from the "Normal School," and had teaching credentials—and I wanted to live and work in Pittsburgh. I would settle for Indiana or Johnstown if I had to. We Elgin siblings were not totally bereft of finance resources. Dad and Mum gave us change for our tithe at church, and an occasional extra quarter. We never had the luxury of a regular allowance, however. Hitchhiking, thus, took on more urgency. It offered an exciting escape, within the restrictions that War had imposed upon it.

My interest in holiness while hitchhiking paralleled my physical development. Church and Sabbath activities started taking on more importance and interest, as did awareness that I needed to practice Jesus' teachings and serve God more intentionally in weekday life. (My family moderately and reasonably observed the Sabbath, as stipulated in Commandment Number Four, "to keep it holy.") Although Sabbath-observance theology did not make a deep impact on me at the time, the longer I lived and the more religious I grew, the more I became convinced that it had something to do with the brand of personal holiness Jesus had experienced at the age of twelve. Holiness and human life are integral, I decided. To behave better I needed to believe more, believe in God; and believe in Jesus and in the truth he taught. I concluded that the message from the Luke passage is that maturity resulted from being in the right place, in the right company, and in the right mind.

Growing into my teen years, I occasionally pondered what kind of a teen turbulence Jesus had gone through. My Sabbath School teachers, including my Aunt Zelda Elgin, thought that they had quieted my spiritual curiosity by assuring me that since Scriptures offer scarce information about Jesus' youth, God intends that human beings do not need to know a lot about what kind of a child, adolescent, or young adult Jesus had turned out to be. His habits, particularly his travel ones, were quite different from ours. If he had done any hitchhiking, his rides would have been on donkeys. He could possibly have done holy talk with the owner or loaner of the animal, or people who welcomed him in his travels. The only Scripture about Jesus between his birth and his adulthood can be found in an incident that could, on a more cynical reading, be entitled, "Parental neglect." He was twelve years old and had accompanied his parents to Jerusalem for the Passover. At the end of the feast they started home, believing he was elsewhere in the caravan. He was instead back in the Temple dazzling the teachers. When they found him four days later, his mother expressed her displeasure. (Cf. Luke 2:41-51.)

My spiritual wisdom and understanding were expanding minimally by benign treatment by my parents. They contributed more to my spiritual growth by personal example than by Scriptural precept; it was happening as a result of their expectations of us, and our family involvement in church life. My preparation for church membership located me on a higher spiritual platform. It started when I was a year younger than Jesus at the time of his Passover experience; I was eleven years old. My one-year older sister and I, and a cousin, John Clark, met with the elders, shared our reasons for becoming Church Members, heard our personal confessions of faith, and accepted us into United Presbyterianism.

The bottom line of my spiritual deposit, as far as human input is concerned, relates to the fact that I had been born into a Christian family. Unlike Jesus I had not been circumcised when I was eight days old, and unlike me he had not been baptized when he was three months old; he was probably thirty years old when he received baptism.

Taking showers with my peers after basketball games and practices relieved any anxiety about uncircumcision. Shower room observances suggested that in our small town few, if any, boys had had foreskin removal. Many of us had been born in a bedroom at home, a midwife and the local hometown doctor assisting our mother with the birth. Like Jesus, my religious upbringing began by entering into the religious tradition my family had followed for generations, namely, the Presbyterian track. We participated in weekly Sabbath School teaching and Church worship. For Jesus the observance happened on Saturday in the local Synagogue, and the once-a-year Passover trip to Jerusalem. We had summer Vacation Bible School Sessions and the already alluded-to Youth Group meetings on Sunday evenings. I grew up believing in Jesus, loving Jesus, and wanting to be like Jesus. At the age of eleven and twelve I took on that challenge more intentionally, and I started becoming sassily critical of my parents' minimal practices of piety, nothing of the extent to which my grandparents had. (My one Grandma had died before I had been born, and the other died when I was five.)

Holiness took on a deeper meaning for me around the age of fourteen. Our Sabbath School Class studied the Bible diligently. Teachers Plum Clark, Stanley Schall, and Ward Williams—all church elders—held high expectations of us. We were told to remember that Jerusalem was the location of the Holy Mountain Zion. What difference does the location make? The answer: it means that some places are holier than others. We also memorized the Ten Commandments with, "Remember the Sabbath Day to keep it holy." Some of we boys developed unholy thoughts about the Sabbath—which we were told is the same as Sunday—because we could not play ball, attend a movie, or hang out at a department store. (Of course, there was no shopping mall in Elderton. And TV was not yet available.) During the two years our family lived in Gastown with Grandpa Smith, Sabbath observance became oppressive. We were not allowed to read the comics in the *Pittsburgh Post Gazette* until Monday. Grandpa kept the Paper in his room until then. I developed ambivalent feelings about Grandpa's holiness.

My early childhood education and subsequent hitchhiking and engaging in holy talk benefited from a habit (mentioned earlier) that my mother described as my "gift of gab." The gift, I became convinced, had laid a foundation for my wanting to talk religion in a variety of situations. Sabbath School, Worship, Communion (the Eucharist of the Lord's Supper), Sabbath Evening Youth Group, summer Vacation Bible School, men like Calvin Frye and his wife and his daughter, Gertrude, righteous Aunts and Uncles, and other family members and friends—my Grandpa, to some extent—all contributed to my religious commitment and my desire to hitchhike holy. The Eucharist (Communion or the Lord's Supper), and Paul's writings about his conversion ushered me into increasing commitment to Christ and his Church. I began also to realize that "To whom much is given, of that person much is required." (Luke 12:48.)

My spirituality made another expansive advance when I became fifteen and began participating in a summer church gathering, the Westminster College, New Wilmington (Pennsylvania) Missionary Conference; and attending Youth Conventions. I also volunteered to teach in summer Vacation Bible School. My religious understanding was growing, to use a Biblical phrase, "...in many and various ways." (Hebrews 1:1.) Mention should also be made of the many holy saints in our United Presbyterian church, beginning with the Pastors and elders. They recognized my maturing spirituality and holiness, and they complimented and encouraged me in their growth. They also gave me increasingly challenging responsibilities in the life of the congregation. While in college I wrote, directed, and acted the major role in a Holy Week drama that involved a number of our combined community Church youth organization members. Our sanctuary was packed on the Sabbath evening that the play was presented. (As a Pastor, I wrote and produced several.)

I soon became aware that I needed more understanding of the meaning of holiness. My pastors offered as much help as I was willing to ask for or accept, or was spiritually ready for. A college youth group also gave breadth and depth to my spiritual growth. Eventually, in seminary, I would gain a broader knowledge of both the will of God, and especially of God's holiness. The Hebrew word "qadosh" translates as "holy" in English. As used in Scripture, it implies an association with God; or in other religions than the Judaic-Christian one, with a cultic or national deity, a "higher being" or some power that transcends capacities or capabilities. The antonym of "qadosh" is "chalal," in English "profane." "Holy" applies not only to persons and their vocations, but also to objects such as garments, vessels, places, the Temple, the Temple esplanade, Mt. Zion, the city of Jerusalem, and offices held and acted out in the Temple, in worship and sacrificial services. Christians often use the word in conversation about our holy books: "The Holy Scripture" or the "The Holy Bible." As a child, many of us learned and were taught to obey our Church's interpretation of the fourth commandment, "Remember the Sabbath day (for the Jew, 6:00 p.m. Friday night until 5:59 p.m. Saturday night) and keep it holy." The Church, for the most part, transposed the Old Covenant "Sabbath" day to the New Covenant day, Sunday.

The Old Testament Temple—the one that Solomon built after his father, David, had been denied the privilege—had a large gathering place, "The Holy Place." A smaller room beyond the Holy Place housed the sacred Ark of the Covenant, and other holy objects or utensils; it bore the name, "Holy of Holies." "Holy" is used elsewhere in the Bible for both persons and paraphernalia. Jesus addressed God as Holy Father, and Paul even called the Law "holy." The books of both Kings and Chronicles ascribe special powers that belong to the Ark because it is holy. Persons assigned the duty of transporting the container for the tablets of the Ten Commandments to its final resting place in the Temple (that Solomon had built and dedicated) became increasingly impressed about the holiness of the contents they were responsible for. (Later Solomon desecrated that holiness by his idolatrous and bigamous behavior.) Along the route to Jerusalem the party experienced an alarming demonstration of the Ark's holiness. Once when a bump in the road caused the oxen to make a sudden shift of position, and the Ark began moving out of its base, "Uzziah reached out his hand to the ark of God and took hold of it.…The anger of the Lord was kindled against

Uzziah; and God struck him there because he reached out his hand to the ark; and he died there beside the ark of God." (1 Chronicles 13:10.) David in turn became angry about holiness, <u>i.e.</u>, at God, for striking Uzziah. The power of holiness made the king leery of future responsibility for the ark. He stored it in the house of Obededom. The caretaker and his household had an immediate increase in his personal welfare. Upon learning of the good fortune of the ark's protector, David changed his mind, and with a singing and dance ceremony that embarrassed his wife, he had the ark brought into the Holy City where it belonged. David eventually had it ensconced in the Holy Temple, in the section called the "Holy of Holies." (2 Samuel 6.) Holiness is not to be taken lightly.

Angels are unequivocally holy, except Lucifer. Finally, the word also applies to the Eucharistic or peace kiss. The Apostle Paul closed his litany of final messages and greetings in his first letter to the Corinthians with the admonition: "Greet one another with a holy kiss." (1 Corinthians 16:20.) I regularly take Paul literally when observing the Eucharist or Communion.

Another understanding of "qadosh" connects to Jesus' teaching about life abundant and eternal. In John 6 he says—fifteen times with slightly different nuances—"*Ego eimi o artos tes zoes….*" Translated, "I am the bread (artos) of life (zoes—as in zoology)." One of the nuances, and in fact, one of the toughest of his sayings, follows: "Unless you eat the flesh of the Son of Man and drink his blood, you have no life in you." Later when many of his listeners could no longer tolerate the teaching and had left the circle, Jesus asked the Twelve Apostles why they did not join them; Peter replied, "Lord, to whom can we go? You have the words of eternal life."(John 6:53.) Life eternal on the basis of that verse may be defined as, "…living a holy existence here and now with a sense of the everlasting presence of God, and a desire to do God's will and work for God's kingdom."

From the foregoing it should be clear that holiness matures in essence, and offers more assurance of an eternal quality about life, as a believer matures in Christ; the converse is equally valid and true. Holiness sets a person apart from the world for God. When I hitchhike I regard my ride and my time with the driver and others as an opportunity to encounter the "Imago Dei" in every human being and every event, or as an ancient prayer says, with "…the treasure stored in every human life." If someone tells me, "I have no awareness of being holy," I respond, "Well, you should develop one." It becomes a holy person's accountability to increase in holiness, and humbly to expose it.

Hitchhiking has frequently enshrouded cars and drivers and passengers and highways with wonder and awe and appreciation for the heavens and the earth, and all that is in them. A new appreciation of meaning in phenomena that may otherwise appear mundane develops. One does not need to search the heavens and the earth, however, to see and appreciate holiness. Just pinch yourself to assure you that you are a living person with thinking and feeling, or spend five minutes alone with God, and you could experience the holy. In his first letter to the Corinthians, Paul speaks of the human body as holy: "Do you not know that your bodies are members of Christ? (Paul was admonishing the Church to avoid fornication by avoiding worship of the ways and things of the world, and especially by having sex with a prostitute, male or female.) Your body is a temple of the Holy Sprit within you, which you have from God, and that you are not your own. For you were bought (Sic, made holy) with a price." You have accountability to God: "Therefore, glorify God with your body." (1 Corinthians 6:12-20.) This kind of glorification incarnates holiness. It can happen while hitchhiking.

In one of Israel's lowest national ebbs during their Babylonian Captivity, the Prophet Isaiah attempted to persuade the people of God to think holy. Keep up hope, for one day you will be heading back home on holy terrain. Isaiah prophesied:

> "A highway shall be there,
> > and it shall be called the Holy Way;
> the unclean shall not travel on it,
> > but it shall be for God's people;
> > no traveler, not even fools, shall go astray.
> And the ransomed of the Lord shall return,
> > and come to Zion with singing;
> everlasting joy shall be upon their heads;
> > they shall obtain joy and gladness
> > and sorrow and sighing shall flee away." (Isaiah 35:8-19.)

The class in systematic theology about the "holy" has now ended.

The background on holiness moves the tale ahead to a return to the road; time has come again to hold out a thumb. I was sixteen when I began the practice seriously, regularly, and more distantly. I was without a car and with no prospects of owning one until I had gone to College and started working. I had not yet made a total commitment to ministry, but I came to a radical decision, to which my parents responded, "Good Luck!" The end of my high school junior year approached, and I had decided "No more digging potatoes or picking pickles or mowing graves or pitching horse manure." (I was not yet habited to using dirty words, and in fact, I never became so habituated.) I was maturing into a career minded guy—about to be a senior in High School. I was going to attempt to go "big-city" in search of a job. I went to bed one night, determined to get up in the morning, put on my Sunday clothes, and head for Indiana. (I could have gone to Kittanning on the search, but then I would have to ride with my dad morning and evening, and he left the house early. I preferred Indiana over Kittanning for many reasons.) I decided that since our little Elderton High School ended its academic year in mid-May I ought to have an advantage over the city boys; the big Indiana High School would not close for two more weeks. After a sleepless night at the end of my Junior year, I arose early, drank a glass of milk, and against my Mother's insistence that I eat breakfast, I walked out our front door onto Route 422 and stuck out my thumb.

The journey toward the work force began with a less-than-promising omen. I must have waited fifteen minutes before a car finally slowed down and stopped. The driver motioned for me to come and "Hop in." I thanked the stranger for stopping. I was a bit nervous so I did not introduce religious talk. He complimented me on how clean I looked, and wanted to know about my reason for going to Indiana. I said, "I am looking for a job—one that pays." He chuckled. We had an interesting conversation about our families for the next fifteen minutes, and by that time we had arrived in front of Alex Stewart's hardware store on Philadelphia Street. The man pulled the car over to the curb. I opened the door and exited, thanking the driver for the ride. He responded, "It was a pleasure talking to you. Good luck on getting a job. One that pays well." I thanked him again, slammed the door, and headed for Troutman's Department Store.

As I passed the Stewart Hardware I spoke to Alex; he was settled on his traditional bench in front of one of the large display windows of his hardware store, and he was wearing his red suspenders. He had not lost any weight since I had last seen him. I said, "Good Morning, Mr. Stewart." He responded, and gave me his friendly grin. I stopped and asked, "When is Jimmy coming home again?" He responded, "Never know." (Cross-country flights before World War II were formidable journeys.) It came to me that I should ask Mr. Stewart if he hired boys for the summer, but then I thought of how dirty hardware stores can be. My cousin and best friend, John Clark, was a "hardware son." His Dad, and Granddad before him, had owned a family hardware business in Elderton for many years.

I wanted to work in Jimmie Stewart's hometown, even if Jimmie did not travel from Hollywood to Indiana frequently. I said good-bye to Mr. Stewart and headed across the Railroad Tracks for Troutman's.

I stopped and admired the well-dressed mannequins in the windows, then screwed up my courage and headed into the store. It was cool, kept that way I knew without being told, not by air-conditioning, but by large fans. A tall redheaded man stood near the entrance. I held out my hand and greeted him, and he responded warmly. I told him my mission. He immediately broke into a broad smile. To my surprise, Mr. Peck said, "I am delighted that you stopped by." He went on to explain: the (mechanical) Elevator Operator had quit yesterday, suddenly, and the store needed someone to run the elevator. Would I be interested? Of course, I would. I signed papers, was given a quick lesson in elevator operation on the spot, and spent the rest of the day in my new job—earning fifteen dollars per week. How I bragged to my peers! I had a job in Indiana! So began my city work career.

When summer ended, I was ecstatic when the management offered me Saturday work during the next school year. The regular elevator operator wanted weekends off for the next nine months so she could be home with her family. Having my driver's license the next summer, I was elevated to delivery boy, and in-store selling on Saturdays. My salary increased to twenty dollars per week. Hitchhiking posed no problem. Military service veterans were enrolling in mass numbers at the local College. My skills in provoking host drivers to talk holiness improved. Those who regularly picked me up dubbed me "The Holy Hiker." The dubbing, plus increased responsibilities in my church, had the effect of making me search more seriously for God's plan for my life. Was being a minister a possibility? Hardly!

Upon graduation from high school at the age of seventeen, I began facing up to turning eighteen by another year. The prospect of military service was head of me, unless the Axis powers capitulated soon. However, they were still advancing fiercely in 1943. During the first semester of school the male population of my senior class had dwindled from six boys to four; the four had joined the Navy, with the guarantee that they would receive their diplomas whether or not they had finished their Senior High School year. I decided after I had graduated that my time had come to enlist in the United States Army Air Corps Reserves. I asked for a day off at Troutman's so I could take the train to Pittsburgh and sign up. I did not want to be drafted into the Infantry. The Assistant Manager of the store told me to take off, and my salary would not be "docked." I traveled to Pittsburgh, went through the tests, took the physical exam and was accepted into the Air Corp Reserves. I worked at Troutman's the rest of the summer, hitchhiking to work, and talking holy talk when it appeared appropriate. In September I received orders to report to the Virginia Polytechnic Institute by the fifteenth of the month. My hitchhiking would suffer drastically. My salary would improve by fifteen dollars a month.

My train ride to Virginia introduced me to "Jim Crowism," and I became convinced that segregation was out of sync with Jesus' teaching. I believed, "All people are God's children no matter their color," but I also shared some of the racist attitudes of my parents and peers. I had seen black people before, but I had never been able to satisfy my curiosity about the mythology connected with the toughness of black skin. I felt strange when the black people who had ridden with white people from Pittsburgh to Baltimore suddenly had to move to their own coach. When I arrived in Virginia, I began to see evidence of a phenomenon that I had not had much acquaintance with: that black and white do not mix. I would experience it a lot more at Virginia Tech.

I checked in at VPI, was assigned to my dormitory barracks and was issued GI-clothes. I had no fear that I would be rooming with a "Negro." My roommate turned out to be a tall, redheaded, skinny guy who resembled my tall, redheaded, skinny brother. In fact, VPI had no black students, not even, or maybe, especially not any, in the Cadet Corps. I was presented with a schedule and began my military career. I had my first siege of homesickness Sunday morning when the Church Bells rang. I assuaged it by finding my way to the First Presbyterian Church. I was the only Army Specialized Training Reserve Program guy in attendance. I was proud to go to church in my uniform. The next nine months turned out to be among the toughest of my life

A classmate, Andrew, a Richmond Cop's son, became one of my best friends. I admired his southern accent and I envied his physical strength. He could cross the PT Obstacle Course Wall twice while I struggled to climb over it once. On a couple of occasions Andy and I hitchhiked to a nearby Women's College for a Saturday night dance. He was unabashedly biased. He had warned me before we had even had our first experience on the road that he would not enter a car driven by a "Nigger." I chided him for the use of the "N" word and he laughed. I was tempted to break up our friendship. He eventually proved that he meant what he had said. One Saturday we were thumbing to Roanoke for a Thanksgiving Season gala. I was happy about the break; the socialization would help me with my homesickness. We walked from the campus to the east edge of Blacksburg. A clean bright car pulled off at our begging. I ran ahead of Andrew. As I approached the vehicle, I said to myself, "Oh, oh, no!" My buddy came close behind me, and as soon as he had caught a glimpse of the driver, he swung around and headed back to our original location. I thanked the man for stopping and added, "I want you to know that I would have enjoyed riding with you, but my companion is a racist!" He said, "Thank you. I understand." I closed the car door, and he drove off. Andrew and I spent a glum Saturday night. We did not make the dance. We never hitchhiked together again.

The ASTRP contingent mustered us pre-Air Force members out of VPI in late May, and by mid-June most of us were "Active Duty" Airmen. I was sent to Keesler Field, Mississippi. After Basic Training at Keesler I was stationed at Scott Field, Illinois. There I met a man whose friendship resulted in a relationship between us like that between the future King David and King Saul's Son Jonathan. Scripture says, "Jonathan loved David as his own soul." (1 Samuel 18:3.) My best friend, Robert Will, from Pittsburgh, and I occasionally hitchhiked on weekends to St. Louis, but only on the days when we had missed the regular army shuttle; that occasion arose when too many other GI's had also missed it. Robert became embarrassed if I introduced religion with a driver who had offered us a ride, and he asked me not to do it when he was in a car with me. Ironically, he and I attended Base Chapel services regularly.

When a three days' leave became available to both of us, my buddy and I decided to hitchhike to Chicago. We had been told that Illinois folk and military travelers were friendly toward GI's, and we should have no trouble making it to Chanute Field. Once there, we could easily obtain a ride to Chicago on one of the B17's that flew to and from Midway Field as frequently as taxis travel between Manhattan and the Queens. The report proved accurate. We fared well on rides to Chanute, and from there we had no trouble obtaining a seat on a B17 to Chicago. It was my first airplane ride—but not the last one I would receive while hitchhiking. Once on board and in our hammock-like seats, and when Robert wasn't looking, I sneaked in a holy moment of prayer.

In less than an hour, we arrived at Midway. We caught a GI bus into the City Center and found our way to the USO, where we loaded up on tickets for a movie theater, the Symphony, special foods, and a workout facility. On Sunday we attended worship at the Fourth Avenue (United)

Presbyterian Church. We returned to Scott Field by a GI bus late Sunday night. (We chose not to risk Sunday Night B17 hitchhiking.) The next morning we showed up at Building T-424 to teach our Teletype Class. Robert sniffed at me when I related to him that some weekend I wished we could hitchhike the whole way by highway to Chicago. I guessed that he feared that I may turn religious with our driver. I think he would have entered the car if the driver happened to be black.

The relationship between Robert and me lasted until he died in Los Gatos, California in 2006, and although we had seen and visited each other occasionally over the years—in Ohio and Seattle and California and Florida—we never hitchhiked together again. Robert, an inimitable stand-up comic University Ph. D. in Science, taught for several years at the Foothills Community College in Santa Clara as a Horticulture Professor. His grave might have shaken with laughter if I could have penetrated through the soil—he warned me never to call it "dirt"—with George Bernard Shaw's classic comment about grief over long-term friendships that end in death: "It isn't so much that I grieve over losing old friends, as that I grieve over the loss of the man I used to be." I still miss Robert, in spite of his threat that if we ever were successful in obtaining a ride while hitchhiking together and I started talking religion, he would request the driver to pull off the highway and let him exit the car.

Upon my discharge from the Air Corps in late 1946, I registered for the January 1947 winter term at the Indiana University then known as the Indiana State Teachers' College, today named Indiana University of Pennsylvania. For one and one-half years I hitchhiked from my home in Elderton to Indiana, and when class schedules permitted, I rode with friends. In my senior year I rented a room near campus. In 1949 I graduated with my B.Sc. In the meantime my "call" to ministry became firm, and I subsequently registered at the Pittsburgh-Xenia Theological Seminary. My understanding and knowledge of holiness became more educated, and also more practiced. Weekends home in Elderton were so short that if I went there I would have to travel by bus. My Middler and Senior years, however, opened more opportunities for travel. I was frequently hitchhiking Routes 420, 40 and 66, and lesser known ones. And I was talking holy talk, much more credibly than when I had begun at age sixteen.

I always felt that I was traveling in a special class and timetable when I was on Route 66. I have already introduced the romantic feeling I had upon hearing and dancing to the Hit Parade 'hit,' "You can get your kicks on Route Sixty-Six." When our son lived in Oklahoma and we traveled to visit him, and later him and his wife, I was quickly reminded that the Route had originated and opened in Oklahoma in 1926. I had read about it many years earlier in John Steinbeck's Great Depression novel, *"The Grapes of Wrath."* Steinbeck writes of its importance during the migration movement occasioned by the economic tragedies of the Depression. He records:

> "...66—the long concrete path across the country, waving gently up and down on the map...over the red lands and the gray lands, twitching up into the mountains, crossing the Divide and down into the bright and terrible desert, and across the desert to the mountains again, and into the rich California valleys.... 66 is the path of a people in flight, refugees from dust and shrinking land...66 is the mother road, the road of flight."*

Through the years I have had kicks-after-kicks, and rides after rides, hitchhiking Route 66. Once on a trip to Arizona, Marjorie and I drove to Oatman just to travel on it. Besides its "66" fame, Oatman has established itself as the city where donkeys freely roam its downtown streets. In addition it has the Hotel where Clark Gable and Carole Lombard spent part of their honeymoon.

The Chapter will close with an account of one of the most exciting hitchhiking kicks of my Seminary Years (1946-9). It happened shortly after my last Seminary year had begun. It took place on a beautiful sunny Saturday in November. The Ohio Church with whom I had spent two years as a Summer Seminary Intern had invited me to come to St. Clairsville for the weekend and take part in their 125th Anniversary worship. I decided to save either the Church or myself (in case they did not reimburse me for expenses) some money. About noon, after a morning class, I rode the trolley to Mt. Lebanon, and from there I took a city bus to the western boundary of Pittsburgh. I had decided that if I did not arrive in St. Clairsville by 7:00 p.m. I would phone the Pastor to come and find me, with the instructions, "Just look for me on Route 40. If I weren't along the highway hitchhiking, I would be in a car going all the way to St. Clairsville. You could not miss me, because if necessary, I would do my toilet behind a pole or a tree."

At the end of the Pittsburgh public transportation line I started hitchhiking. I began on Route 19 headed for 40. I obtained a couple of short rides, then a long one to Claysville. Surely Western Pennsylvanians would be heading out for Wheeling for Saturday-night shopping. I stood there for a while, familiar jitters of anxiety slowly knocking on my heart's door. Shortly, a shiny gray car slowed down; it pulled off onto the shoulder, and a black hand from the back seat signaled me to come and enjoy the ride. The rear right door opened, and the wave became firmer. As I came nearer to the car, I discovered six black hands from three big Black men. (My VPI Richmond friend, Andrew, would have turned around immediately and started walking back toward Pittsburgh!) As I entered the vehicle I was met with broad smiles and happy voices. The car pulled back onto the highway, and I located my backpack and myself in the back seat. The car smelled so new. The men had obviously sprayed themselves with expensive cologne. All offered handshakes and told me their names. I told them mine. From then on we addressed each other by our first—Christian—names. The vehicle was a large Cadillac.

The men were on their way to a church convention in Columbus. We immediately lapsed into holy talk. We had arrived at Holy Spirit theology when flashing red lights caught our attention; a police car was summoning Michael to steer the car off the road. A patrolman came toward us. Michael searched around in the glove compartment and came up with official looking documents, and his license. The cop asked him to step out of the car. All conversation had suspended by this time. The car was quiet. I was preparing to step out and start hitchhiking toward Wheeling. James cautioned against that plan. He saw no reason for the stop and mentioned, "racial profiling."

Michael returned to the car smiling, the Highway Patrol car pulled out in the direction of Wheeling, and Michael said we were to follow it to the Wheeling Police Station. He himself was still confused. He reported that pulling him over had to do with the tags, and the title; they were temporary because the car had been in Michael's possession less than a week.

Arriving in Wheeling we turned south off Route 19-40 one block, and followed the Patrolman into a designated parking stall. I thanked the men for the ride, hurried out of the car, and wished them well at their convention. They accepted my gratitude, apologized for the interruption, and wished me the best. I headed back up to Route 40 and started hitchhiking west. For a long time, drivers ignored me. The Ohio River flowed south ahead of us. I was wishing I were walking Main Street in St. Clairsville, Ohio. I began to think that I needed to find a telephone and phone Pastor Frank. A half-hour passed, and I was still walking and stopping, walking and stopping, and even beginning to offer holy "importunity" prayers. Shortly a car appeared and it slowed down. It was large, and similar to the one I had just left--a shiny gray color. The driver pulled off a few yards in front of me; a man exited the rear passenger-side and waved for me to get in. I suddenly overcame my afternoon fatigue as I realized who was offering me a ride: my three travel companions of half-an-hour ago. When I arrived at the car, all four of us laughed. They joked about their short imprisonment. James, my recent back-seat companion, hugged me, slid into the car first, and invited me to sit in his seat; he slid over to the one behind Michael. We headed toward St. Clairsville, and Michael spoke of some technicality about the license plate. James interrupted, "Now, Mr. Reverend Vernon, you have probably enjoyed your first, and hopefully last 'racial profiling' experience." Michael added, "That is your penalty for climbing into a car with three black guys!" We all laughed.

We discussed race the remainder of the trip to the First United Presbyterian Church of St. Clairsville, located prominently on Main Street (then also Route 40). I told them about my experience in Blacksburg with Andrew. One of the men said, "How we pity the poor guy!" Another said, "I hope he is still alive." I agreed, but I would not count on his having become more tolerant. By that time we had arrived in St. Clairsville, and when we neared it, I pointed out the Church. Michael found a parking place across the street. As I gathered my briefcase and suit bag, all three of the men left the car and came to the street and hugged me. I thanked them for our time of holy travel together. They smiled and offered thanksgiving when I said in reverent relief, "Never again will I be able to say, 'I have never touched black skin!'" They took my name and address, re-entered their car, and headed off for Columbus.

I walked across the street to the Manse. The Montgomery's were waiting for me. They had not seen how or with whom I had arrived. Frank greeted me with, "How was your bus ride?" I responded, "I can hardly wait to tell you!"

*   John Steinbeck, *The Grapes of Wrath*, p. 160.

CHAPTER II

Castle Connections:
Queen Elizabeth II at Balmoral,
and Helen Carnegie Miller at Skibo

"Those who wear soft robes are in royal palaces." (Matthew 11:8c.)
*"Do not neglect to show hospitality to strangers, for by doing that some
have entertained angels without knowing it."* (Hebrews 12:2.)

Confident of my hitchhiking skills, secure in a holy profession, engaged
to a beautiful Pittsburgh-Xenia Theological Seminary Kansas coed, winner
of the 1952 Jamieson Academic Scholarship from the Seminary Class,
ordained a United Presbyterian Clergy, installed as the Pastor of the United
Presbyterian Church in Cadiz, Ohio, and accepted as a post-graduate
student at the New College of the University of Edinburgh, Scotland,
I, the Reverend Vernon Gibson Elgin, B.Sc., B.Div., and M.Div., sailed
out of Hoboken, New Jersey, on the Holland-American *S.S. Ryndam*
on a beautiful day early in September of 1952. I would leave the ship in
Southampton, England, and head for Edinburgh, Scotland. I would enroll
for a year of post-graduate study at the New College of the University
of Edinburgh. The year would afford me my first study-travel adventure
outside mainland U.S.A.

The *Ryndam* a new, tourist class Holland American Line ship, offered
only a few First-Class Cabins. A significant number of those on board were
single twenty-something's; many of them of Dutch extraction, going home

after a time of study or travel in the United States. A large contingent of American students made up the Passenger List, several of them headed for Utrecht in the Netherlands, Oxford and Cambridge in England, Glasgow and Edinburgh in Scotland, the Sorbonne in Paris, Tubingen and Goettigen and Berlin in Germany, a few for Italy, and some for Scandinavia. Upper Sun Deck political and theological discussions took place regularly during the crossing. Many of my new Dutch friends and acquaintances extended me gracious invitations to visit them if I toured the Netherlands. They gave me their addresses and phone numbers; email was not yet in use. Several of them extended me their hospitality, in case, or when, I hitchhiked in the Netherlands. Several of them eased my anxiety about solo travel in Europe with assurances that drivers frequently take in riders.

The slow-boat crossing required almost eight days. One day early in the voyage I stopped by the Bursar's office to investigate whether a Chaplain would be offering worship leadership on Sunday? The answer was "No." I offered to conduct it. The Bursar enthusiastically accepted my gesture, and added that the main Mid-Deck lounge could be set up for such an event.

The next day a notice was posted on the announcements board, and a passenger, whose profession was church organist, volunteered to play the portable miniature electronic organ. As I prayed and pondered my responsibility, I chose to reflect on a Psalm that I had based my sermon on the previous Lord's Day; it had a nautical reference. The words—from Psalm 107—seemed salutary for ocean travelers:

"Some went down to the sea in ships,
        doing business on the mighty waters;
    they saw the deeds of the Lord,
        his wondrous works in the deep.

. . . .

Let them thank the Lord for his steadfast love,
        For his wonderful works to humankind."
                                            (Vss. 23-43 selected.)

I rewrote the sermon and prepared the worship service. Sunday arrived. The attendance stretched the lounge capacity, some attendees standing through the approximately forty-minute gathering. We listened, we spoke, we prayed, we sang, a man played the organ, and I preached. For the rest of the sail I received occasional kind compliments for my homily. (I speculated whether any of the worshipers had pondered if my sermon had been a "warm-over.") My service also swelled my list of potential Hollander hosts.

The arrival of the boat in Southampton aroused tears of both happiness and sadness. We had arrived at a destination that would either return the British—and after arrival in Rotterdam, the Dutch—home; or would introduce students and tourists to a country where they would be privileged to visit or hitchhike through, or travel for study at some of Britain's finest universities. By the time that the boat had docked and passengers started leaving the ship, I became engaged in a good-Samaritan duty. I had made the acquaintance of a German "war bride" who was taking her four children home to spend time with Grandma and Grandpa. I helped her with luggage and children, and as a consequence, we missed the *Ryndam's* scheduled Boat Train to London. The young mother and I had to wait some hours for the next one.

The delay put me in a travel ambiance that I had never before experienced. A boat arrived from the British West Indies. Hundreds of passengers streamed into the customs and waiting rooms. We quickly became a racially mixed crowd. The newly arrived and the leftovers began filling the train. As I settled into a coach seat, I experienced a language surprise: the black persons were speaking with a British accent. I was accustomed to that race in the United States speaking either southern or with a distinctive African American drawl. I delighted in hearing the citizens from the British West Indies.

We soon filled up the train and left for London. I saw the German mother and her children off for her train to Germany, and headed for my connections—as instructed by the lady with whom I had made a reservation for my second night in London—for the Victoria Station. Upon arriving at Victoria, I collected my luggage and took it to "Hold" and processed it for eventual travel to Edinburgh. I planned to spend almost a week in London. I headed out of the Station to find a taxi to take me to the Bonaventure Hotel, where I had a reservation for one night.

A taxi was hailed for me, and as I entered it I pulled off one of my first "ugly American" faux pas. I enquired, "What model-year is this taxi?" With a slight tone of effrontery, the driver answered, "1952!" I had my second "stupid" moment when we arrived at the hotel: I paid the taxi driver three pence. They looked high valued; they were bright shiny copper. I had not yet made an exchange of money into pounds, so I handed the driver a dollar. He offered the bill back with the comment, "Here, you need this pittance more than I." I apologized and gave him three dollars. He smiled as he thanked me. I wanted to ask him why the city was so dimly lit and why the cars headlights were fixed on "dim." But I feared another ignorant-American embarrassment.

We arrived at the Bonaventure Hotel in ten minutes. My welcome at the Hotel Desk was courteous and sincere. (I paid with a credit card!) As I was about to head up to my room, the Desk Clerk spoke to me: "Sir, I have one ticket left in the front row of the Drury Lane Theatre for tonight's performance of 'South Pacific' with Mary Martin and Ezio Pinza. You can still make it if you do not linger too long at tea. It is much more economical to see it in London than in New York. It just opened a few days ago. The cost is one Pound. I can charge the billet to your account. " I paused only slightly, and then said, "I will take it!" I went to the room, took care of my toilette, and returned to the Dining Room.

My dinner seating arrangements treated me to another British innovation, a post-War one, I was later told. (It proved amazing how many inconveniences or adjustments I would discover in the next nine months that would be defined as "post-War" inconveniences.) Without either hesitation or consultation, the hostess ushered me to a table already occupied by a man. She moved the chair for me to be seated. As soon as I had sat down, I introduced myself, and the man said in a delightful London accent, "My name is Johnny Walker." I blinked! Johnny Walker, my tablemate at my first British meal! Without commenting, I shook his hand. I was not, and am still not, convinced the man was telling the truth. He welcomed me to London. I had Fish and Chips, and we had a delightful conversation. He was amazed that on my first night in Big Ben City, I had a ticket to "South Pacific." He had been trying for weeks to obtain billets for him and his wife. I told him I would not forfeit mine. I also suggested they may want to try going singly. We both laughed.

After I had eaten I headed for the hotel lobby. I exchanged a few dollars for British coins and pounds. A bellhop obtained a taxi for me. I was introduced again to wartime austerity by the subdued street lamps and car lights. Upon arriving at the Drury Lane Theatre I dug out some pounds' currency for paying the taxi driver. I must have given him the right amount or more; at least he kept it. My seat was comfortable. At times I could almost reach out and pinch Mary Martin or Ezio Pinza. I stayed awake for the whole production, and quietly sang along on "Some Enchanted Evening," and "Gonna Wash That Man (I sang 'Gal') Right Out'a My Hair..." At the intermission, while tea was being sold in china cups, and biscuits (cookies) could be bought, I chatted with the theater audience members sitting beside me, and others near by. Upon hearing my accent, they welcomed me to Great Britain.

My theater good-fortune launched a week of London lush. When I transferred the next day to the B&B that I had reserved while still in Ohio, I was immediately impressed with Elise, the Matron, and with the brightness and cleanliness of the room; and the convenience to the Tube, (Subway). The boarding place was only one block from Victoria Station. During the rest of my stay in the Capitol of the United Kingdom, I buzzed to as many of the London favorites as I could manage—and afford—in fourteen-hour days. One of the essentials had to be The British Museum, where I could pay a respectful nod to the remarkable Elgin Marbles. As I feasted on their artistry and history, I suffered a twitch of guilt, instilled in me by my "World Civilization" College professor's comment: "Remember, Class, that Lord Elgin, with a little assistance from the Ottoman Empire, practically stole them!"

My first Sunday in London began with a holy observance: I worshiped at Westminster Abbey, in a Chapel. The Cathedral nave was undergoing repairs for the Inauguration of Queen Elizabeth 2 the next June Second. Features of the Anglican Service unique for me, a Presbyterian, were: kneeling at the altar and receiving the elements from the Dean of the Cathedral; a disc-wafer placed in my open hand as the bread, symbolizing Jesus' body; drinking real wine from a "common chalice"; sharing the sacrament with mostly Anglicans, mostly English no doubt. As my week in London drew to an end, I reconciled my frustration over having only "scratched the surface" of this remarkable city, with the reminder that I would probably visit again while studying in Scotland. It even entered my mind that I could possibly hitchhike between Edinburgh and London. The day finally arrived for me to say good-bye to Elise after I had eaten breakfast and paid my bill; and to head for Victoria Station, claim my belongings, and board the train for Edinburgh. Elise had expressed her hope that I would have enjoyed her B&B service enough to stop again when I was in London. I assured her that I would. She suggested I make a reservation. I wanted to express my appreciation with a kiss, but I had been taught that British folks are reserved. I eventually learned that only a few are.

Arriving at the Station I located a "Blue Cap." He claimed my luggage from the holding service and checked it through to Edinburgh. Once on a coach, I found an eight-seat compartment occupied by only four passengers. I settled in with my typewriter and journal. The train pulled out of the station. I spent the time traveling North reading, watching the English and then Scottish countryside, conversing with some of the more gregarious fellow coach riders, writing notes for my journal, exploring politics and culture and the differences between English and Scottish customs, and then merging into holy topics. The comments confirmed my information that Presbyterian Scots give the impression of being more pious than the Anglican English, but perhaps not quite as habitual and devout as the Roman Catholic Irish. One of the familiar biases about Scotland that I heard expressed constantly by the English and other United Kingdom Citizens was, "It is so cold up there—and gray and bleak. And the people are so proper!" I had a Pavlovan reaction to the perception: I shivered. (After a year in Scotland I had a different opinion about the English forecasts. I leaned more toward concurring with the Scots' judgment on the lower country's bias about the northern country's weather and citizens: "It's just the English snobbery.")

Between typing, talking, and window gazing as the train headed north, I became impressed with the English, and then Scottish, countryside. Green pervades. Walls separate neighbors. Backyard gardens are prevalent and well manicured. Upon arriving at the Princess Street Station in Edinburgh—in the dark—I was amazed at how quickly the approximately thirteen-hour trip had passed—I immediately conscripted a taxi, presented him with my baggage claims, and we drove up to the famous Princess Street. I became a bit apprehensive when the driver had to dig out his Edinburgh map to locate Vandeleur Avenue. He seemed confidant, however, as he headed out toward the east coastal area. Then he drove directly to it. Upon our arrival, Annie came out to the taxi and greeted me, along with her daughter, Leslie. Her military service son, William, was away in training. We all began carrying in luggage. The taxi driver picked up the footlocker and put it on his shoulder. By this date I had learned how much to pay taxi drivers and how much tip was adequate. Because of the amount and weight of my luggage, and my request for him to follow Mrs. Thomson with it, I gave him an extra Pound. He appeared grateful.

Annie took me to my room at the back of the house. A fire burned in the small fireplace. Because of the hour, the luggage was quickly stacked in whatever space could be found for it. Annie had tea ready, with cucumber sandwiches, soup, scones, and biscuits (cookies). I ate lightly, again expressing my delight in being their (paying) guest. She was amazed when she poured tea that I did not drink it white, with milk. After a few moments of becoming further acquainted, and questions about what time I wanted breakfast, I headed for "slumberdom." The fire still burned, providing both charm and heat, and alleviating some of my surface homesickness. I decided: no unpacking until morning. Annie had informed me that a German student would be arriving in a few days; he would occupy the front bedroom. He faced the street, I the garden. I gave myself a quick wash and headed for bed. A knock came on my door. Annie asked, "What time shall I "knock you up" in the morning?" I paused, as I pondered an appropriate answer. I negotiated an hour that proved convenient for both her and me. I told her I would shower in the morning. She was a bit taken aback, but said there may be sufficient hot water left in the tank heated by the living-dining-social room fireplace to accommodate me. I turned out my light and lay down under the bed covers, thinking of how romantic it felt—with light in the room from the fireplace. I knew, of course, that I would awake to ashes in the morning. Annie provided a small heater to take the chill off the room, but she did not hesitate to remind me that the fireplace was to provide most of my heat. Even it was to be used wisely because coal was still rationed, again a wartime disadvantage. My closing thoughts settled on one of my favorite verses from the mouth of David, a verse I had often repeated and would say a lot more in the next few months: "Who am I, O Lord, and what is my house that you have brought me thus far?" (2 Samuel 7:18.) The bed was a bit shorter and narrower and softer than I was accustomed to, but I was determined to adjust to it. I offered a quickie prayer, remembered Marjorie and the Cadiz Church, and then fell asleep.

Annie knocked me up at an appropriate time. I showered—with almost enough hot water—and after dressing, I headed to the table in the room that Annie, her family and guests spend a lot of their time. It was a dining room, living room, library and social room in one area. It had a large fireplace and a pleasant dining table bay-window view of the garden and their still-buried bomb shelter. Annie's single-story concrete blockhouse had a small cooking kitchen, a large front bedroom where she and Leslie slept, and across the hall another bedroom which the German student would occupy, with the bath, and my bedroom behind his.

The hot breakfast of porridge, toast, bacon and tea satisfied me. Annie had almost forgotten that I was not a tea-milk drinker. No coffee was offered. (I eventually bought a jar of Instant Coffee and she provided me hot water to make it.) At the conclusion of breakfast, I was reminded that my payment did not cover weekday lunches, but for a fee Annie would fix them. I thanked her for the warm breakfast, and then I headed for my room and started unpacking and putting away my clothes and personal items.

As soon as I had made the room reasonably comfortable and tidy, I walked up to the wide coast-road boulevard and caught the double-decker bus to the castle drive on Princess Street. From there I hiked up the hill to the New College. The College stands approximately half way up the hill. The Royal Mile leads down behind it, beginning at the 10th Century Edinburgh Castle at the top, next to the small St. Margaret's Chapel, centuries of years old. A large esplanade extends out in front. The annual music festival, "The Tattoo" is performed there. The "Mile" down from the Castle features book stores, several of the other buildings of the University, St. Giles Cathedral, the John Knox House, other buildings of cultural and historical importance, and it terminates at the bottom at Holyrood Palace, the British Royalty's official residence when they are in Scotland. During the time I was there, and still today after her long reign, it is the house where Queen Elizabeth and her husband, Prince Philip, Duke of Edinburgh, reside when in the Nation.

The first term of the New College year would begin in two days. I found my way to the office of the Registrar, Erna Leslie, with whom I had had registration correspondence. I introduced myself, "Vernon Elgin, from Ohio," and before she could respond properly she cleared her throat, "Accchhh," and continued, "We'll hae nae 'o that here; it's 'ElGin' in Scotland!" Miss Leslie pronounced the name with a guttural "g" rather than a soft "j" g. I was pleased, because the hard "g" is the common pronunciation in Elderton, Pennsylvania. It is also used in the name of the famous Lord who had obtained the Marbles, and of course, for the name of the ruined Cathedral, Elgin in Aberdeenshire. In addition the pronunciation prevails almost universally. Of course, I would have to make a holy hitchhike to Elgin. And I did—two or three times. A framed picture of the ruins hangs on the side of my desk.

Ritual and ceremonial worship attended the formal opening of the New College year two days later. Orientation sessions followed, and afterward, we students headed down the Royal Mile to the University bookstores. Lectures began the next day. With both professorial and student guidance, I had settled on a course schedule. I signed in for a five day-week of classes. I was excited when they began. I felt privileged to be sitting under world-famous theologians. I also felt the chill of the classrooms, which only exacerbated as winter advanced. I became friends with several American students, all male; and with other Internationals from Switzerland, Greece, and Africa. Some American students' wives monitored the classes, my wife being one of them when we returned to Scotland in 1956.

My housemate—his room and amenities matched mine—arrived on schedule, and we became friends. He was from Berlin, a student from both Goettigen and Tubingen Universities. He would take graduate classes in History at the main University Campus. We soon became hitchhiking buddies, and when we had to wait for a kind driver to pick us up, or to find a ride or wait out the schedule at the Ferry Dock he taught me German hymns and I taught him, "I Come to the Garden Alone;" and the lyrics to a hymn or two set to his favorite tune, "Ode to Joy." When we traveled about I became amazed at how Harald substituted the lard he received in care parcels from Berlin for butter, which, I discovered later, had been not only a wartime necessity for Germans but a bread spread staple. On weekends I was either out holy hitchhiking the highways of Scotland alone, or staying in the city for special events, like hearing famous preachers or world-renowned lecturers. Occasionally I was invited to friends for High Tea. Hitchhiking became relatively easy. Conversation became even easier when I introduced myself, starting, "Elgin (using the Scottish pronunciation) is my name, Vernon Elgin. I am from the United States, but studying at New College." It was unnecessary to identify the city.

One of my earliest "Holy of Holy" visits took place in worship at St. Giles Cathedral. Stopping by once in my first days at New College for a look—it is only a few blocks from the School—I slipped into the Queen's pew. I imagined myself a holy royal. St. Giles holds among other historic distinctions, the occasion when perhaps Scotland's most famous Reformer, John Knox, reputedly tossed his stool from the pulpit in the direction of the pew where the visiting Roman Catholic Queen Mary was sitting. Knox was railing against her Roman Catholic heretical dogmas. Holy hitchhiking confronted the student with no seating problems in most Edinburgh Churches, of for that matter, in almost any church in Scotland. Vacant pews or chairs abounded. So did closed restaurants and cafes or pubs. Obtaining a meal or even local fast food, like a kidney pie or fish and chips—or a hot haggis pouch—required a diligent, and usually futile search on a Sabbath. Many of the churches held evening services, with attendance significantly reduced from the morning numbers.

I enjoyed my classes at New College, but I looked forward to weekends with joy and relief. Off I went hitchhiking with my backpack, a sandwich that Annie had fixed—in lieu of her not having to feed me weekend teas—and an apple and a thermos of tea. Later on in his studies, Harald joined me on occasion. He found it too economically burdensome to go with me every weekend. I soon learned a trick that facilitated my Scottish hitchhiking, especially if I were going north: the Firth of Forth dock. In the 1950's the only way across the Firth was by Ferry. A railroad bridge crossed it, but none for cars. I obtained a Ferry Schedule. I could take a bus from my "digs" to Princess Street, transfer to a Ferry bus, and be at the Ferry Auto Parking Lot in less than a half hour, if I were lucky with the buses. My hitchhiking by mouth began at the Ferry. I invariably proved lucky, almost as fortunate on Saturdays as weekdays.

Cars were often more filled on Saturdays and Sundays, as families traveled together on weekends. Occasionally they were willing to squeeze an American into their auto, as a driver once said, "As a novelty!" Upon arriving at the Lot, I took a quick survey of the situation, and I was soon at the windows of the most fancy cars I had ever seen. I was promptly, asking the driver if he—occasionally a family member or two was in the auto—could give me a ride. I quickly learned the trick to ask about a destination not too far from the ferry, even though I was going farther. Once having ingratiated myself to whoever was in the car, I enquired if they were going farther. (I hadn't been untruthful, as I was not stopping where I had suggested I was headed!) What a way to see Scotland. And the price was right. I kept hoping that one-day when I would be riding along Loch Ness the Monster would take a flip. It never showed. I became increasingly skeptical about the mythology.

The preceding background will serve as preparation for the drama of the two most celebrity hitchhiking episodes that Scotland afforded me. As noted in the Chapter Title, I call the episodes "Castle Connections." One castle belongs to the British Royal Family: Balmoral. The estate is located in North Central Scotland, and has long been the retreat of Royalty for rest, for hunting and fishing, and for entertaining. The other castle featured in the narrative is Skibo. Andrew Carnegie purchased the estate several years ago, after making his wealth in America. He became rich, not only because he was a smart planner and hard worker, but also because of the healthy American economy, then the number one economy in the world. I felt privileged to connect with his footsteps.

My connection with Queen Elizabeth on this occasion was more with her Rolls Royce limousine tire tracks than her footsteps. The episode happened at Balmoral Castle. On the afternoon of the Balmoral excitement one of my North Carolina friends, Robert Hall, also studying for the Ph. D. degree, and I were in the countryside. We were not aware that the

Queen would be in the area until we stopped in at the Crathie Store, near Balmoral. We first took a quick look at the Crathie Church, next door to the store. When at Balmoral the Anglican Queen and her family and guests become Presbyterian. The Store Manager said she regularly attended worship on the Lord's Days when she was in residence. "As a matter of fact," he said, "she should be traveling by within the hour." She was scheduled to arrive at approximately 3:00 p.m.

Robert and I hiked down to the entrance at Balmoral Road. It was a sunny afternoon in Scotland. Cattle were grazing in the fields. We could spot castle turrets down the road. We posted ourselves and waited. We kept a constant watch on the road coming from the South. (The Queen would travel from London to Edinburgh by train, then travel to the Castle in her Rolls Royce Limousine.) Her train had been in Edinburgh on schedule that beautiful May 1953 sunny afternoon. Near three o'clock we caught sight of two large black cars a mile away. The cars had to be the Queen's. We kept our eyes on the vehicles, and our gazing paid dividends.

The black limousines approached the Balmoral Road. The first car turned in; it bore License Plate No. 1. Robert and I stepped as close to the passing vehicles as we considered appropriate. We did not want to arouse suspicion of us as either Paparazzi in disguise, or roadside bombers. The auto slowed down, the horn blew, and a lady wearing a hat started waving. The lady was Queen Elizabeth. We presumed that the woman beside her was either Princess Margaret or the Queen's Lady-in-Waiting. Both Robert and I gestured politely, snapped as many photos as we could, snapping even after the Queen's limousine had gone by and the second car approached, probably bearing Prince Philip or other members of the Royal family. We had concentrated so intently on the first limousine that the second one drove by before we had thoroughly investigated it. Thus, we could not identify the passengers. We speculated that one of them could have been Prince Philip. However, the Queen of Great Britain of the United Kingdom had greeted us!

When the cars had disappeared into the trees that surrounded the Castle and its environs, we left the scene, returned to the store for a cold soda and listened to some Royal anecdotes told by the Store operator. Both Robert and I had twice before seen the Queen: once before when she had come to Edinburgh for the marriage of the Earl of Dalkeith, along with several members of her family. The ceremony had taken place at St. Giles Cathedral. Rumor circulated that the Earl had once dated the Queen. We were amused at the Edinburgh folk who had carried ladders to the

Church environs. When the royal and wedding parties were arriving, the ladders were opened and placed in polite locations. I said to myself, "The next time...."

After finishing our sodas, we headed back to the highway and stuck up our thumbs. Amazing hitchhiking luck complemented our excitement over our close-up encounter with the Queen. It proved to be the closest connection to Royalty that I had ever had, or would ever have. We felt privileged to have shot some close-up photos. We hoped that they would serve as proof that we had been at Balmoral and had seen the Queen. We could hardly contain ourselves with anticipation. Robert turned to me and asked, "Well, Vern, what does it feel like being a Paparazzo?" I responded: "Probably the same way it feels to you, Robert! Except you have the black hair to go with it!"

Once developed, the photos pasted a sheath of comedy on our experience. Since my days in Edinburgh were soon to end, I took the film with me to have it developed on the Continent. I located a fast but expensive developing service in Paris. Otherwise, the film could not be processed until I arrived back in the U.S.A., probably two months into the future. I was excited to see the results. I paid the price and had them developed. What a disappointment, considering how much the developing cost me! The shot with the car closest to Robert and me had been taken so fast that the camera had caught only the back end of the Rolls Royce, a faint glimpse of Queen Elizabeth, and five cows on the other side of the lane, their heads sticking through the fence. Well, after all, Elizabeth was their Queen, too. Like Ms. McGuigan's comment about the Elgin Marbles, the cows were British, and Great Britain belongs to the United Nations, so "they belong to everyone." Good Global logic, eh?

As will be noted later, I heard the Coronation service June 2 over the radio of a Greek bus passing along the Corinthian Canal. Before I had left London I had bought a souvenir booklet of the ceremony and had familiarized myself with the Order of the service. The event was steeped in historical references, religious tradition and ritual. The book opened with poetry from John Masefield, the British Poet Laureate at the time, framing a photograph of the beautiful Queen, decorated with a tiara and jewels. Masefield entitled his piece, "Lines on the Coronation of Our Gracious Sovereign."* The closing stanza reads:

"Now that we crown Her as our Queen
May love keep all her pathways green,
May sunlight bless her days;

May the fair Spring of her beginning
Rise to all things worth the winning,
That very surest of our praise
That mortal men attempt.
May this old land revive and be
Again a star set in the sea,
A Kingdom fit for such as She
With glories yet undreamt."

The souvenir book related that the Archbishop of Canterbury would preside, and several other Archbishops would assist him. As the Queen's entourage arrived at the West Door of the Church (Westminster Abbey) she and her train of attendants would be greeted by an Anthem based on "Psalm CXXII," "I was glad when they said unto me, 'We will go into the house of the Lord...' Peace be within thy walls, and plenteousness within thy palaces."

The oath that the Queen would swear to uphold concluded with the Question, "Will you to the utmost of your power maintain the Laws of God and the true confession of the Gospel? ... Will you maintain and preserve inviolably the settlement of the Church of England, and the doctrine, worship, discipline, and government thereof, as the law established in England? She would be presented a Holy Bible, "To keep your Majesty ever mindful of the Law and the Gospel of God as the Rule for the whole life and government of Christian Princes...." The Gospel lesson would be read from Saint Matthew 22., 15ff., including the words, "Render therefore unto Caesar the things that are Caesar's; and unto God the things that are God's." Hymns were to be sung, symbols of her office to be presented, investures to take place, and the St. Edward's Crown would be placed on Elizabeth's head, followed by a Benediction. Archbishop Geoffrey then would charge both her and Prince Philip to keep the faith during her reign. The Eucharist was to be observed, the peace of God and his Son Jesus Christ extended, and the Abbey Choir would conclude the ceremony by singing the "Te Deum Laudamus." As the Queen recessed from the Chapel, according to the program rubric, "There shall be sung by all assembled the National Anthem." Then, "FINIS."

What a holy day it would prove to those privileged to attend, and even more special for those with seats in the cathedral! As I absorbed some of the beauty and majesty of Longon, I kept wishing I could be in London at the time, but I would be on the Continent. Following my perusal of the Service, I offered my own brief prayer for Elizabeth. I knew that the Queen would never know unless I wrote her, that such pieties for her coronation would be offered by a touring American along the Corinthian Canal in a Greek bus.

The Elgin family of Marjorie, one and one-half year-old Mark, and the Ph. D. Candidate himself, returned to Scotland in September 1956. I had resigned my position at the Cadiz Church, the family had packed our household goods, we had stored our car, borrowed money, and other members of our family drove us to New York to board the SS *Queen Mary I*. (Pianist Liberace, and his Mother and Brother George and wife, were also passengers!) The Ship Bulletin Board announced a Liberace Concert at sea, approximately halfway over the Atlantic. I kept recalling my first crossing of the Atlantic, and I kept recalling my leading worship on the Lord's Day, but this crossing did not include a Sunday on the seas. I kept imagining what might have happened if there had been one, and no one had offered to officiate worship, or if only the Ship did not have a Chaplain, and if only I had or could come up with a sermon to preach...well, dream on. A concert by the Maestro was announced and "Y'all Come" was extended to the entire ship. The venue was commodious, but the crowd was more desirous than space could accommodate. Marjorie set out for the Concert, Vernon stayed back with Mark. Marjorie returned to our cabin shortly; she had lost out by being at the end of the line. Ship authorities shut the door when she was only three or four persons away from entering.

The family spent an enjoyable nine months in Scotland; that is, two of them stayed nine months. With our money running out, the decision was made that Marjorie and Mark would return home. They obtained passage on the *S.S. United States*, and I accompanied them to London—on the train—and bade them good-bye. I returned to Edinburgh and remained a year and a quarter. I continued preaching, receiving a call almost every weekend. I received a stipend and was reimbursed for travel expenses. On occasion I hitchhiked, and on occasion the experience turned out to be holy hitchhiking a foreign highway. I did not resume holy hitchhiking seriously as I had done my first time in Scotland; I was too busy doing research, and writing my dissertation, and trying to live on our meager savings, that I had little time for travel. Besides, I had already hitchhiked almost every road in Scotland in 1952-3. This time I was riding the train and bus on weekend assignments. The stipends I received for my services helped us pay our rent, about fifteen pounds ($35.) per month.

In the middle of the summer, I received a request from the Church of Scotland National Office to preach at Dornoch Cathedral. A Cathedral?

I had never heard of Dornoch, but I did not hesitate to accept the honor. I began to wonder if my warmed-over sermon with some embellishment could challenge a Cathedral Congregation? I decided it could, so I did some embellishing.

Saturday morning before the Sunday I was to lead the Dornoch Congregation in worship, I packed my clergy shirt, a clean pair of under shorts, my books and a briefcase and headed north. I took along pages of my dissertation. The day was pleasant, the train was comfortable, and the company in the compartment did not bother me. I had some sleep, I read up on Dornoch, and soon the train pulled into the station. The Clerk of the Congregation, Alexander Hamilton, met me. He helped carry my luggage and we headed out, walking to his home. Alexander did not own a car. He carried my lighter-weight bag. Upon arriving at his home, I discovered that he and his wife, Marie, operated a "Mom and Pop" store in the basement of their home. The Ice Cream Machine caught my attention immediately. I commented on how rare they are in Scotland. He had a tale to share. He was closing the shop one Saturday night, and Jesus and Satan showed up at the freezer. Satan tried to destroy it, Alexander declared. Jesus assured him, however, that the Devil had only done temporary damage. Have faith, and soon the machine would be repaired, and a significant source of his income would start flowing again. He asked me to be discreet about the incident. I promised him I would.

Alex then said that he and I would walk over to the Cathedral so I could become familiar with the setting and review worship procedures. We had another brisk walk. The Cathedral immediately stunned me; I had a deep feeling of humility. Time had arrived again for me to remember David's prayer when chosen as Israel's shepherd to replace Saul (previously quoted): "Who am I, O Lord, and what is my house that you have brought me thus far?" (I have frequently quoted those words when I have a challenge before me for which I have felt inadequate or undeserving.) I wanted to start preaching right away to the saints Biblically, historically, theologically, with whom I felt a mystic communion. After all, I say in the Creed, "I believe in…the communion of the Saints."

The Cathedral exterior immediately charmed me. The gargoyles at the ends of the roof dated to the eleventh century. The interior was traditionally Basilica, a long nave beginning a third of the way into the church and ending in the chancel, and a transept that completed the cross shape. The rectory for clergy preparation, dress and privacy looked and felt accommodating. Alexander brought me out of my reverie when he turned on the amplification system and it let out a screech that set my teeth on edge. From the control room he requested that I go to the lectern and pulpit for a voice tryout. He made some adjustment. He rejoined me, convinced that the preacher could, and would, be seen and heard adequately. The light oak colored Table of the sacrament, sitting on the nave level, rather than in the chancel—another one holding sacramental symbols sat appropriately in the chancel—reflected the rays of the late afternoon sun in the colors of the stained glass-welded windows. The chancel glass complemented the nave and transept for rich beauty and clarity. Typically, the seating was austere: wooden chairs, without cushions. The setting would surely have power to inspire esthetic inspiration in an atheist. More than fifty decades later pop-singer Madonna would exercise cultural class when she and her then partner, and the father of their infant son, would choose the Cathedral for their son's baptism. (The day after the rite the couple was married at the nearby Andrew Carnegie Skibo Castle. They have since divorced, and Madonna has attempted adoption of two Malawian Children. She has had some problems with the law, as of 11/09.)

Alex and I returned to his house—after a final check of the Public Address system—satisfied that we had meticulously taken care of all the details necessary for a flawless worship the next morning. Marie was preparing High Tea when we arrived. My sense of smell guessed that our entrée would be roast lamb, with the appropriate browned vegetables, including Brussels sprouts. My smell proved accurate. When dessert time came, Marie apologized that she could not embellish her Scottish trifle with ice cream; the machine was currently not working. I told her that Alex had shown it to me before we had made our trip to the Cathedral, and I had remarked about how fortunate they were to have such a machine in their store. She remarked that Alex had been so patient about having it repaired. Alex interrupted with a bottle of Scotch to "embellish" the trifle. He said that a repairman was coming on Monday. The weekend preacher missed the soft ice-cream treat. I vowed to myself not to bring up the "soft ice cream maker" topic again. I was, however, in luck with a remarkable future sermon illustration. Marie's trifle tasted great, as delicious as any I had eaten in Scotland—or had myself attempted to make—even without soft ice cream.

Bedtime at my host's household came earlier than usual for me. I needed, however, to take a few minutes to look over and make changes in my sermon that would adapt it to Dornoch. I also wanted to familiarize myself with the order of service that Alex had provided. In addition I needed his opinion about my success at hitchhiking back to Edinburgh. I needed a day off on the highway, and I could manage my wardrobe in my backpack as I had on so many previous occasions. I would make enquiry at breakfast, which, I was informed, would be served at 7:30 a.m. Worship was held at 10 o'clock.

If Jesus had visited the basement store that night, Satan had paid no attention; the Devil was too busy in my room, making my night miserable. Whether the cause was trifle or tea or lamb or a broken down ice-cream maker, I spent one of the most "insomnial" nights in the Hamilton's Guest Room that I had ever experienced before. I could not blame my wakefulness on anxiety or fear or insufficient preparation. My discomfort could be blamed on the hardest, lumpiest, padding-less bed I have ever lain in. The springs sprung so close to my back that I could count every one of them; there were twelve in the set. Few times have I prayed more feverishly for rest and for a quick end to the night. How could I stand in the ornate pulpit, in that reverently holy and aesthetically elegant sanctuary, and preach my leftover sermon? My lack of creative and fresh homiletical preparation would surely become awkwardly transparent. I could suffer a repeat of the rejection and threat of assault that was inflicted upon Jesus when he went home to preach in Nazareth. (Luke 4:16 ff.) How truthful would God expect me to be at the breakfast table when Alexander or Marie asked, "Did you sleep well last night?" I could possibly fake a choke and take a minute to return to a speaking voice, and the subject would have become irrelevant. I suddenly remembered that Jesus had told his disciples not to be anxious ahead of time about the answers they would give when brought before accusers for trial; the Spirit would supply an answer in case I were asked about my night. I prayed, "Come, Holy Spirit, come." Daylight was dawning. It was 5:00 a.m. Rising hour was 6:30. I groaned as I reminded myself that I had to spend another night with Alex and Marie.

Kippers were on the menu for breakfast. As with anchovies and kelp, kippers stayed in my taste for at least twelve hours after I had eaten them. I ate more toast than usual and apologized for not being able to finish the fish. I spoke of how delicious the toast was; it had been made from homemade bread. My uneaten kippers suddenly became the cat's breakfast.

Alexander and I left for the Cathedral shortly after eating and teeth brushing. The day surely dawned as one of Scotland's finest. Alex did his pre-worship chores, the organist arrived and we went over the service. I went to the vestry to make my "personal spiritual preparation," as Alex named it, and had either suggested the devotions as kindness or as a need. Either way, he was considerate in allowing me some time alone—with God. I feared lest I may fall asleep in the pulpit and end up like the proverbial preacher "Who dreamed that he was preaching, and he awoke, and he was!" I needed an injection of the faith Jesus had often instructed his disciples to exercise.

At 9:45 the Cathedral began to come alive, not only with the sound of music, but also with the chatter and laughs and voices of the arriving congregation. Alexander, who filled several positions essential to the smooth functioning of a cathedral, summoned me from the rectory, picked up the pulpit Bible, took his position in front of me, and entered into his role as Church Beadle. He preceded me into the sanctuary and placed the Bible on the Chancel Lectern. I felt that I looked adequately clerical for a cathedral; I had dressed in the robe hanging on the vestry door, and had placed my personal stole and cross where they belonged. As I had anticipated, and as Alexander had affirmed, approximately fifty parishioners were in attendance to hear my exposition of John 1:1-14. Hopefully they would think that I was preaching this sermon for the first time. The truth was that each week I revised it!

Worship started well. Folks seemed to give rapt attention to my Gospel exposition. Then suddenly Alexander's ice-cream nemesis showed up: the sound system became demon possessed. A screechy whistle and intermittent buzz became so unbearable that Alexander had to turn off the system. I spoke more slowly and loudly, but my voice barely held out until the Benediction. I did not encourage conversation, as my voice was already on the wane. After I had greeted the last person, I retreated to the vestry.

I was waiting for Alexander when a knock sounded on the door. I opened it to face a tall handsome Scot in uniform. He introduced himself as Ian McTavish, Helen Carnegie Miller's chauffeur. He extended a personal invitation to me from her: to come to Skibo for afternoon tea. He would "collect" me at Alexander's house at 3:00 p.m.

I had temporarily forgotten that Dornoch was Carnegie country, and that Skibo Castle was located in the area. I managed in my surprise to close my mouth, collect some spit, and thank Mr. McTavish for conveying the invitation. I would be delighted to accept. I requested him to thank Mrs. Carnegie Miller and tell her that I felt honored, and I would be ready to leave when he came to Hamilton's for me. I had had a few castle connections before, but never an invitation to tea with the owner.

I set out in search of Alexander to tell him of my fortune. He said he had just heard about it from Ian, and that Ian had just returned from talking with Mrs. Miller, and travel plans to the Castle had changed. She had met a retired clergy friend in the Cathedral Circle Drive. They had had a conversation. She had invited The Reverend Haimish Beckwith, and his wife, to join us for tea. They would call for me at Alexander's and take me with them to Skibo. Fine. I then became curious. I asked Alexander, "Was the lady in the blue chiffon dress and feathered hat Andrew Carnegie's daughter?" Alex asked, "How did you guess?" I smiled and shrugged my shoulders.

We walked "home" together, and Alexander filled me in on some of the history of Dornoch and the Cathedral. It was interesting, but I was sleepy. After a lunch of cucumber and salmon spread sandwiches and hot chips ("French fries" in American English) and biscuits (cookies)—Marie had obviously and thoughtfully suddenly come up with a menu that would not spoil my appetite for afternoon tea—I asked to be dismissed from the table. I enquired of my hostess whether she had any objection to my relaxing on a soft chair in their parlor. I obfuscated for my deception, like being able to rest better vertically after such a good tea. She gave me "leave" of their house. Did that include a different bed tonight? I was tempted to ask. I went to the parlor and took off my collar and rested. Marie awoke me at 2:30 p.m.

Beckwith's arrived promptly at 2:45. I immediately recognized them. Alexander made a formal introduction. I bade the Hamilton's farewell, entered the car with the Beckwith's, and we headed for Skibo. Haimish had interesting data to share about Dornoch that I had not yet heard. The few kilometers we traveled to the Castle were covered quickly.

Upon our arrival at the Skibo gate, a sentry waved us through. After going a few yards into the Castle grounds, it became necessary to weave around a Circle turn-around garden drive. Glancing about, my eye must have suddenly increased in pupil size. High up on a pole in the center of the Circle "Old Glory" was waving gently in the mid-afternoon Scottish breeze. I blurted out, "Oh, say can you see...." And Fiona Beckwith interrupted with, "God save our gracious Queen, God save..." We both laughed over our spontaneous patriotism. Mr. Beckwith pulled the car up to the wide steps leading to the large front doors of Skibo Castle. Ian was standing there ready to park our car.

Helen Carnegie Miller's Lady-in-Waiting came down the marble steps to meet and welcome us. She took us into the Great Hall (the Madonna marriage setting), where Mrs. Carnegie Miller was waiting to greet us. The Beckwith's shook her hand and greeted her with a verbal "Good Day," and I followed with the same gesture. I was wondering if I should kiss her hand, but she satisfied my quandary by reaching out her hand in a shaking position. She spoke kindly and complimentarily about my sermon and about the joy of the service. She and her Lady-in-Waiting ushered us inside to a most beautiful grand room. I pondered: was it the Castle parlor, or was it the tea room? In any case, it had to be one of the most elegant rooms that I had ever stepped into. Mrs. Miller began pointing out several salient features about the artifacts that she had inherited with the house (she was Carnegie's only offspring), and the native woods. We stepped back into the Great Hall, and we were oriented on the imported glass, the architect's redecorating touches, and the dignitaries who had once been welcomed into the house—including an American President or two. After a few other comments about the Mansion, Mrs. Miller led us into the drawing room where the tea table was set. She asked me about my wife and family, my ministry, and my studies at New College. The Beckwith's offered anecdotes as we shared the tea of sandwiches, biscuits, tarts, fresh fruits, and other sweets. I was suddenly becoming drowsy and feared that I may fall asleep, or say something disjointed or disconnected, or miss a question directed toward me. I asked about the grounds, the gardens, the animals, and the maintenance required. I received impressive answers.

Perhaps sensing my fatigue, Helen Carnegie suggested a walk around the gardens. We all were ready for it. She offered several unique comments about the Castle and its grounds and barns. The information proved intriguing. Details were provided on the number of bedrooms and baths at Skibo, on European dignitaries who had slept there, and on the size of the Castle Staff. She also scanned the history of her Father and Mother. He loved both Scotland and America, she related. She loved New York. I had several questions; raising them helped keep me awake and rational. I glanced across the gardens toward the Front Gate. Details were given about the Gate's design, the history of her Father's purchase of Skibo, his birthplace, some of his entrepreneurial excursions and world travels, and other family details. He had had a major voice in much of the Castle remodeling. She related that she had lived many years in New York, and that she had raised her three children there. (I regretted later, that as a Pennsylvanian and a Presbyterian, I had failed to ask her if she had any Pittsburgh connections.) No mention was made of her children's father. She was a grandmother. Family members occasionally accompanied her to

Skibo for summer "holidays," and when they were children they had spent a considerable amount of time there.

Our walk led around rose beds, perennial bushes, giant trees, pens of fowl and birds, and a variety of flora. In one turn the flagpole at the entry drive came into view. I stopped. Was I experiencing an anomaly or a fantasy? Was my fatigue skewing my reason? Old glory had disappeared, and the Union Jack was flying. I commented to Helen about it. (She had given permission for the informal and casual use of her Christian name. I did the same with mine.) Helen laughed, and said: "Vernon—by the way, Father would have been pleased with your Scottish surname—you were neither intoxicated with patriotism nor condescending to imperialism by your observation. Here is the situation: Father loved both the United States and Scotland so equally, that, even though Skibo is in Scotland, he did not want to show favoritism between his two nationalities. To install one flag above the other would betray a citizenship bias. So he had two flags sewn together—back to back!" And she concluded with, "Oh, say, may those two flags wave forever and together in unity and harmony, o'er the lands of the free and the homes of the brave. And God save the Monarchs of both!" We all concurred, and I thanked our hostess for her perpetuation of her Father's character and will. The sentiment raised chills on my back that beautiful sunny afternoon; I was walking grounds once walked by an American-British-British-American entrepreneur whose Scottish heritage and discipline and prosperity had made significant contributions to American industry and culture, and to many institutions in Scotland as well.

The long walk terminated at the front entrance to Skibo. Hamish's car was there. Tea and visiting time were over. As we said our cheerios to Helen and her Lady-in-Waiting, I reached out my arms to her, and she placed her cheek in front of my lips, and I gave her a kiss. She warmly accepted my expression of appreciation and admiration. I could not recall ever having kissed anybody so famous before, unless it had been that day in Indiana, Pennsylvania, when Jimmie Stewart's Mother happened to be in the hardware store as I stopped to say good-bye to Jimmie's Father, Alex, before leaving for Scotland. The Stewarts had surprised me with gifts from the hardware store's merchandise, including a small pocketknife that I still cherish (but never try to pass Security with on either foreign or domestic flights.) I gave Mrs. Stewart a kiss of gratitude, and she gave me one in return. I did not kiss Alex—Stewart, that is.

I had forgotten about an afternoon nap until we had arrived at Hamilton's front door. I suddenly felt exhausted. I thanked the Beckwith's for the ride, and I expressed a hope that we would meet again while I was still in Scotland; or perhaps sometime they would visit me in America. Hamish responded, "America? On a retired Scottish Pastor's salary?" They offered best wishes on my dissertation, and drove off. As we headed back into the house, Alexander and Marie wanted a running account of the Skibo visit. They had only been there once, on a tour, and Helen Carnegie Miller was not present. It had been in wintertime. I summarized my afternoon.

Marie prepared a light tea of eggs soufflé and sausages, and, especially for the American, a tossed salad, deviled eggs, and tarts. I apologized for not being hungrier, and the couple understood. And, they said, they had a surprise for me. Alex had gone down to the shop to tinker with the ice cream maker, and a miracle had happened: it was working. They had quickly frozen a few quarts. I woke up. I gorged my stomach on ice cream. I stayed up and talked until 9:00 o'clock. When I brought up the subject of hitchhiking back to Edinburgh, both of them again encouraged me. I had another dish of ice cream, and went to bed. Remarkably, I slept until Marie 'knocked me up' the next morning at 7:00 a.m. Following a substantial breakfast, I packed my shoulder-pack and prepared to leave. I said goodbye to Marie in the kitchen. Alex walked me to a lorry stop. As we shook hands, I offered a brief benediction, incorporating thanks for the ice-cream maker miracle. Alex responded sheepishly: "Marie doesn't know this, but the repairman couldn't come tomorrow. So he stopped by today while she was at a neighbor's; he broke Sabbath law and fixed it. Isn't that a miracle?" I said, "It's one hell of a miracle!" And we both laughed, and parted, doubting that we would ever see each other again—at least not in this world. Too bad!

*Masefield, John; *"The Coronation...Souvenir Programme,"* "Lines on the Coronation of Our Gracious Sovereign," p. 2.

CHAPTER III
_____

Four French Flights From:
A Flaming Truck Cab;
Christmas Eve Candle Wax;
Sheep on the Tarmac;
The Chiropractor's Maid.

"(The God of Daniel) is the living God,
enduring forever.
His kingdom shall never be destroyed,
and his dominion has no end.
He delivers and he rescues,
he works signs and wonders in heaven and on earth;
for he has saved Daniel from the power of the lions."

(Daniel 6:26-7.)

While hitchhiking in France on two different occasions I experienced four traveling adventures that had flight in common. Two of them occurred at the end of the first break from classes at the New College of the University of Edinburgh in Scotland, the Christmas-New Year's holiday time; the third and fourth happened after I had finished the academic year at the New College of the University, and was hitchhiking through France toward Israel.

The New College Christmas-New Year suspension of classes and lectures lasted more than three weeks. Part of the School Administration's logic could have been to save fuel, which was still rationed in Britain as a result of World War II austerity. New American students—and possibly other internationals—tolerated double deprivations, both food and coal rationing. The Scots—students and staff and Professors—had adjusted to the inconveniences. Several of us internationals, as well as some locals, wore "long johns" and double plies of wool sweater. On many occasions we never took off our outer coats during classroom lectures. Professors donned black gowns, which might have provided them a wee bit more comfort. The fireplace in my boarding room kept me warm most of the time, but landlady Annie occasionally reminded me of the coal limitations. Several professors had small electric heating devices in their University offices.

As the first term moved closer to its finish, the challenge of pursuing a Ph.D. degree began to occupy my mind more pervasively. I signed up for the program and was accepted into it; the Reverend Professor Doctor John Bailie was assigned as my Advisor. Professor Bailie, who had taught at the Auburn Seminary in New York some years, was a favorite among the American students. One reason for his popularity stemmed from his openness to students' questions during his lectures, and his amenability to classroom discussion. His teaching style reflected his time in the United States. He was also more personable than some of the other faculty; he and his wife occasionally extended "open house" to the American students. During the evening together the Professor shared anecdotes from his career that kept the group laughing continually. We American students loved Dr. John Bailie. I felt most privileged for my dissertation assignment with him.

In the few days following my acceptance as a Ph.D. candidate, I set about seriously making my plans for a three-week trip to the Continent. When the day of the beginning of the Winter Break arrived, I was packed and ready to depart Edinburgh. I was planning a hitchhiking tour of France and a brief excursion into Switzerland. Finally the day for departure arrived. I bade Annie and Leslie and Harald good-bye. I headed out on my usual route toward London: from Vanedleur Avenue to the Rt. 1 coastal highway south, and hitchhiking to England. I landed in London after an amazing hitchhiking record. I had even entered into occasional holy discussions. Once in London I headed for the B&B operated by Elise. I had obtained a reservation by mail, and we had worked out a front-door key arrangement in case I turned up late. I arrived at the B&B before Elise had turned out the lights. She welcomed me warmly.

My scheme for reaching the Continent worked out as easily as my hitchhiking to London. I took the train to Dover. The day advanced cloudy, and the white cliffs had hidden behind the clouds. The North Sea appeared to be misbehaving. The Ferry to Calais quickly loaded with passengers and cars. I started searching for a ride, hitchhiking first by mouth, rather than by thumb. My planned Phase 1—getting a free trip across the Sea with a driver who was traveling alone—failed. The time for the Ferry to leave was shortening. In order to leave on the boat I had to purchase a ticket. That contingency had not been part of my budget. I had not given up on obtaining a refund on my ticket once I had boarded the Ferry and located a car driven by someone who would take on a passenger.

As soon as I had boarded the Ferry I disregarded my bad luck at the car waiting area and headed to the lower car decks. I set out in search again for an auto with the driver as the sole occupant. Good fortune prevailed. I located a late model BMW with a driver who had laid back his head. Was he sleeping or sick? I wasn't too concerned. I tapped on his window and he perked up. I asked the mustached driver if he would give me a lift to Paris. He replied that he was going only as far as Rouen, but he would be delighted to have an American ride with him and keep him company. I reflected a moment on his quick perception of my nationality, and then I accepted his offer. He even offered to accompany me to the Bursar's window to redeem the fare that I had paid; he had no passengers traveling with him. We headed up the stairs for the ticket window together after I had placed my one piece of luggage, a fatly packed backpack, in his car. The refund transaction was completed without argument, and I was reimbursed. The two of us went to the Lounge. He bought enough tea and biscuits for both of us; we began a friendly acquaintance, at the same time watching as the boat moved farther out of sight of the Dover dock. Our crossing was choppy, but we were soon in Calais, and we headed for Rouen. The trip was pleasant. We had many interesting conversations, including discussion about the Anglican Church. By the time we arrived in Rouen it was dark. I found the Youth Hostel, bade my driver-donor farewell, paid for a night's lodging and went to bed.

I was up and out on the highway early the next morning—a chilly one—and after a croissant and coffee, I started hitchhiking my way south through France. I netted good fortune, not only free transportation, but on occasion a free meal, and on two chilly nights, overnight accommodations.

The first night was with a young man and his wife and children on a large farm; he had given me a long ride. Perhaps the American flag draped over my wrist had helped. Five years ago Pierre had spent a year in the U.S.A., in Iowa, learning the technique of "Confined Hog Raising." He had gone there on a scholarship from the Agriculture Ministry of France. His "payback" was not only to experiment with the technique on his own considerable family enterprise, but also to help other French hog-raisers. He said, "As you say in America, I am having the time of my life." I thanked him for the first of lucky nights I would enjoy in France. Pierre said, "I am pleased to do a favor for a person from a nation that has been so kind to me." I told him that his accountability to his family and government was considerable payback to the American farmer who had helped him.

Infrequent discussion of holiness emerged from my brief acquaintance with Pierre. He admitted that he had once had a very superficial relationship with the Church, Roman Catholic, of course. His best gift to me was a clue that had little to do with "Qadosh" but with hitchhiking in Europe: go to Lorry (truck) Stops and beg, and if it is morning, look for how many empty carafes are on the table. French truckers drink plenty of wine with their morning croissant; they are happy to give lifts to hitchhikers, he offered. "Even ones who don't speak French?" I asked. He came back with, "Did you never hear that the French are the best hand-talkers in the world? Even better than Jews." I said that I had heard the French boast before, and I would appreciate it and try to respond correctly. The next morning Pierre drove me to a Lorry Stop near his farm, and we bade each other farewell. "Remember," he said, "Lorry Stops. And empty carafes." I thanked him again, and he reached over and kissed me on both cheeks, then drove off.

I decided to follow through with his advice. I started searching for a ride with a trucker. I went into the café, bought a cup of coffee and started mingling with the eaters. My poor use of the French language presented a pitiful handicap, and my attempts at hand talk elicited laughs. I spent a half hour trying to communicate with some of the men—no women except the waitresses. Finally I found someone who expressed interest in a driver wanting company, and desirous of practicing speaking English. I asked him why I was having trouble persuading someone to give me a ride, aside from my awkward French. He said that there had been a recent murder of a driver by a hiker, but I should keep on trying. The word of the murder might not have yet spread universally. Drivers did not appreciate that kind of publicity, so they had done little talking about the incident.

We boarded his rig and he took me for one hundred fifty kilometers. I kept advancing south slowly, in cold weather. Night was moving in.

After a while, another vehicle stopped, an auto. When I reached the car, the driver opened the door and yelled out in American English, "Where ya' goin'?" I told him Montpelier. He said in broken English, "Long way off...not goin' that far...but I'll take you as far as I'm goin.'" I said, "OK." I moved up to his car and entered it. He seemed affable. He also seemed humble. He perceived that his poor use of English would prove embarrassing to him. I retorted, "I am a French language moron." He laughed. We had gone only a few kilometers when he started humming "The Star Spangled Banner." He pointed to me. I began to insert the words, and as he sang along, I was amazed to discover that he knew most of my national anthem, in English. I gave him a word of appreciation. He responded, "Thanks to TV and the Olympics!" I told him he had better stop the car so we could engage in the proper protocol: step on firm ground and stand at the side of the road, face west, and salute. He laughed. Our singing altered from patriotic to folk. He wanted me to teach him "Oh, Susanna...." and "Old MacDonald Had a Farm," and "Jingle Bells." I had a request of him: "Frara Jacque...." It was the closest I could come to pronouncing it. He knew what I had in mind. Then we turned "holy" to Christmas Carols. He knew a few words to "Away in a Manger" and "Silent Night." I asked him if he knew the tune "Fauxbordon," and he did. He sang a hymn to it, in French. He then confessed to me that he had taught choral music in elementary schools. After we had traveled a number of kilometers, he apologized for his poor English and expressed regret that he was not traveling farther. He also encouraged me to resume "Lorry-Stop Hitchhiking." He went ten kilometers farther south than the road to his house, in order to drop me off at a mammoth "BMP Truck Stop." I thanked him. He told me that he was bringing his wife and family to Disneyland in two years. I suggested that he look me up, if he could find me. I informed him that I lived in a part of the U.S.A. that was a long way from Disneyland. I gave him my current address. We wished each other the best of luck. His name was Lavoir. I was sad at leaving him, not only because he was so affable, but also because it had turned dark, and I was turning apprehensive.

As soon as Lavoir had driven away, I started checking with truck drivers. None of them spoke English, or at least none admitted to it. However, they understood my pidgin "Ou alle vous?" I had decided that the only way I was leaving the Lorry Stop at this hour of the night was in a truck going either to Montpelier or Marseille; or to one that may park for a few hours of the night and had sleeping space for two. I finally met luck. A driver who seemed safely sober—he had only one empty carafe at his table—indicated that he was headed for Montpelier, and yes, I could sleep in his cabin bunk if I chose; he would probably not sleep again until he had arrived in Montpelier. How fortunate! We went to his rig, and I decided to sit in the cab at the beginning of the trip. I told him that perhaps I would climb up into the bed later. "OK," he said in English. Ferdie, the driver, started his big motor and pulled out onto the highway. The night was black and the highway was busy, mostly with trucks. I was groggy. Ferdie assured me that he had already had his nap at the last stop. I nodded peacefully off to light sleep. I should have stayed awake; I was about to be jolted into a French flight.

In less than an hour erratic driving awakened me, and I sensed that Ferdie was anxious. Maybe his wine consumption was wreaking its havoc. He seemed to be searching for something. He suddenly slammed on the brakes, pulled the rig off the highway, turned off the motor, raised the hood, shortly closed it, re-entered the cab, and steered the truck back onto the highway. He said nothing to me. But he appeared uncomfortable. I was satisfied that we would be arriving at our destination in a few hours. I knew it was needless to ask Ferdie about his vehicle concern. I lay my head back and anticipated more rest.

Before I could doze off, I realized that the engine was making an abnormal sound. It was not performing "on all cylinders." I smelled an odor like an overheated radiator. The noise grew louder, and "crankier." Emergency lights flashed on the dashboard. The motor stopped. Sufficient power was available, however, for the Ferdie to steer the behemoth off the road. As soon as it came to a stop, he motioned for me to evacuate the cabin immediately, and move away from the crippled rig. I grabbed my backpack and headed out onto the highway. I had only walked a short distance away from the vehicle when I heard a loud swishy boom. I looked back and discovered that the cab was engulfed in flames. I shuddered. I saw Ferdie move away. I satisfied myself that he was a reasonable distance from the fire. He had not been able to contain the fire before it struck fuel. If I had stuck around or returned to the fire, I would only be in the way, and might have met with a worse fate. Meanwhile, the reduced and slowed-down night traffic allowed "gawkers" a comprehensive view of the scene. Someone, no doubt Ferdie, began placing torches around the wreck. Where was the fire department? Where were the gendarmes? Cars were traveling in both directions very slowly. One with red flashing lights soon appeared, and stopped.

I watched from a distance as the fire subsided, and I observed that fire extinguishers were in action. I suddenly realized that I was feeling cold, and I walked a few more yards. I really wanted to avoid the scene, and I wanted a ride. Gendarmes started arriving from both the north and the south. Eventually the scene went dark, except for flashing red lights and individual flashlights. Promptly a car slowed down; the driver had apparently caught sight of my thumb, and he drove off to the side of the road. The passenger door opened. Two men were inside. The driver invited me into the auto. As soon as our doors had closed, the two men asked if I had any idea about what had happened. I told the men that I had just left the truck, that it had developed trouble a few kilometers back, but that the driver had hurried me out of it, and I moved a good distance away from it. I was certain that the driver was safe. The driver, whose English was efficient, enquired whether I needed medical help. I told him I had evacuated the truck just in time. He wanted to know if I had any clues as to what had caused the conflagration. I told him I did not, except that the trouble had appeared to start in the engine or around the radiator. They gave no hint that they suspected me of any culpability in the fire. I had convinced them that I had safely and innocently survived my first French flight. Both men laughed softly.

The driver—neither of the passengers had shaken my hand nor offered their names—said that were traveling only a few kilometers, and that there was rail service in the next city, where we would arrive shortly. The city has a railroad hotel located on the main line that went to Montpelier and Marseille. Both men recommended that I spend the night there and take the train to Montpelier in the morning. It was too dangerous for me to be hitchhiking French highways this hour of the night. I could easily arrive in Montpelier before noon, and then I could enjoy Christmas Eve with whomever I was visiting. A few more questions were raised about the accident, but I had little further to offer.

We arrived at the Railroad Hotel and I checked in, and within thirty minutes, after I had checked out the morning train schedule, I was in bed, asleep, but not before I had prayed: "Oh, Jesus, thank you for my escape from a French Flight—out of the cab of a burning truck. I pray that the driver is OK. Bless Marjorie.… " Surely a holy presence had been with the driver and me in the flight from the truck. What an Advent gift! I felt anxiety about the driver, but I quieted my fears by remembering my last sight of him: a distance away from the conflagration. "Lord, I hope…" I prayed. I slept well and responded promptly to a wake-up call. I showered and dressed, lounged in the Hotel dining room over coffee and croissants, and was ready to go south when the train arrived. I phoned my Montpelier contact, Madame Prousant, and gave her the details of my arrival. She gave me the good news that she would meet me at the train. I thanked her and told her that I had an amazing flight tale to relate. She responded that she was anxious to hear about it. I was amazed at her ability with the English language.

Madame Prousant held the position of Librarian at the Reformed (Protestant) Seminary in Montpelier. Two Columbia, Georgia, Presbyterian Seminary students who had become friends on the *S.S. Ryndam* during the September sailing had spent time with the Madame during their tour of southern France, and they had stopped in Edinburgh on their way home to the U.S. The Columbia Seminary had a close relationship with the Montpelier Institution; they had Professor and Future exchanges yearly. The students told me about Madame Prousant and her close contacts with their American Seminary. Her husband, a brilliant young theologian, had died shortly after the Second World War as a result of an illness related to his activity in the French Resistance movement. The Nazis had imprisoned him for some time.

The Seminary students had given me Madame Prousant's name and address and phone number, and they were certain that she would be willing to be of assistance to me if I were to visit Montpelier. She was appreciative of the contribution Presbyterians in the United States had made to the Montpelier Institution. Her French Protestant missionary parents—her Father was clergy—had spent their careers as missionaries in the Cameroon, Africa. She shared an apartment with them. I had written her, and she had related all this information to me in her response to my letter received before I had left Edinburgh.

The train arrived in front of the hotel on time. I boarded and found a comfortable coach seat, and had a comfortable ride to Montpelier. The train arrived on time. As soon as I exited the coach and was on the platform, I caught sight of a sign with my name, and a beautiful woman holding it. She was obviously the Madame. We met with a handshake and an embrace, and left on foot for the nearby Hotel where she had made a reservation for me. She apologized for not being able to accommodate me at her home. She repeated the information about the compactness of her living accommodations. I told her that I understood, and that I had not expected her to take in an American stranger. I just felt most fortunate to be in a foreign land with Christian acquaintances on Christmas Eve Day, and for a short time thereafter.

Madame Prousant had worked out a comprehensive schedule for my visit: that evening, Christmas Eve, I would have a light supper with her parents and her, and afterward we would attend services at her Reformed Church; we would then participate in the midnight mass at the Roman Catholic Cathedral. She had purchased the necessary tickets. On Christmas Day I was invited to have early-afternoon Christmas dinner—of duck— with her and the family, and we would spend the afternoon listening to Handel's "Messiah" broadcast over the Radio, Station BBC, London. Her schedule sounded as if it promised me a concentrated, yet spiritually refreshing and relaxing holy experience, one of the best since leaving the U.S.A. Especially significant was the fact that I was visiting the land where John Calvin had been born four-hundred-fifty years ago, and I planned on my way back North to stop in his city of many years of work and ministry, Geneva, Switzerland. (The year, 2009, was the five-hundredth anniversary of his birth.)

After a simple Christmas Eve supper with the Madame and her parents—not the oyster soup tradition of my childhood and youth—we started walking to her Church. The aging parents kept up to our gait. By the time we arrived, the Church had filled. We located seats in the balcony. Madame Prousant had a surprise for me: a professor and his wife, and their young son, who had been friends on the *S.S. Ryndam,* were waiting for us. They were spending a year in Montpelier, where he was a visiting professor at the University. Ours was a cheerful reunion. Another cheer was deserved for our location; it offered us one of the best views in the house, in the right front balcony. As I gazed around the simple but attractive interior, my eye caught sight of a large unlighted Christmas tree loaded with candles in the chancel opposite us. It was amply decorated, but not one candle was burning. At the moment I had no clue, but I was not long away from my second French Flight.

The Church service began with pageantry that involved live animals and climaxed with an infant human. The most dramatic moments—and most frightening for me—arrived when acolytes started putting flame to the waxed candles. Nightmares of the truck ablaze returned. I sat tense. Finally the whole church was filled with real candlelight. The scene was impressive. I had never experienced one like it. The heat began to permeate the balcony. I had always wanted to officiate a live-candle gesture at a Christmas Eve service in an American Church, but the local Fire Department said, "Absolutely not! Your fire insurance will be cancelled if you do!"

I looked around the balcony area, but I did not see any fire extinguishers—metallic or human. There surely must have been gallons of water available nearby! The service moved beautifully. Colorfully robed clergy and liturgists led us. The Christmas Message was delivered, the choir sang, the animals behaved, the congregation joined in singing French carols from a hymnbook. Occasionally during the service the Madame softly whispered interpretations to me. Her calm assuaged my homesickness. To add to the heat, and to accentuate the hazard, candles had been passed out to the worshipers for lighting during the singing of "Stille Nacht, heilige Nacht." The incandescent lights were extinguished. Ushers lit the candles of aisle-seated worshipers, who passed their light to a neighbor. The Service ended with blazing illumination and accelerated heat. Many of the balcony worshipers had removed capes and coats, all of us controlled and confined to where we were intended to be on this holy night. In a few hours Christmas Day would be here, and here I am in France, and my closest loved ones would be celebrating approximately eight or nine hours later in Kansas and Pennsylvania. Jesus Christ was being honored and praised in many parts of the world. The creed said, and I spoke it in English, "We believe in one Holy Catholic Church." Hallelujah for the holiness of our unity. I had hitchhiked thus far to enjoy it. Words came back to me, "Who am I, O Lord, and what is my house?" I soon dismissed my fear over the burning candles. In fact, as the service was closing, I was planning on how I could persuade the elders in Ohio to have live-burning candles at Christmas Eve Services in the Cadiz United Presbyterian Church in 1953. Of course, we would have to bribe the Fire Department! Unlikely! I concluded that I needed to absorb as much of the holiness of this service as I could; live candles would not be lit on a Christmas tree at the church in Ohio.

As we left the Church and went out into the chilly night air, the Christmas tree candles were still aflame. I presumed sentinels were watching over it. We went out into the chilly night. The American Professor and his wife and son joined us, and we headed for the Prousant home for coffee and cookies. The Madame's parents tuned in to a BBC Christmas Eve service in English. After food and fellowship, she and I accompanied the Professor and his family to their bus stop and waited till their bus arrived. We then headed for the Cathedral.

As in the service at Madame's Church, a sell-out crowd had already gathered at the large edifice. We were ushered to our seats. Madame had selected well; we found ourselves in the second row. I enjoyed the beauty and dignity of the pomp and ceremony and music of the service, and I opened myself to as much of the spirit as I could understand. I nevertheless felt nostalgic about the special past Christmas Eve services that I had help create and choreograph and conduct "back home." As the choir assisted beautifully with the mass, I consoled myself with the reminder of God's special event in Bethlehem heralded by an angel choir. The Birth of Jesus the Prince of Peace could not have been celebrated in any more holy and sincere a manner. At the climax of the service, the large tree with candles was spotlighted, and acolytes in robes began the lighting. I quietly breathed a prayer that they would prove as steady of arm as the lighters at the Protestant Church. They met the test, and the Cathedral showed off its splendor when electric lighting gave way to flaming candles. At the end of the benediction I said to myself, "I have just survived French Flight 2B." (2 A had happened at the Reformed Church.) As we left the Church I assured the Madame that I could find my way to the hotel, if she would be safe making her way home by herself. Both were only a block or two away. She said that she had taken the walk home alone on Christmas Eves for several years, and she was more concerned about me than herself. I felt assured of her safety, and after going over the plans for Christmas Day, we parted with a hug and a "Good night."

Christmas with Mme. Prousant and her family unfolded as she had planned. She had come for me at my Hotel and we walked to the home she shared with her parents. It was simple, comfortable, and modestly decorated. The love expressed by its occupants helped forestall any homesickness and loneliness I might have felt on the occasion. A deep, seasonal spirit united me to the humble and holy presence of the devout, holy people. Madame had alerted me to the fact that she and her family observed reverent silence during the "Messiah" broadcast. I complied. The time together with Handel's music without interruption by conversation proved a holy experience. I wrote in my journal of the blessings of my first foreign Christmas Observance. I had experienced mystic communion, not only with devout French friends, but also with Joseph and Mary and their baby—except that they had spent the night in a cattle-shed. As soon as the broadcast had ended, I presented modest gifts to Madame and her parents: "real" Parker fountain pens from the United States. I went to bed early that night, earlier than I could ever remember retiring on Christmas

Night, but probably not as early as when I was a child living with my parents and siblings. Before I slept, I said, "Thank you, Heavenly Father, for a double French flight from burning candles." And seemingly, God and I in unison said, "Amen."

Madame Prousant came to the Hotel the next morning to accompany me to an appropriate hitchhiking spot—a lorry stop. She pushed her bicycle while I walked alongside. The stop was located on the main road leading to the French Riviera Highway. She and I chatted along the way, and I was overflowing with the joy of my Christmas 1952 with her and her family. She flattered me by saying that it had been one of their most memorable Christmases since her husband had died; they had never before entertained Americans on the Holiday. I reciprocated by repeating that I would never forget my Christmas in Southern France, including the flight from both a potential Protestant and Roman Catholic Christmas Eve candle-wax fire. She laughed and said, "I risk it every year." I told her that I hoped she could have an American Christmas some time. She hoped so, too. I again expressed appreciation for her and her parents' hospitality; and for steady-handed waxed candle lighters at both churches. We both chuckled and hugged and separated. She took off on her bicycle, and I stuck out my thumb.

My third and fourth French Flights took place at the end of my academic year in Scotland. I planned a major excursion across France to Greece and then to Israel. I checked my luggage through to Southampton, and arranged to have it held for the late July sailing of the new ship, the SS United States. In the meantime I would travel light, with a medium-size backpack. As soon as the term was over, therefore, I bade my friends farewell, said a tearful good-bye to Annie and Leslie and Bill and Harald at the house, and left Scotland with the part- sentimental, part-academic thought: "I wonder when and if I will ever see Edinburgh again. I want the Ph.D., so I expect I will return in a few years."

I headed for the Princess Street Station. I would make my last 1953 trip to London by rail. When I arrived at Victoria Station I made arrangements for the Southampton pickup of my baggage by the "U.S. Shipping Lines" for travel on the SS United States, the same sailing I would take in July. I had one last night at the familiar B&B. In the morning Elise had a small gift for me. I was lucky that it was small and flat—embroidered handkerchiefs that she herself had made.

I followed the same transportation schedule to the Continent that I had taken at the Winter Break. I arrived at the Ferry Dock too late for car solicitation; autos were already driving on board. I decided to try to spot drivers in the refreshment lounges, and if not successful there, I would head down to the car dock and see if I could awaken a sleeping driver—in a big, comfortable car. In the meantime I began to enjoy a cup of strong French coffee. A man also drinking coffee came and sat down at my table. We began talking, he in a British accent. He introduced himself as Arthur. He was driving to Rouen. I asked him if he had room for a passenger. He said he would be happy to have my company.

I silently thanked God for my good fortune in obtaining this ride. In the course of our conversation, Arthur expressed interest in my Ph.D. Dissertation topic. I outlined some of my themes that I was beginning to research. After some choppy waves, and not too soon for me, the Ferry's speaker system announced that we were about to dock in Calais. Arthur and I returned to the Car Deck and settled into the luxury and comfort of Arthur's car. Ours was one of the first to leave the boat. We drove onto a well-paved, smooth French highway.

I momentarily entertained a concern about how good hitchhiking would be after Rouen. My worry was brief, for as we headed to the Cathedral city and sped along, meeting and passing several other cars— most often at the speed limit, sometimes a little more—I manipulated conversation toward Church and Faith. I was disappointed that Arthur had no connection with either, and showed little interest in further discussion of personal religious experience. My dissertation on miracles had lost its appeal to him; he had been interested primarily for academic discussion and an opportunity for him to express his skepticism.

Arthur partly compensated for my disappointment later. He related that his elder son, on the day of his confirmation for church membership, had said something to the effect that he believed in miracles. The conversation went no further. Arthur trusted medical science and the chemistry of healing more than alternatives. (His son became a physician.) He finally admitted that he was a professor at an English University, and he had decided to take a break when an opportunity arose for him to travel to the Continent. He was driving the BMW to a new purchaser. He offered that he occasionally engaged in new car delivery service, and once in a while he rented a car for a few days while in France. He informed me that he had been divorced for several years, but he had a special French friend in Rouen.

We arrived at our destination too soon. Arthur was willing to take me through the city—it was on his way, he said—to an Eastern suburb.

I said that since I was in Rouen, and if it were not too complicated for him or presumptive of me, I would like to spend an hour at the Rouen Cathedral. He was delighted to deliver me there. He stopped directly in front of the magnificent Church. He refused my suggestion for the two of us taking an hour tour of the Cathedral together. I claimed my backpack, and we bade each other good-bye and went our separate ways. I had mixed feelings about our not traveling together farther, but they gave way to my anticipation and exclamation: "What an introduction to France!" Following my hour in the Cathedral I headed for the Youth Hostel, where I spent the night. The next morning I took a bus to the intersection of the major highway heading south, and stuck out my thumb.

A shiny sedan approached, with two passengers. The driver pulled off to the side of the road, rolled down his window, and called back to me in his native tongue. Any communication beyond "Bon jour. Parlez vous Francais?" was, at this point, beyond my French Language expertise. Oh, yes, I had memorized, "Ou alle vous..." or something like that—"Where are you going?" I hurried to the car, hoping that it was traveling non-stop to Paris. The passenger door opened, and an attractive woman stepped out and began to enter the rear passenger space behind the driver. She welcomed me to come and enter their car.

Both she and the driver spoke slightly more English than I spoke French, but they perceived by my accent that I was an American. It was agreed that we could engage in communication in each other's language and receive a brief education as we traveled together. We had a delightful beginning. However I conceded that their English was so much better than my French that I would be willing to forget trying to communicate in their language. For the next several kilometers, therefore, English became our exclusive language of conversation. I thought it a strange question when the Monsieur asked, in English, "You like to fly?" Perceiving that he meant, did I prefer flying to driving, hitchhiking or rowing, I answered positively. He said something like, "Tres bon; we fly." I was confused, but my confusion turned out to be short-lived. In a few kilometers, the driver—who told me his name was Avide—turned onto a graveled side road. I muttered some concern, and the man smiled and said, "Don't worry." As I was wondering if I were being kidnapped, the Madam reached up to me with a map and pointed out where we were.

Shortly we pulled into a field occupied solely by a barn and a flock of sheep. The car stopped alongside the building. The husband and wife—I assumed that they were married to each other—walked toward the big door, unlocked it, and started sliding it open. A small plane came into sight. The two went to the Piper Cub-sized craft, and started pulling it out on the grass. They locked their car doors and led me to the plane. I was beginning to comprehend what was in store, but I was nevertheless apprehensive. The couple was taking me on a plane ride. I had no reason to suspect that I was being kidnapped. I wondered if the pleasure would interfere with my plan to arrive in Paris before nightfall. What if the plane crashed? What about my identity? Would my passport survive? And how about the "Black Box"—if the plane carried one?

The wife—whose name I learned was a common French one, "Gigi"—scrambled into one of the two back seats. Avide helped me into mine, then climbed into his, turned the engine's key, and amazingly the plane started without prop assistance. As the plane taxied the field, he looked over at me with a captivating French grin, and said, "We fly." I looked around for a parachute. Avide perceived my anxiety and leaned toward me and said, "They are under the seats." The wife called my attention to the map, which now rested on my lap, to identify places of interest. My enjoyment of the couple and my comfort with the flight began to increase; I breathed deeply, exhaled, and said, "God, be praised." I perceived that I was not being taken way off my course toward Paris. If any impediments to our flight arose, I prayed that I would flee them.

After approximately one-half hour, we arrived at a less populated area, and Avide indicated that our flight was about to end. Fortunately our course had followed the route I had been hitchhiking. He indicated that we had covered one hundred kilometers. The plane began descending. I looked for a runway, but all I saw was a hay field, similar to the one from which we had taken off. The sheep occupying it began to scramble. They seemed alarmed and perhaps scared by the noisy plane over their terrain. Avide swept the field once, and the sheep scattered. He repeated his scare tactic, and the ewes and rams cooperated. He turned to me and smiled, appearing satisfied with his having created an instant landing space. He put the plane down smoothly, with only one or two bumps due to rocks hidden under the grass. He taxied to one end of the field and then back toward a building big enough, I surmised, to be the plane's home-away-from home. Avide laughed when I told him my guess. He and Gigi would return the next day to the spot from which we had flown.

The field we were landing on belonged to his father-in-law, and he and the two were planning an overnight visit with_them. He turned off the engine, hopped out, came to my door and helped me exit, followed by

Gigi, We all enjoyed a big stretch; each of us kissed each other—on both cheeks—and then said our good-byes. I headed for the highway, which Gigi indicated extended the same route that I had been hitchhiking. I yelled back at them, "Don't expect this kind of hospitality when you come to visit me in the United States!" They laughed again, and waved good-bye. I headed for the road, saying to myself, but far enough away from the waving couple that they could not hear me, "I have just survived my third French flight—in the air, with a hayfield as the tarmac and animals and buried ruts or protruding rocks our only threats to a safe landing!" The sheep had cooperated. Now they were beginning to return to the area where we had landed. I walked over to the highway, exulting over the flight. I headed south; I would re-visit Paris on my return hitchhike through Europe after my time in Egypt and Israel, and places in between.

I obtained several rides going south. I spent the next two nights in hostels, stopping relatively early in the evening. Daylight was extending, and I was making the best of it. I was not going to risk another nighttime flight from a flaming truck. I may not be so lucky again.

I was on the road by 7:00 a.m. in the morning. I draped my American flag over my wrist and gradually knocked off the miles of the long haul to Marseille. I was fortunate to find a ride with a family who were planning to bypass the city. They dropped me off on the Riviera Route. I headed for Cannes and Nice. The weather reminded me of Florida. For some reason—I later learned it was a provincial holiday—hitchhiking along the beautiful Mediterranean proved disappointing. It was pitiful compared with my first couple of days in the Country. I gave moderate credit to the American flag for the short rides I obtained. Most of the to-and-from Marseille drivers ignored me. One auto gave me a horn honking. I followed the car a few yards with glares and I let out an epithet, "Why didn't you stop, @#%*?"

It took me until early afternoon to come within a few miles of Cannes. My disappointment disappeared when a clean shiny car pulled off to the shoulder of the road, and the driver—a handsome young Frenchman probably my age or younger—motioned for me to come and enter the car. He stepped out and put my backpack among many of his belonging in the trunk. Back in the car, and in traffic again, Larois—he wanted to be called by his American name, Larry—introduced his Father and Mother; and I told them my name. Larry reached around and shook my hand, as did his parents. They were returning from a short vacation weekend trip to Marseille. They lived in Cannes.

"Where are you from?" Larry asked. (He had a quasi-American accent.) I told them about my American residence, and my studies in Scotland. I continued, "I am a Protestant Priest, a Presbyterian Clergyman." Larry laughed, and after he explained my comment to his folks, they laughed also. He congratulated me on my profession, and lightheartedly addressed me, "Father." He turned around and grinned. I asked him about himself. He filled me in: he was a Chiropractor, one of thirteen in all of France, and the only one between Cannes and Nice. He had studied at the world-famous chiropractic school in Davenport, Iowa. He had an Office in Nice, and his practice included patients—and an occasional tourist—from several miles along the Riviera coast. He asked me where I was spending the night. I told him I was planning on locating at the Youth Hostel. (Larry regularly translated parts of our conversations to his parents.)

When we reached the outskirts of Cannes, Larry made a generous offer. He had talked to his parents, and he said that they had all agreed that he had better housing to offer than a Youth Hostel: I could spend the night in his chiropractic office. He had a comfortable couch and his mother would make bedding available. He went on: "You will be sleeping in the safest place in southern France. My office is directly across the street from the Communist Party Headquarters for the area. The facilities were bombed a week ago, and ever since, the place swarms with security officers. I even leave my car parked there at night." The location sounded ideal, and who could or would match the price? I said I would be honored to accept the hospitality. Larry responded, "Good. We will take Mother and Father home, unpack the car, have a supper, and as it turns dark I will take you to a spot where you can see the American Navy 7th Fleet. And if you are not too tired, we can travel around the area and take in some night activities. We can also stop by a bar or two." I told him I was overwhelmed with his generosity, and I would place myself completely in his hands, except that I do not drink alcohol—only a little wine. I added, "I would like to experience as much of the ambiance of the French Riviera as you have time and energy to show me." He said, "Very good, Yankee Vern." And again, he humored his parents by telling them what I had said; and how he had made an overnight housing offer to me. They seemed pleased.

We turned off on a side street. Red flags were flying and guards were milling on both sides of the street. Larry parked the car next to the curb and took me inside to show me around. He revisited our evening schedule and wondered if I needed a brief sleep. I assured him that I would enjoy the night tour, and that I could rest tomorrow—at least until he began receiving patients, or kicked me out of his office. He laughed, and said, "I am not a jackass! Besides tomorrow is still a holiday." He concluded, "God will be watching over you." I asked, "And the Communists, too?" He wasn't sure, but he offered, "At least the sentries won't charge; and neither will I!" I thanked him again. He gave me another brief orientation to his office. I congratulated him on the Davenport, Iowa, Chiropractic Diploma hanging on his office wall. I was aware of the reputation of the Institution. (Years later I would live near Davenport and would occasionally drive by the School.) Larry's sleeper sofa looked so comfortable that I was ready to drop on it immediately, but Larry had better plans. And I was ready to be a good sport about them. Larry's parents had waited in the car. They were both napping when we returned.

We entered the car—waving to the Red Sentries, who ignored us—and he drove to his home. I helped the family unpack from their weekend trip, and his mother began kitchen activity. His Father was a physician, and he obviously made good money. Larry showed me around, including his large private bedroom where he had an office-away-from-the-office. The house was expansive and artfully decorated. The artwork, though not all of Louvre quality, was nevertheless impressive. Madame wanted to serve me a cocktail. I said that I preferred a soft drink, if they had something. She promptly came up with a can of Coca Cola and a large glass filled with ice cubes. She made a remark and Larry translated: "Larry became coke-addicted in America." The revelation brought laughs. We sat down to drink, and with Larry helping, his Father told me about the rest of the family. (I gathered that the Chiropractor was having a romantic relationship with a beauty from Nice.) His Mother brought sandwiches and coffee. The sky started darkening. Larry intimated that he and I should prepare to leave. I said "Good-bye" to his parents, gave his mother a kiss and his father a handshake, complemented them on Larry, and we drove off in his comfortable Renault.

We headed down to the Sea. My soul feasted with both pride and prejudice when we arrived where we could see the 7th Fleet ships. The boats were be-flagged and brilliantly lighted. What a view! Some were decked with red, white and blue plastic streamers and bunting. We stopped momentarily by his office. He listened to his messages and wrote his phone number on a pad on his desk. He enquired if there were any other conveniences he could supply—including access to his wine shelf. I could think of none. I asked him where he stashed his coke, and he opened a closet door and told me I could drink as much as I wanted. Moving toward the front door, he said, "Well, then, Monsieur American, we are off to see the French Rivera, more beautiful in Cannes than in any other location." "Including Paris and Versailles?" I asked. He quickly answered, "You don't know your geography. The Seine could not accommodate these boats." He locked his office door and slightly thumbed his nose at the red-uniformed sentries. They had apparently taken the gesture as a wave of honor. They saluted us. We entered the car and promptly drove away. He responded with a sweeping wave.

The sky had darkened. The sights stood out spectacularly. Larry drove to a hilltop parking space for a better view of the harbor. We passed by expensive homes and golf clubs and theaters. We visited two nightclubs. While my host drank "hard liquor," I sipped lemonade. It was long past midnight. We drove a few miles out of the city to a bakery, famous all over France, and even in neighboring countries. We headed for the "Dough Room," where we found the Chief Baker tramping or kneading the dough in his bare feet, a first-time seen scene for me. Larry said the baker does it nightly. They were friends, and, in fact, the Baker was one of his patients. Larry called him to the side of the dough bin and asked him to give me a taste of it—that is, if I wanted it. I wanted a fistful, and that is what the Baker brought me. I ate it all. Larry told the stomper that I was American. He welcomed me again and gave me a brief description of the precise process of baking classical French bread, from the measuring of the flour by the barrel full, to the weighing of the yeast by the pound, to the preparation of the gallons of water-milk-olive oil solution, to the number of workers it took to fill the pans and mix the dough, and the size and temperature of the ovens. I told Larry to tell his friend that I bake the best bread in Ohio, one loaf at a time, in a bread maker. When the Baker heard the translation, he returned to his kneading, and stomped out his laughs in the dough. (I began to understand why he needed Larry's services.) Before we left, our host made sure that each of us carried out a loaf of bread and one-half dozen of rolls. He took time to tell Larry more details about his marketing process, and Larry translated for me. He called one of his workers to provide his visitors with complimentary pastries and hot coffee, obviously not decaffeinated; it tingled my brain and propped open my eyelids.

We headed out of the bakery and drove to Nice. Larry teased me with a quick tour through "sleaze." He asked me if I wanted quick service. I responded with a wry smile, and continued, "I'm engaged, you know! And a student of theology!" He returned with a wry smile. We passed several busy streets, pubs and clubs—including gay ones—and parked in front of a place with a well-lighted marquee and several men and women loitering and seemingly making transactions on the street. Larry said, "Drug dealing; it is rampant in there. And sex is offered upstairs." Larry asked me if I wanted to go inside and observe sexual favoring firsthand; I could even take photos. He offered that for the sake of his reputation, he would have to wait outside—a block away. I told him that I had already walked the famous street in Hamburg, Germany, and I reported to him about the twitch I was at the moment feeling in my conscience as I recalled his earlier comment: "God will be watching over you." He humored me with, "Maybe God has fallen asleep." I quoted Psalm 121:4, "He who keeps Israel neither slumbers nor sleeps." That brief holy moment compensated for not having had many religious thoughts all day. It led to some other conversation about the Church in France, which Larry had abandoned years ago.

Although the night had given way to early morning, Larry had one more stop on our to-see list on the return trip to Cannes: a factory where Asian women sat for hours at sewing machines, making designer bathing suits; the factory stayed open twenty-four hours a day, five days a week. We went into the sewing hall for a few moments. The manager was a patient of Larry. He enlightened me about the producing and marketing of the apparel. He would not talk to me about wages and benefits. Finally, we stopped by a gourmet restaurant for a very, very early, very, very special eggs benedict croissant.

We finally arrived at Larry's office. He parked out front, reviewed the setup again, laid out the bedding, checked to see if he could do any other service for me, and then said, "Good night." As he went out the front door, I called out to him, "God will be watching over you." He smiled and thanked me and added, "And you, too," and then he headed for the street. He had hardly left till the door opened, and it was Larry, and dangling a set of car keys in his hand, he asked in an uncanny teasing voice, "Do you want me to leave you a set of car keys?" I pointed toward the door and said, "Go home!" He laughed and left. I was certain that he would be as safe on his walk to his parent' house as his car would be on the street; and as safe as I would I be on the couch.

I made my bed, cared for my toilette, stretched out under the covers, and finally fell asleep; but not before repeating my nighttime prayers, concluding with King David's old question, "Who am I…?" I fell asleep before I could finish it. As I was having my last moments of consciousness,

I recalled that Larry had told me that I could stay in bed as late as I wished. The day was a holiday, and he had no scheduled appointments.

As I slept, I slipped into a nightmare. A woman was being raped—but not by me—and she was screaming. The scene and the noise proved so close and so loud, and the actions so violent and brutal, that I awoke in panic. As my consciousness became clearer, I began to realize that I was in the midst of a reality as macabre as my dream: a female was screaming loudly. I rose up and put my feet out on the carpet, temporarily forgetting that I was in my typical sleep wardrobe: under shorts. I quickly draped myself in a sheet. The woman was standing in the office doorway shaking her fist and trembling. She signaled that she wanted me to stay away from her. She pointed to the mouthpiece of the telephone she was holding to her mouth, and she said defiantly, "Gendarmes!" She was calling the police. She had a poker from the office fireplace in her hand. She spoke an "Au Revoir," into the phone.

She began dialing another number, and she started talking. After two or three minutes she became a bit quieter. I perceived that she had Larry on the line. She laid the phone down on his desk in the adjoining room, on a table as far away from me as she could, and pointing to it said something like, "Ici... por vous!" "Here, it's for you!" I quickly moved to the phone. Larry spoke to me: "Vern, I apologize for your rude—or should I say 'nude'—awakening. I had not expected that Bridgate would be in today because of the holiday. But since you are up and about, go ahead and shower, and I will be there in an hour. I have told her the circumstances. I am certain everything will turn peaceful. Again, I apologize." I thanked Larry for calling, and I laughed, commenting, "No big deal; it gives me a French Flight to write about in my journal." He laughed. We bade each other "Au Revoir"—I think that is what I said—and we hung up. By this time Bridgate had entered another room in the office complex, and shut the door. I am certain that, if she could, she had also locked it. I headed for the shower. I was aware that the phone rang intermittently, and I heard Bridgate talking on it. I guessed that she was sharing her fright with her family and friends, and hopefully calling the gendarme headquarters with the message, "Never mind!" Occasionally she laughed loudly, and at times she talked softly. I could not hear her but I guessed that she may even be shedding aftershock tears.

One of the rings came at approximately one hour after Larry had said that he would come for me. I was fully dressed. I heard Bridgate talking. She came out of the room and placed the phone on the table nearest the door and nodded toward it. She made a distinguishable remark in English: "Doctor." I picked up the phone. Larry's voice came on, "See, Vern, what I told you about God watching over you, or as you say, over your French Flight. I am sorry that I slept so late. I am arriving shortly." (Larry's command of American English was impressive.) The doorbell buzzed. Bridgate unlocked the night-lock, and in walked my savior. He came and hugged me, and let out a big laugh, and I did, too, and soon Bridgate was smiling. When Larry told her that I was a Protestant Priest, she crossed herself. I awkwardly crossed myself, and blew her a kiss. Larry said, "Thank you, both Bridgate and Vern, for your understanding; and for not attacking each other with one of my letter openers." I laughed. Bridgette had apparently not understood.

Larry said his mother was preparing breakfast, and we would go to his house and enjoy it. I gathered my personal items, and as we prepared to leave, Bridgate came to me and, as Larry translated, she asked me to forgive her. I crossed myself, and said, "You are forgiven. I also need your forgiveness" Larry told her my words, and added again, "Remember, Vern is a Holy Father." She gasped and put her hand to her brow and crossed herself again. I did the same gesture. I said to Larry, "I bet Bridgate has never before seen a priest in his underwear, and she will probably never see another. But don't tell her I said that!" Larry had another big laugh. He promised he wouldn't. He said something to her, and her response took the form of a curtsey. I bowed in return.

I loaded my backpack on my shoulders and held out my hand to Bridgate. She took it, and surprised me with a "bisse." I reciprocated, and Larry and I went out to face the Communists and head for breakfast. We drove away in his Renault. When we arrived at his home, I was still chuckling over my Fourth French Flight: from a frightened Maid. His parents had been made aware of it. I offered details. Larry translated. We could barely swallow our croissants—and the toasted rolls from the Bread-maker. Before Larry and I left for Nice, I asked if I could offer a prayer of thanksgiving. Larry made an enthusiastic response, and when he translated to his parents, they nodded, and his Mother bowed and crossed herself. I prayed and paused for Larry to translate. The family expressed genuine gratitude for my piety. An hour later Larry drove me the few miles out of Nice—to a Lorry Stop where many drivers had their last carafe before Italy. I disregarded the morning imbibing and was soon on my way to Venice.

Future French Flights, I hoped, would be long hops, in Renaults, on a train or a boat or a small plane; or in later years, on Air France. The conveyance was immaterial. What mattered was that the fully dressed Protestant Presbyterian Priest had accepted the offers civilly, survived them safely, and appreciated them thankfully. He was well acquainted with God's holy Word: "The Lord will keep your going out and your coming in, from this time on and forevermore." (Palm 121: 8.)

I coveted divine keeping through my four French Flights as I headed for Italy, thence to Greece via Yugoslavia, and from there to Egypt; and finally, to honor and to spend Loretta's gift of one thousand dollars—as well as for other reasons—to Israel. I did not anticipate that I would be hitchhiking in either Africa or the Middle East. I would in both.

CHAPTER IV

Polizei Block East Berlin Church Entry

"For thus says the Lord to the people of Judah and to the inhabitants of Jerusalem: Break up your fallow ground, and do not sow among thorns. Circumcise yourselves to the Lord, remove the foreskin of your hearts; O people of Judah and inhabitants of Jerusalem, Or else my wrath will go forth like fire, and burn with no one to quench it, because of the evil of your doings.

. . . .

" For I am bringing evil from the north, and a great destruction. A lion has gone up from its thicket, a destroyer of nations has set out; He has gone out from his place to make your land a waste; Your cities will be ruins without habitat." (Jeremiah 4, selected.)

Jesus lamented over his Capitol*: "Jerusalem, Jerusalem, the city that kills the prophets and stones those who are sent to it. How often have I desired to gather your children together as a hen gathers her brood under her wings, and you were not willing! See, your house is left to you desolate." (Matthew 23:37-8.)*

The bleak, foggy, smoky, cloudy weather in Scotland gave way in March to sunshine and warmer days. I had been thinking ahead to my travel plans for Spring Break. What would the weather be like in Germany? My Edinburgh housemate Harald predicted comfortable days, and he invited me to include Berlin in my travel schedule. He would be home by

Holy Week; he wanted his family and me to meet. I would be his guest when I visited Berlin.

By this time my scenario had become predictable : hitchhike the Coastal Route 1 to London; take the Ferry to Belgium and stop for a day in Brugge; spend at least five days in the Netherlands; arrive in Berlin by the Thursday of Holy Week, flying over Communist East Germany from Hanover; leave Berlin on Easter Monday for Hamburg, and travel on the Boat Train to Copenhagen; spend three days with the Sonia Tholsted family, a pen-pal friend of one of my Ohio friends; head for Oslo; take the mountain train to Bergen; cross the North Sea to Britain, and finally, return to Scotland. Was the plan ambitious and costly? Yes, but challenging! Holy hitchhiking and decent weather would help, and I would borrow money if necessary. I had written friends in the Netherlands with whom I had become acquainted on the *S.S. Ryndam*, and several of them had replied with offers of housing and expressions of delight with the prospect of my visit. I felt encouraged. I began to pack so that I would be ready to leave Edinburgh the day the school term ended.

Looking over the German portion of my plan, Harald expressed optimism and encouragement. He assured me that I would find convenient, safe and comfortable hitchhiking, especially in his homeland. I would meet his family when I was his guest in Berlin. I should be able to travel through the Netherlands with ease, and I should enjoy Kobenhavn (Copenhagen) and my time with Ruth's pen pal and family.

Harald warned me: "Don't plan on crossing from the West to East Berlin." He had also shared with me that a historic reconciliation-reunion between his remarried mother (in Berlin) and his remarried father (from Halle) and their families was being planned. The two had not been together for several years, as far as I knew, never. Harald assured me that my visit would cause no problems for the reunion.

New College Classes ended as scheduled, and the day to depart Edinburgh arrived. I need not return to school for three weeks. I had packed my backpack as judiciously and compactly as I considered necessary for me to look and dress decently, hitchhike successfully, and still appear at a variety of engagements acceptably. I would purchase token gifts for my hosts and hostesses in their countries; I already had a gift from Ohio for Sonia. I packed my own small souvenir for her.

Weather-wise, the day I headed out started typically for March: the North Sea blowing up sizeable waves on the shore at the Portobello Suburb of Edinburgh. Annie prepared me a bountiful breakfast of kippers, porridge, and toast. She also surprised me with a lunch of cucumber sandwiches, biscuits and an apple. She might have been compensating for all the American delights that I had shared with her and the household upon return from Christmas-New Year's travels, and for the meals she would not need to prepare for me while I was gone, even though I was paying for them. I anticipated that the same abundant bounty that had arrived for me while I had traveled at Christmas would not be duplicated.

On the morning to head out, I stuffed last-minute snack food and camera supplies in my backpack, grabbed my passport as my last ticket to travel abroad, and walked up the short distance from Vandeleur to Portobello Avenue. I boarded the double-decker eastbound bus, departing at the Coastal Road and started hitchhiking south toward London. Protecting myself as much as possible from the chilly gusts blowing off the North Sea, I held out my thumb, and started praying.

Coastal Road hitchhiking luck did not work out as well at first as I had hoped. However, the traffic picked up. I began hitting on long rides. I had interesting holy talk with many of the drivers and passengers. Toward dusk, I asked the driver of the car I was a guest in to let me off at a lorry stop. He complied with my request. The Station had several vehicles parked around it, and I guessed hopefully that the drivers were having a quick tea and would soon be heading out on the roads. I went into the café and sat at the counter next to a good looking, clean cut (obviously a former or possibly a present) rugby or cricket athlete. I discussed travels with him. I hit good fortune: the young man would welcome my company; he was going to London.

The driver was more amenable to holy conversation than any I had met on the road so far. I was encouraged. In fact, he delighted in "arguing the subject." He said he had become a Christian at the last Billy Graham Crusade in London. We explored his Christian commitment further. He appreciated my comments and advice for his living a more Christian life. I told him that I perceived that he was already doing well, and to keep it up. Time passed quickly. I fell asleep, and when I awoke, we had arrived at a north suburban development that had train service to London. William said he knew where to look for the Tube Station. First, however, he needed fuel. He pulled his mammoth road hog into a "Truck Petrol" stop and started filling his tank. We traded addresses and phone numbers. Back on the highway, William headed in the direction of the factory to which he was delivering his bolts of Scottish tartan material. The station was on the way. He related that he had enough material on board to cut out five hundred kilts. He said he had never worn one, much to his parents' disappointment. I told him I hoped to buy a kilt while still in Edinburgh. I had borrowed one a few times at home for a party, but had never possessed one in my family tartan. "Which one is it?" he asked. "Buchanan," I replied, "because of my Gibson blood. I would like to take home an Elgin one, but they are hard to find. Besides, the Buchanan is so much more colorful with its yellow, green and red, than the Elgin light blue." He suddenly seemed less drowsy: "Buchanan is my tartan also," he offered. "I have Gibson blood," he continued, "but we don't have a tartan." I slapped him on the leg, and burst out: "I have Gibson lineage also; in fact, Gibson is my middle name. I am happy that the Elgin's have a tartan, but it is hard to find." We shared more about our families.

We came to the subway station, and William pulled off the highway. I thanked him for the ride and said that I hoped we would meet again. I located the Station stairs and headed down to the trains. One arrived shortly, and I traveled into the center of London. I had already made a reservation with my B&B lady, Elise, when I had been there in December. Upon arrival I phoned and told her that I had a few places in London I wanted to see, but I would be there for High Tea. Elise said that she was holding a room for me, and that she looked forward to seeing me again.

I traveled by tube and bus and on foot to the few sites in London that I wanted to see, and then headed for Elise's. She had High Tea ready. I ate and then wearily went to bed. She knocked me up the next morning at the time I had requested. After one of her good breakfasts, I headed for Victoria Station. I connected with a train to Dover, where I boarded a ferry to Oostende, Belgium. I surveyed the ferry parking lot and found a Dover car returning to Belgium. The driver was traveling alone and was willing to accept me as his free-ticketed companion, but I soon discovered that he was traveling in the opposite direction from the way I was. The Sea Crossing was rough, but I managed to keep my breakfast.

The boat arrived in Oostende on time. Cars started driving off. I went to where they were leaving and started searching for a ride. My luck prevailed. After several "turn-downs," I connected with Reginald. He rolled down the car window, and when I asked him his destination and if I could ride with him, he told me that he had to make stops in both Belgium and Holland. He was driving first to Brugge, where he had business for a couple of hours, and the next day he was driving to Antwerp. He offered to take me with him. The route sounded good. I had not planned on it, but I wanted to visit Brugge. I settled into his car. We went through Oostende and turned northwest. After we had become better acquainted, and I was asked to call him Reginald or Reggie, he shared that he was driving to Antwerp the next day, and he offered to share overnight accommodations. He had reserved a room that had two beds. He assured me that he was a happily married straight guy. I told him that I was a happily engaged straight virgin. We both had a laugh. I looked forward to the time for conversation that lay ahead of us.

As we became better acquainted, Reginald disclosed that he had a daughter who was studying to be a clergywoman, but in Protestantism; the Anglican Church did not yet ordain women. She was about the same age as I. Our discussion of the Church gathered momentum. He admitted that he and his wife had not been too involved in their congregation, but they were attending worship more frequently, and had started to volunteer their time with the Church. I broached several questions about the effectiveness of the Church in England, and he suggested that it could be much better, but it was improving. We arrived in Brugge in time for me to do a bit of sightseeing while Reginald tended to his business. I bought Reginald's dinner, much to his protest. We spent a comfortable night in the Hotel— each in his own bed! I think he was beginning to think of me as a surrogate son or brother. He paid for my breakfast the next morning. We headed out in his car for a good day, his in traveling, and mine in hitchhiking.

After his business in Antwerp, we crossed from Belgium into the Netherlands, passing Customs without trouble. I left Reginald and headed for Rotterdam. I spent several joyful days in Holland, and I never had to pay for a stay in a hostel or a hotel; nor did I have to spend a night on a public park bench. The itinerary that I had been designed around sharing hospitality with friends whom I had met on the *Ryndam* worked out perfectly. People wined and dined me. One day and night I enjoyed the hospitality of a sister of a member of the Cadiz, Ohio Church I was Pastor of, and she and her driver took me to one of Holland's famous tulip festivals, the Kuekenhoff. The day finally arrived for me to hitchhike into Germany. I had spent a night in Amsterdam with a friend who worked there but lived in The Hague; when he came home for the weekend, I had another night with him and his mother and sister.

Osnabruck was my first destination. I would spend two nights in the home of a Pastor and his family. Their son was one of my best friends in Edinburgh. Derek did not have money for a trip home for Lent and Easter, so he remained in Scotland. His parents were anticipating my visit.

My arrival at the Pastor-family's doorstep terminated one of my most surprising hitchhikes: I obtained a ride in a U.S. Army Jeep, with three military men stationed in Germany. I decided not to bother enquiring if I were legal cargo. The soldiers were delighted to learn that I had spent time in the United States Army Air Corps almost ten years before. They knew Osnabruck, and with an enquiry or two—in German—they soon found Derek's home. Members of the family were surprised to look out in their driveway and see an American Jeep. They soon discovered me, and greeted me warmly, and the Jeep left. I was offered lunch. Besides Derek, the household consisted of Rodelle and Katarin in University studies, but home for Easter Holidays; and Hans, a High School student. His parents revealed later that when they had looked out the door upon my arrival and spotted a military Police vehicle parked in their drive, they had anxiety. I shared with them that I had felt the same way when they had stopped for me.

Derek's "Muter nicht sprecht" English. At the moment when I had arrived, "Fater" was next door in his Church Office. It was the Saturday before Palm Sunday, an extra special day in their church. On Palm Sunday afternoon, the Pastor's Congregation was hosting the District Catechism of Confirmands; so he was extremely busy. Derek's sisters and brothers appeared, and from the moment of our meeting to the moment of my departing, we all felt like family. We were, I contended, "A family in Christ." "Yah," they replied. They spoke communicable English, better than my German, even though I had just finished six months' classical study of the language in Edinburgh.

The highlights of my Osnabruck visit included:

--Herr Pastor Derek Sr.'s insisting when I went to bed Saturday night that I leave my shoes outside my bedroom door. It had been his custom for years that a fairy came by the family bedrooms on Saturday nights and collected the shoes and polished them; the gesture applied also to guests.

--Herr Pastor's preaching and leading of worship on the Lord's Day, and the hospitality extended me by members of his church.

--The Catechism Class examination in the afternoon, with a church full of youth from other congregations in the "classis" rattling off long paragraphs of Luther's "Catechism," from memory. I did not stay for the four-hour session.

--Pastor Derek sharing that he had once been asked to serve on a Committee for Adolph Hitler's Assassination, but he declined. He hated Nazism, but his spiritual priority was to stay with his parish during the troubled wartime in Germany, to protect his family and congregation, to pray for a rapid downfall of Der Fuhrer, and to thank God for their daily bread, of which, during some weeks, his family had little to eat. While they did not always have bread, most of the time they had potatoes and lard

--Sunday dinner with all the family gathered and having such a joyful time; Friend Derek's family responding so hospitably to me, their American Guest, leading me to feel that I was blessing them by being a "Derek" to them all, and how my presence helped compensate for the absence of their son/brother. He would not return to Germany until the end of the academic year. At the end of dinner, I rubbed my belly and commented, "Ich bin vull!" They laughed, and then apologized, and told me why: "Vull" means drunk; a word that sounded to me like "Gemutlikeit" fits better;

--Great discussions with Pastor Derek about the evils of Nazism, and the suffering Germans had endured under it, and the long list of names of persons whose funerals he had officiated, due to the Allied bombings, which he admitted had been necessary.

--The ride I received promptly when I left Osnabruck on Monday, in a Porsche, that would "rev" up to 150 K. per hour on the Autobahn.

--Another ride on the autobahn, in a Cadillac. I was asked to sit in the front-seat passenger place. Two portly gentlemen occupied the back seat. They were engaged in a business discussion. The men were both Americans: one was the International Editor of "Consumer Reports," from New York, and the other was the American in charge of the European Public Relations and publication of "Reports." The two dignitaries were too world-minded to open the subject of holiness; besides they had world business to tend to. They constantly made profane and nasty comments about the "krauts." When we arrived in Essen, the American Editor instructed the driver to drive "the American Christian Pastor" another thirty kilometers and drop him off at a lorry stop. I was most grateful. From there I could more easily find a ride to Hanover, and from there I would take a flight to Berlin. The chauffeur pulled the car to the curb, the men stepped out, and I gratefully said good-bye. They headed into the building, and we headed out.

In route to the lorry stop I asked the officially dressed driver, "Do you speak and understand English?" When he answered, "Yes," I enquired further: "Then, how do you feel as those two men speak so disparagingly about you and your country's citizens?" The driver said, "I have become accustomed to their bullshit. They are both ignorant, typical capitalist Jewish pricks!" Ohhhh...! Holy hitchhiking? I added, "But they are Jewish

Americans, and they probably lost family in the Holocaust." He smiled, patted my knee, and agreed, adding, "I bet I lost as many aunts and uncles and cousins and brothers in the War as they did." I softly said, "I'm sorry." From then our conversation was solemn. As I left the driver at the appointed destination, I thanked him again for his kindness and frankness, and I wished him a happy Easter. He wished me a safe trip to Berlin. We both wished that we were traveling farther together. We exchanged an "Auf wedersein," and he gunned up the Cadillac and waved good-bye. I stuck out my thumb in hopes of a long ride toward Hanover. There I would board an airplane for the flight over Communist land to East Berlin. My hitchhiking proved easy and efficient. I was soon on a plane from the Hanover Airport to Tempelhof Berlin.

Ironic dramas played out in my West Berlin visit. An interesting prelude to it began when I bought the current *Time* magazine. Besides wanting to find out the latest news from the U.S.A., I wanted to keep my mind off such negative thoughts as, "'What if the plane crashes while we are still over communist East Germany?" What a surprise I received when I had settled into my airplane seat and took out my magazine and discovered a photo of Bishop Otto Dibelius on the front cover! He was *Time*'s "Man of the Year." I possessed books in my personal Library back in Ohio written by the Old Testament German Scholar. He was currently the Pastor of the famous Marienkirche in East Berlin. The article reported that the Pastor-Professor-Theologian would be preaching at the Church on Easter Sunday. The Communist Government allowed him to cross the border on the Lord's Day into the Soviet Sector and preach, but with the proscription: "Preach the Gospel, and nothing but the Gospel." The proponents of that policy had obviously not read the Gospel I study and preach! Otherwise they would have seen that the threat to their dictatorship in Jesus' promised coming kingdom and for which he was crucified constitutes the central message of the Gospel. How I wished that Harald would revoke his restriction about a visit to East Berlin! He met me when I arrived at Tempelhof Airport.

The days ahead in Germany, culminating on Easter Sunday, would afford me one of the most holy observances of Easter that I had ever had. Over the years I have told several people that that Easter Sunday 1953 in Berlin stands as the most memorable Easter in my life, and probably will remain so, until the great Easter Morn, or in Jesus' terms, "the renewal of all things." (Matthew 19:28.)

Flying into Tempelhof reminded me of flying into Kansas City, Missouri, in the 1950's: the Kansas City Airport was at that time located in the center of the city. Arriving there at the Advent and Christmas season offered the passenger both an esthetic and spiritual "high." The display no doubt aided business also!

During the flight from Hanover, I kept offering brief prayers for the people who live under Soviet oppression. I had to admit, however, that East Germany produces good athletes and good scholars, even in the field of Christian scholarship. The East German Church's existence and growth has both surprised the western world, and judged it. Churches in the western "free" Germany and other European Nations were experiencing membership and attendance declines. I intended to ask Harald his opinion of the relationships between Church and State in the two sectors. It would also be interesting to hear his East Germany father's views on the subject, if he had time or the will to enter into a discussion of the subject when he arrived Easter Sunday.

As we approached Tempelhof, I became more excited about the drama awaiting me in the former German Capitol. The plane landed, and I was about to enter it. Harald stood out among the crowd waiting to meet arrivals. His mother had driven to the Airport in the family Volkswagen with its convertible canvas roof. The day was too cool for us to do sightseeing from the top of the car. I was disappointed, but would make up for the loss later. Harald's mother and sister and stepfather lived in an apartment in the British Sector.

The next few days drained my energies, delighted my senses, pinched some tears out of my eyes, stirred my imagination, provoked my investigation, and deepened my appreciation for the German character that was reviving from its infection with Nazism. The German economy was healing and progressing in large part because of the American Marshal Plan and German determination; according to the lyrics in the "Sound of Music," in a "most delightful way." The same could not be said of East Germany.

A person could hardly ask for a more holy time for a visit in Berlin. Harald put us through a rigorous routine. Thursday night he and I attended "Maundy Thursday" services in the church commonly referred to as "The Niemoller Church." Pastor Niemoller had been a courageous pastor during the War. Martyr Pastor Dietrich Bohoeffer's steps could be walked in there. Bonhoeffer had been arrested as a suspect in a plot to Assassinate Adolph Hitler. He was charged as guilty, and after a time in prison—during which he wrote spiritual classics—he was executed. One of his most read works is *Letters and Papers from Prison*. Niemoller came out of the War with his health and his profession relatively intact. Worship in the Niemoller Church was a uniquely holy Maundy Thursday event. I keenly and appreciatively sensed the communion of the saints. We attended a Good Friday service, and later had coffee on the Kurferstendam Avenue. Fifth Avenue in New York on Easter Sunday could not have been any busier.

Spending the latter half of Holy Week 1953 with Harald in West Berlin had an even holier meaning for me because of the spiritual change Edinburgh had made in him. When he had first come to Edinburgh he seemed not to be "religious." That spirit changed. Somehow through his University classes he had become involved with a German Student Group, meeting and studying and worshiping with a young Pastor/Clergy/Chaplain leader. Harald hesitated to talk about his experience with me, but our travels together the last few weeks in Scotland had revealed the spiritual change influence of the group. Many weekends he could not join me for a hitchhike because he had to meet on Sunday with his Christian group. (Remember that at the age of fifteen Harald had been inducted into the Hitler Youth organization; he had had little choice. When the Soviet troops belted across Nazi's eastern borders, he went AWOL and headed for Berlin. He had hiked across the terrain for several days without food or covered-over shelter. He finally arrived in Berlin and located his family. He found safe shelter, and was fortunate that when the city was sectored off, they found themselves in the British Sector.) He attended worship with me when we were on the road on Sundays in Scotland, most frequently attending congregations of the Church of Scotland. Since I was a Presbyterian Scot descendant, I identified easily with the Church of Scotland. Harald's spiritual background had been Lutheran.

On Saturday afternoon, the day of Easter Vigil, we participated in a ritual Harold and several University friends have observed since school days: conversational picnicking in the Tiergarten Park. Deep philosophical and political conversation among the young students created a fellowship among them that had a holy touch. One of the most holy happened when Harald shared a bit of the spiritual renewal that he had gone through in Edinburgh. He might have shared even more if I had not been with him. I was asked to share a few minutes of my personal spiritual odyssey. I did. I also called attention to the current *Time* magazine article about Bishop Dibellius. I mentioned that I was disappointed that Harald and I could not go to East Berlin Easter Sunday for worship. Several of the group spoke up, most of them encouraging Harald to take me. He made no commitment.

Saturday night one of Harald's Berlin-American friends came to the Scholtz home for a visit. Harald mentioned that he had thought of going to East Berlin, but he had promised his Mother that he would not risk his life, or mine. The Friend said he crosses to the Soviet Sector regularly, and that he had experienced neither apprehension nor molestation. He said, "Let me talk to your Mother." Harald consented, and the friend left the room. He came back and said that he had convinced her to change her mind, that is, if we had passionately made up our minds to go. We had, and we went to bed that night with plans for the crossing in the morning. Harald set forth the conditions: "Dress shabbily, and when we are in public in East Berlin, speak and act modestly; as softly, as infrequently as necessary, and as un-American as you can." I did not anticipate any problem with either directive, especially with dress.

Easter Sunday in Berlin dawned beautifully sunny. For the first time in many years I had not risen to attend or prepare for a 5:00 a.m. Sunrise Service. We arose at a normal time. Harald had decided that we would leave the house at 9:30 a.m. in order to have a look around East Berlin before going to the Church. He wanted me to see the ruins of the Reichstag Building, the location of the bunker that had been the scene of the Adolph-Eva suicide pact, famous museums in ruins, and other sites. We would have a glimpse at the Wall separating East and West Berlin, but not walk near either it or the Brandenburg Tor. Maybe we—he more emotionally than I—could enter more deeply into the thinking and emotions of the Halle family we would meet when we returned to West Berlin. We were aware that we would not see the prosperity or westernization evident in West Berlin. We may get another glimpse of the partly restored, burned out Kaiser Wilhelm Church, its charred ruined belfry and steeple a reminder of the grief Germany had gone through, and that its leaders had played a role in putting other nations through, most tragically the Jews, "lest we forget."

With Harald's approval of my looks, we traveled East on the underground train; we would return West above ground. Harald instructed: "Don't speak to me on the train unless I speak to you. In fact, sit in the seat on the opposite aisle from me, if seating is available." He kissed his Mother and Sister good-bye, and we left. They seemed to have lost some of their apprehension about our going.

If you can imaginatively join us on the ride on the train, I can clue you in on how I imagined Harald was feeling about how important the day could prove for his family. We spoke very little to each other on the train. Easter Sunday 1953 could etch itself deeply into the Scholtzes' memories, not only as an incomparable Easter, and certainly not because of having an American guest, but also as a major reconciliation of the long separated Father and Mother, former Husband and Wife, Children and Step-parents, and half-Brothers and half-Sisters. Without probing for details, I tried to imagine what was occupying Harald's mind. I knew it was profound, and possibly a bit perplexing. Harald had been born in the industrial city of Halle, and he had lived there until he turned fifteen, when he joined the Hitler Youth organization. His father owned and managed a prosperous toy factory. As World War II escalated, and especially when the Soviet Army began the invasion of East Germany, the business faltered. When the Soviet Sector was designated as one of the occupying nations of the four regions of Germany, Harald's parents agreed on a temporary separation. The factory Foreman, with Harald's Father's approval, took Harald's Mother and his sister to West Berlin; they would be safer there. Harald of course joined them upon his escape from the Hitler Youth Regiment. Upon graduating from the equivalent of High School he began University Studies—at Goettigen, I believe, or Tubingen. Like me, he was awarded a scholarship for study in his field, European History, at the University of Edinburgh, and like me, he was happy to find accommodations at the home of Annie Thomson.

At the end of the war, when severe travel restrictions had been imposed by the Soviet regime, neither of Harald's parents risked going back and forth between Halle and Berlin. In the meantime the former factory foreman and Harald's mother developed a romantic relationship. She eventually obtained an uncontested "in-absentia" divorce from Harald's father, and she and the foreman married. When he learned what had transpired, Harald's father remarried in Halle. Minimal communication had been maintained between the father and his West German offspring.

With the passage of time and change of circumstances, both Mother and Father agreed that, for the sake of their children and their own peace, they should work out an emotional patch-up of their relationship. Easter Sunday 1953—I suppose in part, because of Harald's plans to be home from Edinburgh—was set by mutual agreement as Reunion and Reconciliation Day. As already indicated, Harald had apprised me of the plan, and I offered to move into a hotel or hostel for the time when they would need privacy. Harald said it was not necessary. His mother agreed. An early Easter Sunday afternoon hour, with a Sunday dinner together, was set for the occasion. The time would not conflict with the plan for Harald to take me to East Berlin for worship and a look around. Harald assured his mother that we would return to West Berlin in plenty of time for the gathering. I kept offering to be out of the house for the occasion, but Harald said, "Emphatically no." Perhaps after the dinner, I may even be called upon to lead the group in a ceremony of reconciliation. From the comments I kept hearing from Harald about "...the less ceremony the better," I decided to wait for him to initiate ceremonial rituals, if there were to be any. He never did. His mind was concentrating on the trip to East Berlin with his American guest friend, and their return to West Berlin safely in time for the historical and emotional family event.

When we arrived at the overhead station nearest Harald's home, I gave him money, and he bought our tickets for the subway ride. We briefly talked strategy on the way over—while we were still in West Berlin. He had decided that before and after worship, if we had time, we would tour the inner city area around the Church. When we boarded the train to return, we would buy our tickets separately, and we would not board the train together; nor would we sit together until we returned to the West. If we did end up beside each other, we would simulate an appearance of being strangers. We should attempt to board the same coach, but we should not give evidence of being friends until we had arrived in West Berlin. We would not attract any more attention to the two of us than was necessary, and we would be especially aware of the officials who frequently walked by our compartments and looked for inappropriate behaviors, according to Soviet standards as far as we understood them.

The ride to East Berlin was timely and comfortable. The train had few passengers. We exited at the station nearest the two icons we wanted to see and enter: the Reichstag mall and the Marienkirche Church. We took a brief look at the devastation around the Nazi Headquarters. We could talk quietly and conservatively with each other, but not within the Policemen's viewing or hearing. That self-imposed restriction proved difficult to observe: the Polizei were ubiquitously present.

I had been well prepared for the contrast between East and West Berlin—both by verbal description and by photos. Walking around the setting where damage had been inflicted gave destruction and war a pall that was almost impossible to understand or penetrate. I had a diversity of feelings. I reminded myself, "You were serving the United States Army

Air Corps when VE Day was observed." I had a chill. East Berlin felt like an urban desert: few rebuilt shops; buildings still in disrepair; workmen in torn work clothes wheeling away debris in little carts and wheelbarrows— no heavy trucks or trailers; little street lighting; and few stores open; one deserted American automobile, a Studebaker. But of course, it was Sunday, I said, but I doubted that weekdays looked significantly different.

Contrast rather than comparison defined the prosperity and post-war recovery in the three Sectors of West Berlin. Both Harald and I exercised restraint in making comments to each other. We played the roles of strangers professionally, uncomfortable as it made us feel. Harald finally said softly, "Time to go to Church." I walked beside him part of the time, and behind him the rest.

The Marienkirche came into view. The gray granite structure appeared massive and impressive. We moved toward it. When we arrived at the front door, a Polizei officer confronted us. He spoke to Harald and shook his head, and we began leaving the scene. As we headed back to the sidewalk, Harald interpreted the Guard's words: "All pews are occupied, and the sanctuary is filled to the permitted capacity. No one else is permitted entry!" What a disappointment! Harald would not give up hope, however. He had an idea: walk around the building and hopefully we would find an unlocked, unguarded door. But do not hold out too much hope—which seemed the easier stance in the ambiance in which we found ourselves— because those doors, Harold believed, would also be well guarded.

We did not have to go far or wait long for a surprise. As we approached the right side of the building, a small door opened and a woman came out; she was vomiting, obviously a victim of crowd compaction. Harald led me quickly to the door, and we were undeterred from entering. I said "Thank you," and then made a correction: "Not for the illness, but for the entrance." As far as I could tell, no one in uniform appeared to be approaching to evict us.

A small table inside the door held bulletins for the worship service. We both picked up a copy, moved farther toward the nave of the sanctuary, melding into the standing crowd, pushing politely and shoving softly through the throng. As the Polizei had said, all seating space in the huge sanctuary had already been taken. So had the standing space, it appeared. The service, I perceived, was still doing the opening liturgy. Having studied German at the New College the past six months from a "real" German professor, I soon located myself in the litanies, and I quieted my soul and engaged my voice in congregational participation.

During a choral presentation, I looked around at folk in front of and behind us, and on both sides, and I perceived that most worshipers were seriously and authentically engaged in the service movement. I wondered if my dress code adhered more to a German standard than an American. Actually, I could see little difference, possibly because I was not attired in traditional American Easter finery. Most congregants were dressed as they probably dressed on Monday for work or school or home life. I wondered how many of them were East rather than West Germans, probably a strong majority. I became aware of the differences in our appearances, and for some mysterious reason, I thought back on James' instruction to the Church at worship: "Do you with your acts of favoritism really believe in our glorious Lord Jesus Christ? For if a person with gold rings and in fine clothes comes into your assembly, and if a person in dirty clothes also comes in, and if you take notice of the one wearing the fine clothes, and say, 'Have a seat here, please,' while to the one who is poor you say, 'Stand there,' or, 'Sit at my feet,' have you not made distinctions among yourselves, and become judges with evil thoughts?" (James 2:2-4.) I quickly asked God, "Holy Spirit, keep my mind from wandering at this remarkable Easter Sunday worship." I glanced around quickly, and felt no paranoia. I must have succeeded in looking more German than American.

I perceived that the choral presentation from the balcony sounded purely virginal. I looked up toward the choir area, and I saw the singers: a large group, maybe eighty to one hundred boys, not robed, but dressed in their light blue "Kominsol" or Communist Youth shirts. (The *Time* magazine had reported that they would be there.) The bulletin included the anthem lyrics. For the words that I could translate I decided that the theology was radically disparate from Soviet ideology. As I felt Harald's shoulders next to me, dressed in a different blue shirt, I remembered his sharing with me some of his experiences as a Hitler Youth, and his wandering hungrily through fields and forests escaping the Russians in his push for Berlin. Then I thought of the reunion awaiting us back in West Berlin. My thoughts had not wandered too far astray, considering the drama of the experience.

Bishop Dibelius ascended the pulpit and began reading Scripture. I recognized him from photos on the jackets of his books. His choices of Scripture included Psalm references to life eternal and the familiar Job passage, "I know that my redeemer liveth…" (I prayed, "Lord, give Harald understanding and a good memory, that he may interpret the message to me when we arrive back at his home.") The youth sang in TAB—

Tenor, Alto and Base—in perfect harmony, and with easily discernable diction. The text printed in the worship bulletin was from Handel. A hymn followed, and I could sing it in German; and, because the text was familiar, "Christ the Lord Is Risen Today," I could join with this East German Congregation, and praise God that "In Christ, we are all one." (I vaguely remember that Handel's "Hallelujah Chorus" was sung.)

Time came for Bishop Dibelius to preach. I could understand some of his thoughts, but I could follow more easily in spirit than in Word. I occasionally whispered to Harald for the translation of a phrase, and he whispered a response. I rejoiced in the ecumenicity I felt. I was having communion in the Spirit with the spirits assembled that Easter Sunday in East Berlin, especially when we repeated the "Apostles Creed." I followed in the German language, and I shook softly when we came to "I believe in the holy catholic Church, the communion of the saints...." The Spirit present powerfully in that German—East German—Church that morning spoke, not only in an assured voice of peace inside the Church sanctuary, but also in a voice of defiant mockery. I imagined that the Bishop was the mouth of Jesus as he had addressed the principalities and powers of the nation under whose occupation his ministry was unfolding, but with a power that would trump the evil with good, and would set up a kingdom that would last forever and forever. As the Bishop said that morning—and I joyfully understood and praised God for the truth—the powers of darkness and death had lost their hegemony in Jesus' rising from the grave.

After Bishop Dibelius' short prayer following his sermon, trumpets started blaring from the balcony, and joyful voices rose in a triumphant crescendo of joy and trust. The service ended with the Bishop's raising his hands in a benediction gesture. I held my hands waist-high to receive it: "The grace of our Lord Jesus Christ...." the Bishop began—in German, of course, and he ended with, "Amen." I joined in. The service ended, and Harald and I merged into the massive exiting crowd. Our joy and hope mocked the scene outside the church doors, including the Polizei's' attempts to keep the crowd submissive. I followed Harald out and kept silence. We headed for the train.

We arrived at the nearby station, and since I had German currency, "deutschmark," I went to the ticket booth alone and with as few words and as authentic a German accent as possible, made my purchase. Harald had coached me to say something like, "Nach Berlin Weste," and say the train number. The ticket dispenser apparently understood. I was immediately serviced. Harald was obtaining his billet at another window. Easter Sunday was getting sunnier. The air was comfortable. Children were playful; many of them appearing better dressed than I had imagined; they had probably already attended their Church, and were permitted to spend Sunday in their better clothes. Most youth and adults looked somber. I wanted to yell out, "Come on, people; He is risen." I imaginatively waited for their response: "He is risen indeed!"

In my surveying of the scene and wandering in thought, I had temporarily lost sight of Harald. I glanced to see if I could locate him. I spotted him in what I perceived to be a not-too-friendly conversation with a man in uniform. I was temporarily distracted. I kept my eye on the scene fearfully. A crowd gathered and formed a line at the ticket counter, and my sight of my buddy was lost. I trusted he was heading toward the tracks. I also headed in that direction. A train arrived and stopped. I could not see Harald, but joined those getting on. Suddenly I felt a jolt on my back. My first thought, "These impolite East Germans!" Harald had placed the bump to my back. He came close and said softly, "Other side!" I quickly separated from the boarding passengers and followed him; I had almost boarded a train penetrating deeper into East Berlin! Harald had saved me.

We both stepped onto the westbound train and obtained seats in the same coach car, but apart the aisle from each other. As the train moved out and then stopped, and then moved again, I kept watching the changing scene: from a disarrayed and quasi-dead landscape to an ambiance of color, moving vehicles, bustling people, well-kempt gardens, commercial transactions, and laughter. After we had gone through another stop, Harald came and sat beside me. Neither of us spoke to each other as we rode through several stops. Finally, he shook my hand and spoke, "We are back in freedom. I hope I did not hurt you back there." We both laughed when I responded, "You saved me!" We shook hands again, and I felt like embracing—but not here.

We arrived at the station from which we had departed five hours earlier. As we headed toward Harald's street, we reflected briefly and positively on the service, and on the contrast in topography and demography between the two Berlin's. I offered the comment that I hoped that people who had been at the Marienkirche, and other East Berlin Churches, had received as much new hope and joy from their worship as we had from ours. Harald nodded his head vigorously, and shook my hand firmly. I perceived he had been renewed, maybe more than I had.

We walked to Harald's apartment. His father and wife and two young children had already arrived. Upon seeing each other, Harald and his father embraced, and they wept. So did I. Introductions followed, and then his mother called us to the beautifully decorated dinner table. My eye spotted the chocolate Easter eggs first. I wished Harald had asked me to pray or had prayed himself. Instead, we began the meal with a wine toast. I was gratuitously hosted because I was the first American either family had ever hosted for a Sunday dinner. Harald toasted me in English and I reciprocated. I perceived that most everybody present had understood our mutual courtesies. (I had introduced myself to his step-mother; he was too busy. She appeared younger than his mother, and much younger than his father.) Harald's stepfather invited the gathering to the table, sitting according to the previously distributed nametags. As conversation hushed, Harald took a moment to thank those present for the effort it had taken to make this reunion possible, and we all drank and cheered—even I, the guy without a wine taste. Before we ate, small gifts were exchanged, with the announcement of a prohibition of any further ceremony until after dinner. I perceived that the initial reunion had taken place and that reconciliation was tiptoeing softly and amicably into the hearts of the two families; it became obvious that at least a tentative and fertile forgiveness had become a "fait accompli." The joy of resurrection had triumphed over bitterness and misunderstanding. No further reconciliation counseling or reunion ceremony seemed necessary. If it were, I would not be the one to lead it. I was the fortunate stranger in their midst, and my deepest relationship was with Harald, not the other family members. However, his mother and I had already expressed our love for each other. His father began to make me feel that I had made a significant contribution to Harald's life. I accepted the compliment, which I had done little to deserve.

Harald's mother's cook-for-the-day began placing food on the table. We ate bountifully; I saved stomach room for the chocolate. Conversation proceeded pleasantly and comfortably, at least as far as I could comprehend what was being said. Frequently Harald would translate for me, and he would explain my words of joy and congratulations to his Father's family. Many of them, including his mother's husband, understood me more clearly than the others, and could converse with more ease. Dessert time came, and Harald's Stepfather came out of the kitchen carrying a tray with a plum pudding blazing. All at the table began blowing on it—another family Easter tradition. The fire was extinguished and we began to devour the dessert. I have never tasted better. I concluded that the joy of Easter and the joy of forgiveness among the gathered enhanced the taste. Many of us ate two pieces of the dessert. I dismissed myself from the table and returned with a box of Stover's' Chocolates left from my Christmas presents from America. I presented them to Harald's mother, and she was delighted. She opened them immediately and shared them.

When we had experienced significant "gemutlikeit"—I remembered the correct word from the Sunday dinner a week previously in Osnabruck—Harald's stepfather requested that the family move to the parlor to continue their exchange of gifts. I started to excuse myself. Harald interrupted and encouraged me to remain with them. They had gifts for me. I was overwhelmed. As we prepared to separate from the table, and I intended to retreat to Harald's bedroom, I remarked that I could not recall when I had had a more joyful Easter. I was not feeling sorry for myself one bit—for not having conducted worship at the Cadiz, Ohio United Presbyterian Church. I felt like a parasite on the family's reconciliation, but several of them interrupted to express to me that my presence among them had made a special contribution of joy to their momentous reunion. Harald added a comment about how much my friendship had helped him to adjust to life in Scotland. He asked me if I would offer a prayer. I choked up, but started. He translated, and at the "Amen," several reached for handkerchiefs, and shared hugs.

As darkness began to settle over Berlin, the families began expressing their farewells. They all shook hands and hugged and kissed, even the two husbands. There were tears, and if my perceptions proved accurate, promises had been made that if possible, they would attempt another Easter Sunday reunion in future years. And they wished I could come from America to join them. I thanked them and said I would be praying for them, and I wished they could come to America someday and visit me. Harald interrupted and asked me if I would pray a benediction. "Of course," I said. I began, and I was brief. I left pauses for Harald's translation. After we all had said, "Amen," they surprised me with applause. I was taken aback. I could not recall when I had ever been applauded for praying, but the occasion, rather than my prayer, was worthy of it. A loud chorus of "Amen's" followed my last words. I dismissed myself, as the family continued their parting rituals.

Easter Sunday night the family appeared emotionally and physically exhausted, but also exhilarated. Harald and I seemed renewed, but, of course, we had worshiped that morning at the Marienkirche, and we had heard a classical sermon from Bishop Otto Dibelius. Harald's family was not active in the Church. I perceived that his Mother had some guilt feelings about it in view of a question she raised one day with me. I had shared the Catechism Conference I had witnessed in the Osnabruck Church, and how impressed I was with the youth's enthusiasm and responses to questions about their faith, and about the Luther catechism. She said that she knew Erika should be in a catechism class, and she had gone to a local Pastor to discuss the matter. However, the decision was up to Erika, and she had not expressed much enthusiasm about going. Harald's mother had not pursued the matter. I commented that perhaps both mother and daughter should be praying about the matter, and activate their prayers by further investigation with a Pastor in a local parish Church next year when Confirmation Classes ordinarily start. The response I received was, "Erika has little enthusiasm about church since none of her friends attends." I had nothing further to add, but in my heart, and later in my prayers, I talked to God about Harald's sharing more of his spiritual renewal with his mother and sister. John Calvin said that that is about as much as one can do. You can train up your children in the way they should go, as the Proverb commands, but remember, you may have to wait for the fulfillment of the time factor in the command: "When they are old, they will not stray." (Proverbs 22:6.)

Easter Monday morning Harald drove me to Tempelhof Airport in his mother's Volkswagen, with its retractable canvas roof. I had been privileged on several occasions the past few days while driving around Berlin, to stand up in the car, with Harald standing beside me, and our heads above the retractable canvas roof, as he pointed out scenic and significant sites of the City, like: the Berlin Wall; the Kaiser Wilhelm Church; and the Brandenberg Tor (Gate). It stood at the border of East and West Berlin, and on the Allies side of the Gate a billboard warned in words like this, "Achtung. Sie verlassen nach ...." You are leaving West Berlin for the communist sector. West Berliners enjoyed reciprocal access to the three allied Sectors—American, British and French—without restrictions. However, East Berlin, like East Germany, had restrictions that made you chill as you came near the boundaries. Guards on the West Berlin side alert you to the international dispute and the oppression on the East. The lack of reconstruction and relocation of the war rubble in East Berlin contrasts sadly and starkly with the vitality and cheer of the western sector.

Upon arrival at Tempelhof, I kissed Harald's mother, and hugged Harald—all with a slight patina of sadness but an Easter projection of hope. Would we ever see each other again? (We never have.) They drove off. I went through security and identity. I needed reading material. I had finished the "Otto Dibelius" *Time* issue, tearing out the pages I wanted to save. I stopped at the Newsstand and purchased the current *Time*. (I have forgotten the cover story.)

My intention to read on the flight to Hamburg went awry when my seatmate, a handsome fair-haired young man, introduced himself. Ironically, he was a student of theology in Hamburg, which was also his home. We immediately felt like Older Brother (Vern) and taller, but younger Brother (Bertram.) We immediately scanned several years of our lives, theological positions, and church decline in Germany. Bertram asked where I was lodging. I said, "I will be looking for a Youth Hostel." He came back, "Would you like to come to my Family home and stay with us?" I told him I would be delighted. He said he would have to call his mother first. A young female University student was renting a room from them, but she was not expected back for a day or two. Unless she had changed her plans, a bed would be available for me at his home.

Upon arriving in Hamburg, Bertram immediately phoned his mother, and he returned to me with a smile and good news: "You can stay with us." We headed for a bus, and soon found ourselves at my new "holy" friend's residence. I met his mother and several family members, and we had a light supper.

Bertram and I then left the family for a night in Hamburg. I figured that two theologians could hardly run into ungodliness so obscene and objectionable that the Polizei would take us into custody. Then I remembered that I was in West Germany. Bertram took me to several historical scenes—those worth looking at in the dark. Some of them still showed signs of the destructive bombing of the War. We occasionally discussed Nazism's influence on Germany, philosophically, culturally, intellectually, and theologically. While it had been insidiously evil, Bertram surprised me when he commented that it had also resulted in some good. "Like the Volkswagen?" I shrugged and smiled. Bertram just shrugged. I decided not to broach the subject of the Holocaust. After later discussion with him about his theological training, I wondered if perhaps German Seminary Students struggle under a more rigorous theological course than Americans. I still hadn't heard what I wanted to hear about the Church during the Nazi era.

Most of the shops were closed when we began our tour of the city. Bertram had pointed out the University and his Theological College as we passed by. Classes resumed in a few days. We approached a darkened area of a residential section. However, a bright glow shone above a walled-in section. The illumination gave the allusion of nighttime on the Strip of Las Vegas. A high board on the opening that seemed to be the entrance read, in English, "American military personnel forbidden to enter." (The warning had obviously been the work of American Military Authorities.) Bertram warned me that the streets behind the wall would probably introduce me to a scene that I might never have seen in America. I became more curious. He also added, "Remember: we are on a walk-through, and not a patronizing mission." Now I was becoming apprehensive, but I trusted my host.

Once we had passed through the labyrinthine entrance, we came upon a scene that I would describe as an "Avenue of Marketed Prostitution." I had to admit that at first I was apprehensive about walking the street, and then I felt appalled. I also felt a bit guilty. However, I was there with a young theological student, a future German clergyman. So I proceeded down the avenue with him. I had never seen anything quite like it before. Window-front sex for pay was on gaudy display. The pedestrians were 100% male, the servers 100% female. Both sides of the streets were lined with open, windowless, platform after platform, within pedestrian reach. Nobody was reaching, however, except the females who were beckoning customers. They were dressed in gaudy costume, and their makeup was repulsively exaggerated. Passers-by were permitted limited flirtation with the females, and arrangements for service could be made with their pimps on the spot or in the inside hallways. Occasionally one of the prostitutes stepped off her platform and out into the street in front of her window. The costumes were skimpy, sparkly, and suggestive, and their shoe heels were perilously elevated. The prices were negotiable, Bertram informed me. I asked him how he knew. He replied, "The big boys have told me!" He did not admit to knowing the prices. The private pleasure rooms were upstairs. Occasionally a male customer would step into the hallways and, I presume, negotiate for services, and then head up the steps with his server ahead of him. While Caucasians dominated, the choice of servers included a few Asian and African women. A few gray-haired ladies were also advertising. Gray-haired males numbered disproportionately among the streetwalkers. I wondered how many were in the category with Bertram and me, lookers rather than takers.

The two of us walked down one side of the street, then turned around and walked back. We had minimal conversation with each other during our walk. He assured me that there were Polizei present. He also explained the pimp protocols. After a few more minutes of lingering and conjecturing, we both agreed when I said, "We have come, we have seen, and we have conquered—temptation, that is." Bertram laughed and added, "And without even needing angels to come from heaven to help us!" I nodded in affirmation. Once back in the dark, which seemed doubly dark after leaving the glare of the prostitution promenade, I questioned, "No cameras?" Bertram responded, "Verboten." We took a bus back to Bertram's and went to bed long past midnight.

I enjoyed a good period of three or four hours of sleep before Bertram awakened me with a "knock-up." (I was surprised to hear that expression coming from him.) I couldn't recall having dreamt. I showered and felt cleaner both internally and externally. Bertram's mother called us to breakfast. I was ready. Upon finishing eating, I complimented her by telling her that she had fixed "a breakfast for threshers." I had to explain that American metaphor. After "thank you's" and "good-bye's" Bertram and I left for the Train Station. I was taking the "Ferry Train"—a term I do not use when telling my story without spelling "ferry"—to Copenhagen (in Danish, "Kobenhavn.") Bertram stayed with me until I had boarded, and we hugged on parting. I reminded him that he held in his hands an open ticket to visit me in America sometime, but he would have to pay for his own transportation. We both laughed. That was our last communication, and it will probably hold the record of "Last" until our last days and "the renewal."

In spite of the walk down the sex street, Hamburg had provided a good stop. The saddest part of the visit was that, in 1953, like the Hanover to Berlin trip, I could not hitchhike—or I did not feel safe doing it even if the Soviets allowed it—either to or from Hamburg or Hanover and Berlin; I had to fly. The alternative was a dangerous and very difficult drive, and you were safer traveling with a German, and safest with an East German. The Soviet Union had erected roadblocks with steep restrictions for drivers and passengers. It was easier traveling to Denmark. Mother Nature had set up a few water-blocks, but human nature had learned how to navigate them.

Chapter V

The Mermaid of Kobenhavn, And the Tunnel a Swiss Train Runs Through

"Where can I go from your spirit,
or where can I flee from your presence?"
"If I ascend to heaven, you are there;
if I make my bed in Sheol, you are there." (Psalm 139: 7-8.)

The holy hitchhiking that features in Chapter V took place in two different European locations, and in two different seasons: one at sea level in Kobenhavn (Copenhagen), Denmark in the Spring, the other at snow level in Zurich, Switzerland, three months earlier. Neither hitchhiking nor holiness played a major role in the first; both dominated the second. The two events have neither logical nor chronological connections. Their co-recording at this point serves as a balancer of chapter length.

My first visit to Kobenhavn has already had a prelude. It is recorded in the previous Chapter. I had hitchhiked to Hanover, Germany, flown to Berlin, then after several days in Berlin, I took a plane to Hamburg, and from there I traveled by boat train to Denmark. The Kobenhavn episode resulted primarily because of a pen-pal relationship between a Dane and an American, Sonia Tholsted from the Danish Capitol, and her long-time pen pal, Ruth Giffen, a schoolteacher from St. Clairsville, Ohio. When Ruth first learned that I had received a Seminary scholarship to study in Scotland and would be doing European travel, she encouraged me, if I were traveling to Denmark, to visit Sonia. I told Ruth that I hoped to be there, and I promised her that I would visit her pal. The two had corresponded with each other for several years. They had shared customs and cultural nuances indigenous to their native cultures. However, neither one had ever visited the other.

Sonia, like Ruth, had at one time taught school. She left the profession when she married Paul, who eventually became an executive with the Carlsberg Brewery. She and Paul had two children, Wilhelm and Philip. Wilhelm was nine years old when I first visited the family, and Paul was six. Both were handsome and aggressive youngsters. When Paul retired, he and Sonia moved to southern France near Cannes. She died of cancer shortly afterward. I last heard from him three of four years ago. In addition to the stop detailed in this chapter I have visited the Tholsteds in Kobenhavn two other times when I landed on the plane in their city while taking tour groups to Israel, traveling SAS airlines. Wilhelm became an SAS maintenance supervisor at the Kobenhavn Airport; he visited us once in Seattle. More about his visit will be shared later. He has died since then. Philip had kidney disease, and the last communication with Paul indicated that he was waiting a kidney transplant. His profession slips my memory.

The Kobenhavn time followed a brief overnight stop in Hamburg, Germany chronicled in the previous Chapter. I had put in several days during Holy Week, culminating in Easter Sunday, in Berlin. I traveled on a packed holiday-crowd boat-train to the Danish Capitol. Many of the younger set had been skiing in Germany and Switzerland during the Lent-Easter school break. Beer was consumed in generous quantities. Exhilaration dominated the train compartments. Several of the younger crowd drew me into conversation in English; they wanted the practice, looking to the day when they would come to the United States, and they wanted to arrive with an American accent. Some of them probably were also hoping they could find a prospective host; or someone who would set them up with a date with a beautiful rich American beauty, or a wealthy handsome Casanova. Maybe I could advise them on how to apply for and obtain their "green card." Once a card was in their possession they could look forward to an extended work-stay in the U.S. A., serving in an upscale American Restaurant or hotel maid position, or doing carpentry work and house painting, or finding a job with Microsoft.

I was excited about the train transfer from land to boat to land. It happened more smoothly than I had anticipated. We left Germany in daylight; we arrived in Denmark in the dark. The boat lurched and rolled occasionally. My mind questioned: had the coaches bulged an inch? Or were they too securely bolted to their tracks to dislodge on the Ferry and imbalance it? Occasionally the echo of a train modestly distributing weight to a different wheel could be heard. After a short time on the water, the cracking noise had lost its panic effect on me.

Upon arrival in Kobenhavn the train moved as easily off the boat as it had rolled on. The travel time had passed so quickly, in part because my compartment mates and I shared histories and occupations and hitchhiking adventures. None of them had, or would admit to ever having done, holy hitchhiking; they were interested in hearing about my adventures. They kept asking me theological questions, and I kept offering theoretical answers. They seemed satisfied. All too soon the train arrived in the Kobenhavn Station. (In Germany I had started accustoming myself to pronouncing my host city, and spelling it, as my hosts did.)

Passengers started disgorging the train in hordes. One could have imagined that half the population of Kobenhavn—the younger half—had just spent their spring vacations skiing. In addition to their skis, several returnees lugged bags of sweets and souvenirs, plus poles and boots. (Ski-boarding had not yet become popular.) Skiers would pick up the remainder of their equipment at the Baggage Claim. My luggage was on my back.

I surged with the masses along the concourses. Traffic slowed down at the Terminal entrance, as welcome parties greeted arrivals. Customs matters had been taken care of in travel. I was well inside the Station itself when I spotted a hand-printed sign—held so high that I could not see who was holding it—that read, "Vernon Elgin." I pushed my way through the crowd toward the sign holders. I came upon a tall handsome man and a young lad. I knew that I had arrived in the presence of a senior and junior male Tholsted. They recognized me from the photos I had sent, and started smiling. We reached out our hands and traded shakes. From then on I was Vernon to them, and they were Paul and Wilhelm to me. Pen-pal correspondence had linked us emotionally and physically. I followed Paul along in the crowd until I discovered that he was headed toward the baggage claim area. In accented, but polite English, Paul turned to me and said, "Vernon, we will pick up your luggage, and then we will find a taxi to take us to our residence." He was startled when I turned around and said, "You do not need to walk far; my luggage hangs on my back."

At that moment the little boy—nine years old, I learned—greeted me in precise English with, "Mr. Elgin, how are you?" He held out his hand, and we shook again. I thanked him for asking, and answered, "Thank you, Master Wilhelm, I am just fine. And how are you?" "Very well, Sir, thank you," he responded. As soon as he had answered my question, he had another for me: "How do you know my name?" I told him about his Mother's friend in America, and their correspondence, and ours. He came back with, "I want to visit America sometime. I want to see the Statue of Liberty. And I want to watch the New York Yankees play baseball." I expressed amazement to both the lad and his father at how well they spoke English. Paul admitted, "Wilhelm does better than his father." As our days of being together passed I discovered the truth of the Father's judgment. Paul apologized for Sonja not being at the Station to greet me. She was home putting Philip to bed. Besides, taxi travel would be more comfortable if there were only three of us, instead of five.

Paul hailed a driver who placed my backpack and the "Vernon Elgin" sign in the trunk, and we headed through the crowded railroad parking area and onto the streets of downtown Kobenhavn. I enquired about the "Little Mermaid." I was told that I would see her tomorrow in daylight. I would just have to wait. It would prove worth being patient.

We arrived at the house in probably one-half hour. Paul picked up my pack and rang the doorbell. The door opened, and the beautiful Dane dame named Sonja greeted me with a handshake, a hug, and a kiss. I recognized her from the photo Ruth had supplied. I reciprocated her affection. I later asked her if she had been named after the beautiful skating star, Sonja Heine. She said that, as a matter of fact, she had, in part because she had become a proficient ice skater herself. "And Wilhelm and Philip are both on their way to the Olympics," she added, patting Wilhelm's head; he backed away embarrassed. He was eating a jelly bun and was on his way to bed. He had not ventured any further questions of me; he was too tired and sleepy, I am sure. Before he disappeared, he announced, "Mister, you are going to sleep in my room." Sonja offered an apologetic remark about the room sharing, to which I responded, "I feel honored. Wilhelm, I hope my snoring will not keep you awake." He said that he was not worried about my, "What did you call it?" he asked. I spelled "snoring" for him, and said, "Now, Wilhelm, here is your first English lesson from your American guest. Again, how do you pronounce the word?" He was not sure. I told him we would have an English class at breakfast. He set me straight: "We won't have time at breakfast...!" And he disappeared into "our" bedroom.

The three of us adults sat down to the light meal that Sonia had prepared. I was more sleepy and fatigued than hungry. I presented the adults the gifts Ruth had sent them, and one that I had brought. Sonia had a gift for me to take back to Ruth; fortunately, it was small and flat. The meal turned out to be as much a feasting of the mouth as of the stomach, topped with a rich Danish dessert. We covered several subjects, tastefully combining food with Danish history, royalty and ceremony. Several bottles of Carlsberg sat at the edge of the table, and both my host and hostess had one. I refused a drink, partly on the basis that alcohol bothers my sleep, and partly on the fact that I did not have a taste for beer. Paul offered to bring out some hard liquor, including the Danish national drink, Akvavit. Sonja also offered me wine, and I said, "Thank you, but no; wine gives me bad dreams." She smiled, and assured me that I could drink as I chose. I asked for a glass of ice water. She smiled, and said, "Oh, I forgot. Ruth had written that you Americans drink more ice water than just about any other liquid." "It's cheaper," I added. We all had a laugh. I was yawning frequently. Sonja was sensitive to my fatigue. She again apologized that I had to sleep in the room with Wilhelm. I assured her that the arrangement was fine. My brother and I had slept together until I joined the Army Air Corps at age seventeen, and we had remained friends—most of the time. She and Paul both responded politely, "Oh?"

Sonja showed me their bathroom, and the intricacies of flushing the stool. I assured her that I would have no problem; I had lived in Scotland and traveled Europe enough that I had become accustomed to plumbing idiosyncrasies. She explained the hot water arrangements for a bath. There was no shower. I thanked her, and I added, "I am a morning bather. I just need to wash my face tonight." Sonja said that I could rise whenever I wakened, as long as it was after daylight. We agreed that that was a comfortable schedule. She planned to start out in the morning on our tour of their beautiful city. She would take me to see the "Little Mermaid" and other waterfront attractions, and several other Danish icons, including the Queen's palace. She was already aware that I could stay only two nights this trip, and I wanted to go to the Tivoli Gardens sometime—if it were convenient. She said we would do that tomorrow night. I thanked her and kissed her, and I said "Good night" to her and Paul. They reiterated how honored they were to have an American guest. I said, "The pleasure you feel compares with the joy I have in my first visit in a Danish home. I am humbled. Thank you." They nodded and headed down the hallway to their room.

When I went into "our" dimly lit room, I discovered that Wilhelm was still awake. He raised his head off his pillow, and said, "I was just waiting for you." I apologized for taking up some of his space for two days, and for keeping him up so late. He responded with another supply of questions about America. I told him that he could ask two, and then we had to go to sleep. His first question was, "Do you like yogurt?" I said that was not a very American question, since not many Americans eat yogurt, but it was becoming more popular. And yes, after visiting in Holland, I have come to enjoy it. I asked him if he likes it. He said, "It's my favorite food. You will have some of momma's homemade yogurt for breakfast." I said that I would look forward to it. (American Pizza had not yet crossed the Atlantic, or into Denmark from Italy.) "Now what is your second question?" I asked. He said, "Do the girls like the boys in America?" I paused, and said, "Oh, that is a hard question. Do they like each other here in your country?" He had a cryptic answer: "Very much." "I think that the same happens in the United States," I commended. "Now you may save the rest of your concerns until tomorrow, and we will have fun questioning each other. I have a lot I want to ask you about. OK? " He said, "OK, Mr. Vernon. I love you." I told him that I loved him, too. He yawned. I asked, "Wilhelm, do you pray a bedtime prayer?" He answered quickly, "We don't pray at our house. Do you?" I said, "I pray a lot at my house. And at God's house. Here is one prayer I pray before I go to sleep." And I led in the old standby, "Now I lay me down to sleep..." After I said the "Bless you's" and the "Amen," Wilhelm, with a yawn mumbled, "Oh, Mr. Vernon, that is nice. Will you teach me that prayer?" I told him I would, but tomorrow; and I said a final "Good night."

I undressed down to my underwear and turned out the light. The boy once again punctured the dark quiet of the night with, "Someday I want to go to America and get a job." "What kind of job?" I enquired. He quickly said, "Fly an airplane." I congratulated him, adding, "I am sure you will some day." (And he did.) He persisted: "Then maybe I can come and see you, and Aunt Ruth." ("Aunt Ruth" was the name the boys had been taught by their Mother to call her pen pal.) The lad had one more suggestion: "Maybe I can come and live with you." I said, "We shall see." I bade him goodnight. He was still not prepared to let go of the day. He asked, "Mr. Vern, where is your nightshirt? Don't Americans wear nightshirts?" "Some do," I responded, "but most wear pajamas." He asked, "Why aren't you wearing pajamas?" I told him that I did not have room in my backpack for a pair. He asked, "Why did you not bring a bigger backpack?" I paused for a minute, and then answered, " I was afraid it would be too heavy to carry. Now, Wilhelm, I think we had better both go to sleep. Otherwise you will not be able to get up and go to school tomorrow." He continued, "Oh, that is right. And I don't want to miss school tomorrow; one of my friends is bringing pastries for his birthday." "That sounds good, Wilhelm, and I know you don't want to miss it. So I am saying the last good-night now." With a bit of a grumble, he said "Good night," and turned his head toward the wall. Soon we were both asleep. I heard him snoring.

The bed was comfortable, with a large comforter to keep me warm. I started thanking God silently, and in the morning I recalled that I had only gone as far with my prayer list as Marjorie and my parents and my Scottish Landlady. I am sure I dreamed, but on awaking in the morning, I could not recall any details. It was 7:00 a.m., and I was wide-awake, ready to see the "Mermaid." I discovered that Wilhelm was dressed and making his own bed. I greeted him and asked him if I had snored too loudly. His answer came quick and curt: "Yes!" I headed for the shower...or... bath.

I approached the kitchen breakfast nook. Paul had gone to his job. I met Philip, and of course, greeted Wilhelm. He reminded me of my promise: gifts. I had forgotten what it was. I had small pens for each of the boys. I went to the bedroom and dug them out of my backpack. They thanked me for their gifts from America. Sonja had prepared a Danish breakfast of pastries, bacon, oranges and cereal. And her homemade yogurt. Four bottles of beer also graced the table. When I reminded her that I do not care for beer, she said, "Fine. Never mind. The boys and I will have a little for our afternoon snack," and she paused and smiled, and continued, "And maybe we'll drink part of yours." She smiled again and winked. She poured herself a healthy glassful. The boys had left for school. I asked for a glass of milk.

Sonja tidied the kitchen, and we headed out for our city tour. Our first destination was as planned. The "Little Mermaid" reached out a hand to us, or so Sonja interpreted. I held it, stroked it, and kissed it. And Sonja took my photo. We visited churches and museums. She had planned to take me to their church, but time did not allow. We saw more of the city the next day. I spent the end of it answering Wilhelm's questions, and teaching him and his younger brother some American folk music. They seemed to enjoy it. When I went to bed that night, Wilhelm was either still awake, or he had set his inner alarm to wake. He had another string of questions about American sports, food, and girls. I finally told him I was too tired to go on, and he thanked me for keeping him awake for a while.

The next morning Sonia took me to the train, lamenting how short our time together had been. I said that I hoped I could return. She hoped so, also. Paul and Sonia never made it to the United States, but a mature, married and divorced, and father, Wilhelm once paid a visit. More details about his time with us will be written about later. Sonia bade me farewell, and I boarded a train that would take me through Sweden to Oslo.

When we arrived in Goteburg I was tempted to leave the train and spend a day in Sweden, but I decided I could probably make that stop sometime in the future. Besides, Oslo had two or three attractions I wanted to see. I spent a busy day there. I had no hitchhiking, but a bit of holiness as I visited two churches famous for their architecture; and a famous museum of Viking lore and culture. From Oslo, I took the train across the mountains, through ski country and winter wonderlands to Bergen. From Bergen I traveled by ferry to Scotland, and resumed my studies. I soon began making plans for my long summer venture through Europe and Africa to Israel. (I experienced my first seasickness on the North Sea Crossing.)

Three more visits with the Tholsteds took place in the 1970's and 1980's. The reunion that I cherished most involved no hitchhiking. It resulted, however, in a Super Holy Sunday. I arrived at the Kobenhavn Airport early on a Sunday morning on SAS airlines. I was leading a group on a tour to Israel. Wilhelm, now grown and holding a job at the airport in aircraft maintenance, was not working that day. We had a long-day layover in Kobenhavn. Paul and Sonia met me at the airport. Except for a significant exception, my agenda for the day was taken up with visiting churches. Before that activity could begin, however, I had a YMCA mission to perform. I belonged to a fraternal group called, "The International Organization of Y's Men of the YMCA." The International Executive Committee was meeting at a Kobenhavn Hotel the Sunday I had the few hours of layover at the Airport. My local Club had commissioned me to extend official greetings from Washington, Iowa to the body. Tholsteds took me to the Hotel for my meeting. I gave my five minutes Y's Men's greeting, and then we headed out for churches.

Our first stop was the Church of the Danish Royalty. As I had expected, I found the architecture classic and beautiful. The Queen had not yet arrived for the service, or had left early, or for some reason was not attending church that day. We drove next to the Church of Tall Ships' Sails (or some such name.) The crossbeams of the nave of the church supported chandeliers in the form of tall sails. The scene was inspiring. We visited another large cathedral. We ended up finally, at the Tholsted's family Church, where morning worship was nearing an end. My hosts then took me to their home. Wilhelm, who had married—and Philip, who was nearing the age to—stopped by for a quick bite. Lunch was celebrated with the opening of a bottle of "Alborg Jubiloeums Akvavit." I turned convivial and drank some. Wilhelm bade me good-bye, and said he hoped to see me sometime in the U.S. I extended him an invitation to visit the Elgin's if it would prove practical. Paul drove me to the Airport, where I rejoined my waiting tourists, and a few hours later we left for Greece, on our way to Israel.

A few years after my last time in Kobenhavn Wilhelm, now a divorced man with two children and still working in maintenance at the Airport, flew to Alaska on a part business-part pleasure trip. The time was the early 1980's. He flew to Seattle for a visit. He brought along a bottle of Akavit, which sits in our storage shed, waiting to be opened when a dignitary comes to visit. One of the days Wilhelm was with us happened to be my skiing day. Although not a skier, Wilhelm was happy to ride with me to the mountain. He found plenty of persons to talk to, especially "ski bunnies."

My last visit in Kobenhavn happened in 1980 on a tour-group trip that I led to the Vatican, Greece, Russia, Egypt, and Israel. Our eighteen year-old Son, Paul, took three weeks out of his senior high school year to travel along. As had happened before, we had a layover in Kobenhavn. A young man from our Congregation, my future Attorney, Clint Johnson was studying in Denmark. Clint also came to the airport to welcome us. Paul Tholsted met all three of us and took us to their home, where Sonia had prepared a Danish dinner. Paul, the Dane, returned Son Paul and me to our Hotel, after dropping Clint off at his residence. It was nearing nine o'clock p.m. Son Paul and I had time to walk in the rain from our Hotel to the nearby Tivoli Gardens, more to meet my curiosity than his; he was tired after a sleepless flight from New York. We stayed until the Tivoli lights signaled their midnight closing. I have not visited in Kobenhavn since.

The second event of this Chapter, to which the first has neither a hitchhiking nor a holy connection, relates a winter-wonderland Switzerland climb. The Kobenhavn visit occurred during the spring break from my studies in Scotland, the Swiss episode had taken place on my previous mid-December early-January holiday. It happened sequentially to an episode previously shared, my French Flight from the Christmas Eve wax-candle lighting.

Recall that on my winter New College holiday, and my hitchhiking to southern France, I had spent Christmas Eve and Christmas Day with Madame Prousant and her family in Montpelier. When I left that metropolis, I started hitchhiking north, my destination being the Swiss City of Geneva. I wanted to visit the iconic places connected with the Reformation principals: John Calvin and John Knox; and then I wanted to travel to Zurich, if I had time.

I had shared my plans with a New College friend from Switzerland, Heubert Mueller, and he had encouraged me to stop and spend a night with his parents, near Geneva. I took Heubert up on his offer. After two days of hitchhiking north from Montpelier, I located the Mueller's; I also discovered that their ability to converse in English was even more deficient than my ability with German. We spoke in the deeper language of the Spirit and the simpler language of hands. I ate well and slept well the night I spent in their home. After an incident that had happened before I had gone to bed, I am sure Heubert's Mother did also. Frau Mueller had a group of women in the parlor, holding what I understood was a Church Committee. Herr Mueller and I occupied the dining-living room. At one point, while I was writing in my diary and reading about John Calvin's life in Geneva, and Herr Mueller was quietly reading, his Frau walked through with an empty wine bottle, heaved a huge sigh, and wiped her forehead with her apron. When she walked back through the room with a full bottle and headed for the parlor, Heubert's father made a comment, and they both laughed. I politely laughed at their laughs. I wanted to say, "Presbyterian Church (U.S.A.) Committee meetings aren't that convivial!"

I went to bed before the ladies had left, so I have no idea whether Frau Mueller made another visit to the wine cupboard. However, when I showed up at the table for breakfast, she gave no appearance of a hangover. While at the table I reported to the family about my family and fiancé, my hometown and my current Church vocation. I also obtained helpful advice from Herr Mueller about hitchhiking to and from Geneva. After breakfast he drove me to the town suburbs, and I started hitchhiking for Geneva's City Center. I made it there with plenty of time to see several historical places.

Any time when I become disappointed in or discouraged about the Presbyterian Church, I think about Calvin. Along with Martin Luther he holds the distinction of being one of the pillars that kept the Church from failing, a pioneer of transformation that underlines the truth of Jesus' words to Peter, "On this rock (sic. of faith), I will build my church, and the gates of hell shall not prevail against it." (Matthew 16:18.) No theologian, especially one with Reformation orientation, can enter or leave Geneva without a holy awareness of the spirit of John Calvin and John Knox. The legacies of their spiritual renewal still influence culture—there and all through the Protestant world. Calvin stepped into the shoes of a Reformation Simon Peter; Knox wore them as an apostolic James or John. He related to Calvin as his disciple. After some years in Geneva Knox returned to Scotland and began spiritual and ecclesiastical renewal changes there.

Though he was French-born, John Calvin was Swiss cultured. His father wanted him to become a priest; he studied law. (Recall from an earlier notation that 2009 celebrated the five-hundredth year of Calvin's birth.) Following a short career in law, the French-Swiss Reformer became convinced that God had called him to the priesthood. He set out to study theology, and become a pastor and an author. His iconic work, *The Institutes of the Christian Religion*, was written when he was in his mid-twenties. The Seventh American edition, published almost one hundred years after the first American one (1835), has maintained that the *Institutes* has maintained its status as one of the most studied theological works of all time.

In his "Preface," Calvin stated why he had published the work:
"The Book has been written with this purpose in mind: so to prepare and train candidates in sound theology for the reading of the divine Word that they might both have an easy introduction to it and proceed in it with unfaltering step, seeing I have endeavored to give such a summary of religion in its parts, and have digested it into such an order as to make it not difficult for any who is rightly acquainted with it, to ascertain what he ought properly to look for in Scripture, and also to what head he ought to refer whatever is contained in it."[1]

The 2009 Presbyterian Church (U.S.A.) *Mission Yearbook for Prayer And Study—Center Pages* pays this tribute to the Reformer:
"Calvin insisted that the human mind and conscience are freed for obedience to God through learning. If 'God alone is the Lord of he conscience' and if every person must answer directly to God for obedience to God's will, it follows that an enlightened and accountable conscience depend on an illuminated mind....a mind liberated to

explore the unfathomable mystery of the divine can only lead to the knowledge of God in the human heart through faith….for the Church to be an effective witness in the world to God's mighty acts of salvation, it must have an educated clergy and an educated laity…. Learning is the key to knowledge. Knowledge is the key to truth. Truth sets us free. Freedom serves growth. Growth leads unto wisdom. Wisdom informs faith and instills reverence and humility of heart in the fellowship walk with God."[2]

Awareness of, and appreciation for, the above data, set forth why Calvin exerted such influence on the city of Geneva, if not the whole nation of Switzerland, and the Reformed and Presbyterian Churches that grew out of his teaching and work. He was transformed, and he transformed himself, into a theological giant. As a tribute to his influence, among other reasons, the World Council of Churches, after its formation in the first half of the twentieth century, established its headquarters in Geneva.

My holy goals in stopping in Geneva consisted not only of visiting the buildings and museums connected with both Calvin and Knox, but also to stop by the headquarters of the World Council of Churches. I went by the facilities and a volunteer gave me a quick tour of the WCC complex. I spent the night in the city, and in the morning headed for Olten. I had no trouble either hitchhiking or talking holiness with the older man who gave me a ride. He could speak excellent English. He was not enthusiastic about my heading over the mountain pass for Zurich. It was a scenic route, he informed me, but it could turn treacherous.

I left his car at the turnoff. A young man was standing at the side of the road hitchhiking on the main road. He gave me the opposite advice from what I had received from the older man. He recommended I take the shorter route. The weather was clear, the road was well traveled, the scenery showed off the non-Alps area of Switzerland at it best, and the highway department took constant care of it. Since I was wearing a warm ski-jacket and had gloves and a stocking cap, I concluded that I was adequately clothed for Pass travel. I decided that I need not be overly cautious. I also had along a pair of fold-up boots. I bought a bag of chips and stuck it in my pocket and headed for the scenic route. I became more encouraged when the young hitchhiker quickly obtained a ride.

My hitchhiking up the Pass began encouragingly. The temperature registered 1C. The rides were short but constant. One driver was willing to talk about Geneva and its theological celebrities, the others wanted to discuss President Eisenhower, Hollywood and basketball. As time and miles passed and the elevation and curves in the road increased, cars nevertheless seemed to hold to the road safely. Unfortunately none of the cars I rode in was going as far as Zurich. However, each of the drivers said that the road we were traveling was safe, scenic, and a "sure bet" for hitchhikers, winter or summer. Besides, the highway was well maintained. The lack of competition for rides, however, began to make me a bit apprehensive.

Low clouds and occasional snow increasingly decorated the scenery. Residents became increasingly scarce. Afternoon daylight was receding. Daylight began to give way to dusk. At one point my courage ebbed, and I questioned an English-speaking driver as to whether I should consider reversing my direction. More traffic was going down the hill than up. His experience was that traffic increased as the end of the workday approached. However, he thought that I should have no trouble reaching the Hostel at the summit. "Then, you should plan on spending the night there," he advised. He insisted that to head down the other side in the dark would be risky, especially since snow was forecast for the higher elevations. "Zurichites" may be driving the highway, but it would become increasingly precarious for a driver to stop in the dark to pick up a hitchhiker.

Shortly after our conversation, the driver turned off the main highway. I thanked him for the ride and the advice. I stepped out into a brisk wind. I mused: oh, if only I could buy a cup of Swiss Hot Chocolate! And eat my sandwich. But I satisfied my appetite with some more chocolate. My prayers began to take on more desperation. I stopped short of bargaining. Visibility of the higher elevations of the mountain was disappearing. Traffic became increasingly spasmodic. Every distant headlight inspired a spurt of hope. I kept wondering, how much farther away is the hostel? Fees were not an issue. The increasing darkness, the beginning numbness of my hands, and the chilling of my feet exacerbated my fear. Fewer cars were going either up or down the mountain. I was experiencing mild panic attacks. When I saw lights on the hills and chimneys with smoke wafting out, I pinched myself to make sure I was not hallucinating.

Occasionally I saw a house, and I began to wonder if I should leave the highway and hike up to it, knock on the door and beg for a bed. I checked the time. Twenty minutes had passed since I had had a ride. If there were residents in the area, the lanes to their houses would soon be slippery. The number of houselights diminished, and the few that glared appeared a distance from the highway. I began gnawing on my last wiener schnitzel roll. I still had candy, but I was saving it for a cup of tea. But where would I find tea? Oh, if only I had chosen to hike a road that offered public transport! Oh, if only a Mountain Patrol Officer or a Highway Maintenance Truck would come by! Or, if only the mountain had a train running through it! I had forgotten that somewhere along the way someone had mentioned to me something about a tunnel station. But how far away was it? I hummed a line from a pop hit of the '50's, "Where have all the people gone?" I began singing hymns. My fingers were numbing and my ears were tingling. "Oh, God, should I turn around and try to pray for a ride back down the highway?" I asked myself. I still had clear enough thinking to realize that traffic headed down was no more promising than cars traveling toward Zurich. I panicked. I pondered: will someone headed for Zurich come along before I freeze to death? My leather gloves and stocking cap seemed to have lost their kindness. A car was coming. I thumbed it as desperately as possible. It passed me by.

In the midst of my despair, I thought I saw a small roadside billboard up ahead. I reached it and read, in French, German and English: "The Summit Ahead." In a few more yards there was a smaller board with the words, "Café Swiss Summit." But how far away was the summit? I reminded myself: "Vernon, you chose to follow a mountain trail to Zurich. And you were advised, 'It is well traveled.'" Suddenly I saw a light by the road, possibly a half kilometer ahead. I hoped it was more than a road sign. I knew I could make it. As I walked, the distance seemed to expand rather than contract. I prayed, "Oh, Lord, let it be a service station, or a reasonable facsimile." (I had already taken care of toilet needs alongside the road. Twice or three times!) Suddenly I thought I smelled coffee! Was I hallucinating again? Just then I arrived close enough to a turnoff road and another billboard to read, in German: "Café Swiss Summit." The hours were posted—in German and French. I translated the words to say, "Close, 5:00 p.m." The hour was 5:10. Maybe the proprietors lived at the Café or maybe they were late closing. Lights were still on.

I turned onto the gravel road and headed toward a building, surely the Café. A dull light or two shone through the cottage-style draped windows. A brighter light showed from a room someplace inside—maybe the kitchen. I approached the door. I tried to turn the knob. It was locked. I knocked. I knocked louder. Was a miracle happening? A man showed up and unlocked and opened the door. He gave me a "Bon jour. Guten Tag." He stood in the entrance as I poured out my plight in English and German "pidgin." Whether he had understood me or not, he had penetrated my desperation. He let me inside. He said something that I interpreted to mean that the nearest lodging could be reached twenty kilometers higher up the pass. I pleaded with him to let me sleep the night on his café floor. He asked—this time in German--something like, "Habst du fare?" I asked what for. He answered something like, "Tren." I asked in very "pidgin" German: "Gehen der tren nach Zurich?" ("Does the train go to Zurich?) He apparently had understood. "Yah," he replied. I felt a sudden survival of hope.

As we struggled further through communication deficiencies, he dismissed himself momentarily. He came back with a pamphlet that turned out to be a "tren" schedule. I think he said that he thought he knew the schedule well, but he wanted to be certain. "Yah," he exulted, and when I heard something like "Sech," I became excited. "Six?" I asked. "Yah," and he pointed to his watch: 6:30. I rattled off excitedly in English, "There is a train at 6:30 p.m." He said in English, "Yes." He added, "I fix you tea." Did he mean "High Tea" or tea and biscuits? It made no difference at this hour and in my desperation. I interrupted, "First, sir, how long a walk to the train? He held up five fingers, and said, "I walk you there. But tea first." "Yah," I responded. He headed for his kitchen. I think I recall saying something like, "Dunke... thank you very much, undt Gotte bless Du." He understood, smiled, and disappeared. He stuck his head around the kitchen door and asked, "W.C.?" I nodded, and he pointed it out to me. He stuck his head out again and asked, "Sie American?" I offered another "Yah." After he left, and I reflected upon his appearance, a question came to mind: "Do you play Santa Claus at a Zurich Department Store?" He was large and ruddy enough, and had a hirsute beard. I decided not to ask any questions. I located the W.C. (I had been in Britain and on the Continent long enough now to know the name Europeans use for restrooms.)

The Innkeeper had no bedroom for me in his Café, but he had plenty of space for me in his heart. As I began to absorb some of the heat of his Café dining room, I had a holy recollection: at least I was not traveling with a nine-months' pregnant woman, on donkeys, and arriving at an Inn that had no space for me except in the barn, and a feeding trough and straw on the floor had to serve as a maternity ward. At least, I would not be called upon to perform like Joseph, doing midwife duties for a woman who "had conceived" by the Holy Spirit and was about to give birth a distance from home, and in the middle of the night. In the short time that the Café operator and I had been together, and while he was fixing me something hot to drink, I had begun to compare him with the Innkeeper at the original Bethlehem nativity.

He appeared with a cup of coffee, a bowl of soup and warm bread and real butter—not the lard Harald had often offered me from his Berlin care packages when we were hitchhiking in Scotland. He also had some chocolate covered biscuits; ah, "Swiss Chocolate," I said to myself. It did not take me long to down part of the soup, drink all of the coffee, eat some of the bread, and gorge myself on all the cookies. (I had been away from Scotland long enough to call cookies by their American name.) I thanked my server and offered him money, telling him how I felt as if I were in Bethlehem, and he was the Innkeeper that had hosted Jesus' birth. The man bowed and smiled and spoke some sentences that I interpreted to mean he felt honored for the comparison. He then suggested that we head for the tunnel. He locked his Café. We headed out in the freezing air, I zipped up my jacket, and we started walking. He picked up my backpack and insisted on carrying it. He explained to me on the way—in French, German and Pidgin English—that the train would emerge from the tunnel on the west and re-emerge on the east. So the mountain was a mountain with a train running through it. And there was a station near the summit. It had been some time since I had ridden a train through a mountain tunnel.

We arrived at the Station within the time frame Chef Kampf had suggested. The train should arrive in about fifteen minutes. The part-time Stationmaster, who lived nearby, sent out a signal for it to stop. If it didn't stop, what would happen, I wondered? I calmed my soul with the hope that Herr Kampf would let me spend the night on his Café floor, and in the morning I could decide whether to head up over the Summit, or back down the highway. I owed Café Operator Kampf a mint—if only I had had one. I handed him a $10.00 bill, saying in English, "You have proved my savior." At first He was reluctant to accept the money, but I finally convinced him he had to. He finally did.

Shortly the train pulled out of the tunnel at a reduced speed, and we were convinced that it was going to stop; we started bidding each other good-byes, "Auf wedersein's." I grabbed my backpack and headed for the boarding area. I needed my flashlight, which I was able to locate after a major backpack search. The part-time Stationmaster made a remark that I took to mean that I could remain indoors until the train stopped. I told him that I wanted to be the first person on it. I need not fear, he said; he doubted that anybody would be leaving the train, and no other passengers were waiting to board. And it would not be overcrowded. And the engineer had had plenty of signals to brake his engine.

An alert signaled imminent arrival of the locomotive. The Stationmaster had turned on flashing red and blue lights. All that was required now was to wait, and trust that the train would come to a full stop. I could buy my ticket from the Conductor. I asked how often passengers came to this station. More often in the skiing season than at any other time, the agent informed me. He then turned to me and asked in German, something like, "Forstayen sie? —Do you understand?" I smiled and said "Yah," and I added a reasonable facsimile of a German "Thank you." I moved close to the tracks, stopping short of standing on them. The train converged on the station more slowly. Before it came to a complete stop and the doors started opening, I said to the Stationmaster: "I have a recommendation for a new name for this train stop: 'The Tunnel Treat,' and for the train itself, 'The Salvation Choo-choo.'" He smiled, and as the Café Operator started leaving, he said in broken English, "Good suggestions, Mr. American, but it will never happen!" I had wasted my breath, except for the fog it made as it came out of my mouth and the triumphant feeling I was enjoying. The Café owner disappeared in the dark. Assured that the Engineer was responding to his signal, the Stationmaster began to turn off the signal lights. The train came to a full stop, steam surrounding the engine. A coach door opened, and the Conductor welcomed me on board.

I entered the coach—it was an open car—and settled into a comfortable seat. The warmth of the car embraced me and gave me back my circulation. The Café coffee, the soup, the human hospitality at after-business hours, the rescue on the mountain that has a train that tunnels through it, and the prospect of arriving in Zurich in less than two hours constituted a miracle. I felt euphoric, I felt revived, I felt blessed, I felt adrenalized, and I felt less guilty about my poor judgment in tackling the challenging mountain pass. I felt alive and awake. Without one holy word—except with the Innkeeper—but with some anxious hitchhiking, I had another holy memory to tuck away in my book notes. I thought of Jesus' comments to the effect that they who show mercy unto one of the least, even the more foolish, of Christ's, have done it unto him. And like the ones who give a cup of cold water to one of the least of Jesus', they will not lose their reward.

As the rail kilometers passed, I began to feel that I could lay my head back on whatever would serve as a pillow—even straw—and dream, dream, dream. In case I could not sleep on the way to Zurich I could mentally organize my day for later recording in my journal. I had words for the caption: "A Holy Hitchhiking Foreign Mountain Miracle!" I slept and I dreamt. It was well I did. A marathon challenge lay ahead of me: seeing Zurich in one day!

1.   Calvin, John; *Institutes of the Christian Religion,* p. 18.
2.   *2009 Mission Yearbook for Prayer and Study,* Center Pages, pp. 3-4.

CHAPTER VI

In Tito's Town Without a Visa

"I was hungry and you gave me food, I was thirsty and you gave me something to drink, I was a stranger and you welcomed me.... **When was it that we saw you hungry and gave you food, or thirsty and gave you something to drink? And when was it that we saw you a stranger and welcomed you?** *Just as you did it to one of the least of these who are members of my family, you did it to me." (Matthew 25: 35-40, selected.)*

The first night I spent in the Capitol of the nation where Tito the autocrat ruled, I found myself in jeopardy: I was in Tito's town without a visa. The year was 1953.The agent at the railroad ticket counter in Venice had failed to inform me that the train to Thessaloniki, Greece, stopped in Beograde, and another one did not depart until the next day. Overnight stays in Yugoslavia without visas were illegal. I did not discover my crisis until the train stopped in Beograde and I had to get off. The dilemma that I faced could land me in jail. My prospects were oblique.

While hitchhiking in Scotland a few weeks before I had left Britain, I had had the fortune on the way to St. Andrews to receive a ride with two men going that direction. As our conversation proceeded, I detected an accent. I soon learned that the two had survived the Hungarian Revolution. They were native Yugoslavians, and they had been working in Budapest at the time of the uprising. They felt that their survival had been a gift from God. (Aha, I mused to myself, an opening for a later holy discourse.) I related that I would be in Yugoslavia in a few weeks on my way to Greece, and I would appreciate any advice they could offer me. One of their first comments issued a warning: "Do not enter the country without a visa; that is, if you plan to spend the night there!" I informed them that I would be buying a ticket in Venice for Thessaloniki, Greece, and so would only pass through Yugoslavia as a transient. The passenger said that he had a cousin living in the capital who is fluent in English. He gave me the man's name, address and phone number, and I gave him mine. He said he would send a letter to his cousin. Our conversation continued with their relating fascinating facts about the recent Hungarian revolution, their escape, and their life in Scotland. Upon arrival in St. Andrews, we separated without having had holy talk. Two weeks later I wrote to the cousin and heard back from him. He wished I were staying a few days in Yugoslavia; he would be glad to give me a place to stay and an introduction to his city and country. I wished I had the time to take advantage of his courtesies.

The New College Spring Term ended and school closed for the summer. I organized my plans for returning to the U.S.A. after travel across Europe to Italy, then through Yugoslavia to Greece. I would stop in Thessaloniki to spend time with the spiritual father of a New College student-friend, go on to Athens, thence to Egypt, and from there to Israel. Italy afforded me these highlights:

--A brief detour of my hitchhiking through the major cities of the Nation took me on a visit to "Agape," a Waldensian spiritual retreat center in the mountains in the central part of Italy. For years I had heard about Agape and had sometime in "daily prayer" incorporated liturgical resources from the community. The center takes its name from the Greek "agape," the word for self-giving love, or God's expression of holy love; the kind of love the world needs a lot more. ("Eros" and "philia" are the other two love-words in Scripture; the English transliterations give a clue to their meaning.) The Waldensians had struggled in Italy for survival, even before the Reformation. Their history has been marked by suffering and martyrdom. A French Church Father, Peter Waldo, began the group in the twelfth century. At the time of the Reformation, they discovered that they believed and practiced religion more like Martin Luther than medieval Popes.

--The hike up the hill to Agape softened as I chatted with fellow pilgrims. I perceived that I had had retreat experience in common with some of them at the Scottish Island of Iona Retreat event.

--A change of attitude toward Italians took place during my days in Italy. I had grown up in a small western Pennsylvania village so parochially

Presbyterian-Methodist that my profile of Italians had this image: "They are the Catholics who live in Pittsburgh and Philadelphia, vote Democratic, eat fish on Friday, worship Mary, and are known as 'dagos'." I was raised a Presbyterian-Democrat, as were my paternal ancestors. Besides "dagos," I also called Roman Catholics "micks," as in Roman Catholic Irish. Both cultural and spiritual effects at Agape moved me to a deeper appreciation for the diversity and piety of the Body of Christ.

-- My spiritual-attitudinal conversion accelerated upon my first visit to the Vatican. I could hardly move away from the sculpture in St. Peter's of the "Pieta." I knelt in one of the side Chapels and prayed, "Oh, Lord, forgive me. Do not judge me according to the measure of judgment with which I have judged Italians—or Roman Catholics."

--A holy hour spent earlier in a church basement had also transformed me. I went to the Milan Church that housed the dark (at that date), worn, brilliant, and inimitable, daVinci's "Last Supper." (It has since been refurbished.)

After those holy conversions, I started hitchhiking to Venice. As I traveled, I read Paul's statement in Acts 19:21ff. He had just survived a tumultuous time in Ephesus. Luke recorded the Apostle's sentiments: "Now after these things had been accomplished, Paul resolved in the Spirit to go through Macedonia and Achaia, and then to go on to Jerusalem. He said, 'After I have gone there, I must also see Rome.'" I had seen Rome, and now I must see Athens; and after that, Jerusalem. (And a few years later, Ephesus and Pergamum and Sardis and other Early Church locations.) I arrived in Venice, had a canal ride, fed the pigeons at St. Mark's Cathedral, spent the night, purchased snack food for the train journey, and the next day I bought my ticket and boarded a train for Greece. Of course, I had to pass through Tito land.

I had a compartment to myself until we arrived in Ljubljana. A massive contingent of soldiers boarded, and the compartment filled. I munched on snack food, read the current *Time* magazine, wrote in my Journal and observed the scenery. The silence of the military passengers amazed me. I found none who could carry on a significant conversation in English. I resigned myself to reading and resting and thinking and snacking. Train officials, perhaps military officers regularly walked through the cars, stopping by our compartment window and gazing. Were they checking to see if we were behaving?

We stopped for fifteen minutes in Zagreb; I looked toward the mountains, where sometime later the Winter Olympics would be held.

When we arrived in Novi Sad the soldiers left the train, as did a large number of the passengers. I waited for new arrivals. Few came on board. When the train pulled out of Novi Sad, the middle-aged English speaking man and I were the only occupants of the compartment. We talked about several matters, including the "forbidden topics," politics and religion. He claimed to be an atheist. He moved to the window seat across from me. He made an obscene request of me. Aha, I said to myself, now is time for that other forbidden subject. The man made a personal suggestion about having some adult fun in the restroom. I told him I was not interested. "Are you sure?" he asked. I said angrily, "Never surer of anything in my life!" Just then a train security officer looked in our compartment window. He paused a few seconds, then moved on. I took out my log and started recording my latest experiences. Conversation between the two of us did not resume. I read; he slept.

After an hour or more, an announcement came over the compartment speaker. The fellow passenger interpreted what the message had been: "We will be in Beograd in thirty minutes, and the porters will be through the cars to collect our tickets. Security will follow, along with customs, and they will want to see our Passports. In fact, the officer may take yours." I asked my interpreter, "What will the officer do with my passport, and how may I retrieve it?" His answer was, "You may get it back as we arrive at the Beograd station, or you may have to go to Security to have it returned." "But I am going on to Greece," I said. "Not on this train, you're not!" he said curtly. "At least not tonight!" "What?" I exclaimed. He explained: "This train does not go on to Thessaloniki. It terminates in Beograd. The train for Greece leaves tomorrow at noon." I looked closely at my ticket. It had two sections: one for Beograd, the other for Thessaloniki. To my amazement I also discovered that the tickets had different dates: one for today, and one for tomorrow. How could I have overlooked the discrepancy? How could the agent in Venice not have straightened me out? As if to console me, my compartment companion said, "Travelers frequently spend a night in Beograd because they have bought the wrong ticket. Good Luck." I looked out the window, rattling with fear and anger.

Two officers, or men of some distinction, came to the compartment window, knocked, and entered. One of them took half my ticket. The Government Customs Official, sensing I was not Yugoslavian, asked in both his native tongue and in English, to see my passport. Handing the document back to me, he said, "It appears that you are not planning to spend more than a day in our country." I asked why he had made that remark, and he responded, "You do not have a visa." I began to explain to him in simple English that the ticket had been sold to me in Venice without that explanation. He seemed disinterested. He said, "See the Customs Immigration desk immediately when you arrive at our Station."

When the train arrived in Beograd, I politely bade farewell to my fellow-passenger and began the business of ticket-confirmation, customs protocol, exploring a one-day visa, and passport processing. At the Customs Kiosk a lovely young woman greeted me in English, and with a charming, "How are you?" I returned her greeting, and said that I was anxious at the moment. I was also angered at the Venice ticket seller for not having informed me that my ticket did not entitle me to non-stop rail travel to Thessaloniki. The woman told me that that mistake happens frequently in Venice. She went on to say that few trains from Italy to Greece follow a non-stop schedule, and that I would have to exchange my ticket for another one tomorrow before I boarded the train to Thessaloniki. "The 'Athens Olympic' leaves for Greece at noon," she informed me, quite clearly and emphatically. I explained that I had no visa, and she said in that case, my passport would have to stay in her office until I presented a new ticket and was ready to depart the next day. In the meantime I was to restrict my movements to the area around the central metropolis of Beograd. "Do you understand?" she asked. I told her that I did, but I was anxious. She said that I would not find myself in any trouble as long as I carried my driver's license with me and as long as I was out of the country within twenty-four hours of arrival. I thanked her and went to the Central Lobby of the Station. I sat down in desperation, to pray and think through my dilemma. I knew that I did not want to spend a night on a hard train station waiting-area bench. I would have to locate a hotel and pay for a room.

An attractive man, probably ten years older than I, sat in the seat next to me. I greeted him in English, and he greeted me in German. He had a kind face. When I told him, "Ich bin American," he apologized for not speaking English. We said a few words to each other in German. Using my modest German vocabulary, I attempted to relate my dilemma. Reason pierced my irritation; it suddenly dawned on me that I had the letter with the address and other data about Adirk, the cousin of the man I had met while hitchhiking in Scotland.

I took out the letter and started looking it over. I showed it to the man I had been talking to, pointing to the Beograd address. He looked it over, raised his eyebrows, and said something like, "Kum mit mier." I hesitated, but at this point I would go anywhere with anybody who I perceived was as honest as this man or who seemed to offer a solution to my visa crisis.

We walked out of the Station together and boarded a streetcar. We sat down beside each other. The streetcar filled; the conductor started it, and we headed out from the Station circle. I took out the letter from Adirk again and showed it again to my guide. He nodded, but I had no clue what he was thinking. After we had ridden ten or fifteen minutes—with frequent stops and passenger departures—my seat companion rose and moved to the front of the car and talked to the vehicle operator. They conversed for several minutes. He turned and pointed me out to the operator, who shook his head as if to say, "I understand." When he came back to our seat, he took out his pen and drew a simple map and made x's on it, indicating where we were, and the street where Adirk lives. I concluded that he was leaving the streetcar before me. He said something to me, which I did not understand and then waved good-bye. As he arrived at the front exit door, he had the operator turn around and wave to me. I waved to him and waved good-bye to the man who had given me the needed assistance. I had a brief moment of comfort; I guessed that the operator of the streetcar knew where I was going, and he would inform me about leaving the car. My helper and I waved to each other, and he left. The vehicle started moving. I rode for a few more blocks, and the driver indicated that I was to leave at the next stop. When we arrived, I was startled with panic that the "next stop" proved to be the "last stop" for this trolley.

The few remaining passengers emptied out of the car and went their separate ways. I went out to the street and stood there until the conductor collected his moneybox and briefcase, left the trolley, and locked it. Before he walked away he pointed me to one of the side streets. He started down another one, turned around to me and shook his head no. He kept on until he was out of sight. I almost stopped breathing. I assumed that the street post he had pointed out was the one I was to be on. I could not read the writing, but it did not resemble the address I had on Adirk's letter. I stood still for a few minutes, wondering which way to turn, what to do. Maybe I should find a bus or taxi back to the City Centre. But no public transportation appeared in sight. I was in a lonely suburban neighborhood. There was no one on the scene; the place was deserted. The area was residential, no cafes or shops or telephone kiosks. And it was getting dark. Had everybody gone to bed? I was becoming more nervous. I had to urinate. Fearing arrest if I did it in public, I nevertheless played dog; I leaned up to a light post and did it on the sidewalk. I decided that nobody had seen me!

I had decided I would start knocking on doors, except the buildings in the neighborhood were large apartment complexes, and the doorbells all seemed to be internal. Night had almost fully arrived. Still no pedestrians! What should I do? If only someone would come along who could make a phone call for me—that is, someone who spoke or understood English. I wished I could cry. I combined my quickie prayers with threatening fears. What does the inside of a Yugoslavian jail cell look like? I wondered. At least it would be warm, and maybe coffee would be available. I imagined how Jesus must have felt in Gethsemane the night before his crucifixion. I was at the point of despair where he had been, and he was less than twenty- four hours away from his crucifixion: utterly alone, and helpless. He desperately prayed, "My God, my God, why hast thou forsaken me?"

In a few minutes I heard voices. They seemed to be coming from the street beside the one where I was. I walked toward it. Three young men emerged. I greeted them in English and German. They came toward me. I called out, "Emergencia, emergencia!" They came closer. I wondered: to rob, to mug, or to help me? I asked if any of them spoke English. None did. I asked for German. One boy said "Bisse." His German was so bisse however, and his accent so strange, that we could not communicate. I took out my letter, written in English, and, in my estimation, worth more than its weight in gold. I showed the "guys" the address. They entered into a noisy consultation. An argument seemed to be going on among them. It must have lasted ten minutes. Finally they said something like "OK," and one of them took off. The other two kept saying, "OK." I was guessing what OK meant: that they would bring my friend to me; that they would find someone who knew what they didn't know about the address; that they would go for a car, and we would travel around the neighborhood looking for the street; or that the single young man was headed for the police station. And what would he learn there: that my passport was at the train station? I did have my billfold, however, and my driver's license.

A few minutes later the young man showed up. He came bearing a map. The three started studying it, and again, an argument ensued. Shortly, however, a moment came when they all lit up with enthusiasm, and for the first time since we had met, all three seemed in agreement. "Ok," the map finder said, and another said, "Kum," and we headed down the street the streetcar driver had pointed out to me. I decided that we were going either to a police station or to a store where the owner would know the location of the address I had, or perhaps to a telephone. Eighty percent of my attitude was confident and hopeful. One of the guys offered to carry my pack. Since my camera was in one of my jacket pockets, my billfold in a secret pouch inside my shirt, I felt comfortable accepting his kindness.

My confidence in the three young men increased when each of them appeared to be showing solicitous regard for my safety and comfort. They occasionally turned on the flashlight and studied the map. They made sure I walked in the light of their flashlight. They cautioned me about the cracked sidewalk. I was feeling fatigued. We stopped in front of a large house with a chain link fence around it and an iron gate at the entrance. Each one checked out the address. They pushed on the doorbell.

At first, there was no response to the ring. My companions tried again. Oh, no, no one at home! Just then a large front door opened, and a figure came down the steps in the dark and started walking toward us. The light at the gate revealed a handsome young man who apparently lived at this address, or who would possibly know where to find it. Could it be Adirk? Without opening the gate the two parties began to talk. The dialogue seemed amicable. The resident drew nearer, and opened the gate and stood in it. The young men showed him my letter, which he scanned, I presumed, to verify the tale he had just heard. Talk resumed between the two parties for several minutes. I was becoming impatient. The man who lived at this address seemed oblivious to me. I was anxious to have my letter returned. He drew nearer, and they talked some more. I grabbed my letter, showed it to the stranger, and I asked, unaware of his linguistic background, "Are we at this address?" The man smiled, and said, in perfect English, "I am the man you are looking for; I am Adirk. Forgive us for taking so long to straighten things out!" He reached his hand out to me and we shook each other's. I was so overcome with relief, that I started shedding tears. We all began to laugh and all talked at once in our native tongues. It was like Pentecost. My guides were anxious to move on. I began to thank them, in rapid English; Adirk was translating. They all offered a handshake. I leafed in my billfold and found three one-dollar bills and distributed them among my saviors. They gave me their best English "Thank you!" that they could muster, and prepared to leave. Adirk thanked them again, and I yelled a louder, "Thank you!" They turned down another street and waved before they disappeared out of sight.

Adirk took me by the arm, shut and secured the gate behind us, and led me into the comfort of a pleasant and well-decorated living-room parlor. I smelled food cooking. Again, I was ready to burst into tears, but instead, I burst into smiles and an almost hysterical laugh. I was not sure, nor did I much care, whether Adirk understood. My tragi-comedy had written another "All's well that—almost—ends..." script. A woman—the family cook or maid, I presumed, showed up; Adirk had not yet made introductions. She invited us to sit down at the large dining room table in another area of the large room in which we had started becoming acquainted. We sat down and the woman served us a bowl of Slavian soup and fresh bread. I wanted to say a prayer of thanks, but I was the guest, not the host, so I decided to wait until I learned whether I was in the home of Orthodox Church Folk, Pentecostal Fundamentalists, Jehovah's Witnesses, or atheists. I was determined to find out before I left tomorrow; that is, unless I ended up in jail!

As we were about to take our first bites, another woman joined us. Adirk arose and began to seat her. He introduced us and told me she was his mother. I also stood up. She reached out her hand and took mine, and in decipherable English she graciously welcomed me. She said she was delighted to have an American visitor come to them. I was their first one. No mention was made about any other family members. As our conversation proceeded, Adirk said he had been waiting to hear from me, and he was apologetic for not being at the train to meet me. I told him about the strange circumstances connected with my travel, my ticket, and my anxiety about my passport. I felt anxiety about being "in Tito's town without a visa." He laughed and made a disparaging remark about the political situation in his homeland. He said his country was not a united nation, and he doubted that it ever would be.

After we had eaten, Adirk announced that we were going into the City to see some sights. Since his home was so far from the station, and since his family was into major repairs in their house, I would be spending the night at the "Hotel Beograd." He apologized. Adirk was certain that my train left shortly after lunch, which meant I would not violate my twenty-four hours of legal stay in their city. So I need not fear either a fine or a jail sentence. I breathed deeply, and when he offered me another bowl of soup, I said yes. He observed that I was eating too fast, and meekly suggested that I slow down. Both Adirk and his mother had traveled in Great Britain, but had never visited the United States. They wanted to know more about me and my family, my studies in Scotland, and football (soccer) in America. Adirk translated the conversation when his mother had not grasped what I had said. Occasionally he had to ask me for clarification.

Adirk's mother wanted news about her relatives whom I had met in Scotland. I filled her in with as much information about their families as they had shared with me, and I briefly concluded, "They seem very happy there; as I am." She then offered brief information about how and why they had first left Yugoslavia—for political dissent reasons; and then Hungary, because they were being sought by Yugoslavian authorities; and how happy they were to be in Scotland; and how fortunate I should feel that they had expressed trust in me by giving me the information they had. I injected, "I am very grateful to them and to God." There was a silence. The housekeeper entered and served us a great dessert. And coffee.

As soon as we had eaten—it was nearing 10:00 p.m.—Madame insisted that we be on our way. Her English proved elementary, but adequate. Adirk's use of English made him sound like a professor, or a future ambassador to the United States. I later told him so, and he was pleased. He said he concentrated on learning English, had studied it for several years at the Gymnasium (High School) that he had attended, and that someday his goal was to come to study at Yale or Harvard. I asked, "How about Ohio State?" He asked, "Why?" It required ten minutes to explain my recommendation, the priority one being its prestige as a major American University, but, "Most important of all," I said, "You could come and visit me. And maybe I could find you a wealthy young Ohio American female beauty." Both Adirk and his mother laughed. I told them about the lucrative coal-stripping industry in the area of Ohio where I was currently living, and serving as a Pastor. No time now, however, for holy talk. Before we had exhausted Adirk's hopes to study in the U.S.A., he suggested that we be on our way, to hear and enjoy the "Songs of the Beograd night." I closed my conversation with his mother telling her how grateful I was for my good fortune of being in their home and meeting their delightful relatives in Scotland, and that I was impressed that they were doing well under the circumstances that they had described. She was pleased to have me share my perceptions. We gathered my backpack. I took Adirk and his Mother's photo. I said that I regretted that I had no gift to give her. She responded, "Your coming is the greatest gift you could have given us." My nose puckered. I kissed her good-bye.

My handsome Beograd host and I left in a taxi for a city safari. He was dressed better than I, but I had done the best I could. We were on our way to enjoy as much of Tito's Capitol as I had energy and interest to see; and then to find the Hotel Room his Mother had phoned about, and obtained for me. As we moved around to various sections of the inner city, I asked

Adirk if we would see a sight such as I had experienced with Bertram in Hamburg. He did not understand. So I elucidated on Brothel Avenue in the German city. He said that those places exist in Beograd, but they are "black-marketed," and he had never visited one. Presuming that he was telling the truth, I congratulated him.

We entered a taxi for the trip into "Beograd Centro." Adirk told me more about his family. He wanted to know about mine. I took out my small portable photo album and showed him several shots, highlighting Marjorie, of course. He was surprised that Americans marry so soon after finishing their graduate education. He would have to work for a few years before a woman would accept his invitation to wed. I repeated my feelings of anxiety about not having my Passport on me. I related that I had been told on the train that I could claim the document the next day at the Customer Service Desk at the Railroad Station as I left Beograd for Greece. "Not to worry," Adirk said, like a New Yorker; "I have an attorney friend to contact if a problem arises." He anticipated none.

We left the taxi waiting in front of the "Hotel Beograd"—its marquee glowing in red neon, of course—while Adirk made arrangements for my room for the night, at his expense. I protested, but he became insistent. He said jokingly, that he "would put on a scene" if I did not accept his offer. I ended my protest when he promised that if he ever came to America, he would attempt to find me. I expressed surprise that the name of the Hotel was in English. Adirk offered a clue: "To attract the Brits and the Americans!" We headed for the registration desk. Adirk had me present my Driver's License and explain where my Passport was. The Hotel Manager was called to enter the negotiation. He disappeared, Adirk surmised, "Probably to call the Immigration Services. Or to make sure your name is not on the list of undesirable aliens!" And he smiled. The Hotel Registrar returned and completed the registration without further interrogation, and with best wishes for my stay in their city.

I was given a room key and we took the "Lift" to the Fifth Floor, unlocked the door and entered. The accommodation was clean, it smelled antiseptic, the bed was firm, the shower worked, the stool flushed, the Hotel offered wake-up phone service, and they provided a complimentary breakfast. There was no television or radio service, but there was a pay-telephone. What more could a person without a reservation expect in the land where Tito ruled? I left my backpack and we headed out onto Tito Boulevard. Adirk did not allow me to dwell on my anxious thoughts. He said we would forget all our troubles and we would enjoy Beograd, limited, as our sightseeing would be at this hour of the night. When he asked me what I wanted to see that may still be open, reminding me that the famous museums would be closed. I responded that the itinerary was his choice.

Adirk came across to me as an intelligent, personable, and diplomatic young man. I was not old enough to be his father, and almost too old to be his Big Brother, but I had reached the right age to be a best friend. I was sure that if the situation were where it could be possible, we would be. In the meantime I concentrated on how valuable we could make our time together regardless of the hour or of what time we returned to the hotel; I could sleep the next day on the way to Thessaloniki. I told him so. He said that he envied me; he had never visited there. He asked me why I was spending time in that city. "For religious reasons," I told him. I had finally found an opening for holy conversation. He was interested. I told him about my Greek friend in Scotland whose residence was in Thessaloniki, and I commented about some of the religious truth I had learned from Paul's letters to the Thessalonian Church. He listened as if he were hearing something he had never heard before. And I began to wonder if maybe he hadn't.

As we walked past some of the important government buildings, I questioned about human rights in the totalitarian nation. He had brief answers: "The human rights situation in Yugoslavia is not good. The Nation is headed for violence, and in some years ahead, possible political separation." He provided volumes of information about the press, the government, family life, professional opportunities, sports, the cost of a graduate education, youth romance habits, the cinema, and the history of the formation of the nation. In some areas, the data were not much different from what I could report to him about the U.S.A. I added some comments about the theater (pre-TV times), the thresholds of a coming computer age, pacifism, and sports. I was curious to know more about Yugoslavia, but I was becoming weary. I asked, "Is it OK if we go back to the hotel?" Adirk was ready.

I invited Adirk to come up to my room for more conversation, if he wished. He immediately accepted my offer. My hotel room had comfortable chairs. We both took off our shoes, and "went at it." Adirk seemed intensive and proved deeply perceptive about our choices of subjects. As the early morning hours arrived, I asked, a bit nervously, "What about religion?" He hesitated and then answered slowly and thoughtfully, "You know, Vernon, from what I know about the vitality of religion in your country, and from what I hear about Europe and the Communist world—I am sorry to have to say this—I wonder if maybe faith isn't a stronger force in the lives of people who live under oppression and suppression than in the free, democratic societies." I responded, "I do not wonder at all about that issue. From what I have heard and read from Czechoslovakia and East Germany, and even the USSR, I had the impression that where faith is harder to come to and to live by, Christ's followers are more prepared to avoid the Peter and the Judas syndromes: denial and betrayal." He asked for an explanation. I reviewed the Apostles' roles, and then I asked if he recalled Jesus' statement about "How hard it is for a rich person to enter the kingdom of God!" (Matthew 19:23-4.) He was familiar with the verse. We discussed Jesus' bias toward the poor and oppressed and dispossessed. I concluded, "In the United States we have impressive church-membership roles and worship attendance, but we tend in our affluence to forget another of the teachings of Jesus: 'Blessed are the poor (in Luke's version of the Sermon on the Mount), (or as in Matthew), "the poor in Spirit," for theirs is the kingdom of heaven.' (Matthew 5:3.) In the U.S.A. we have many people who are 'spiritual,' but not religious, in the institutional sense. Individualism abhors institutionalism." I had to explain that tension to a sleepy Adirk. As he yawned, I said, "Maybe you should crawl into that other bed next to mine, and phone your Mother." He smiled and stood up, thanked me, stretched and yawned, and started to leave.

It was time to say, "Good night!" Before he left, Adirk offered, "I will be here plenty early in the morning to take you to Tito Station; and to make sure that you leave with your passport." I thanked my new Yugoslavian friend, and I assured him that the gesture was not necessary. But he persisted. He left, and I went to bed and soon fell asleep.

Adirk phoned from the lobby at 10:00 a.m. I had been awake for an hour, and about my morning chores. I picked up my backpack and went to the lobby to meet him. When I produced a Visa card to pay my bill, the clerk informed me that there was no balance. "Why?" I asked. She said, "Your friend has already paid it." I looked at him and said, "Adirk, you sneaky scoundrel!" (I wondered if he had understood.) He just smiled. I thanked him profusely, and said that when he comes to visit me in America, I will—I wanted to say, "reciprocate"—but I chose, "I will do the same for you."

As the clerk handed me the receipt, she said, "I must remind you, Mr. Elgin, that when you are going to be in our country for twenty-four hours, you must have a visa." I responded: "Yes, thank you, I know the law. I blame my unplanned stay with you in your beautiful country with faulty ticketing in Italy. I will be leaving for Thessaloniki before my twenty-four hours end. I will be more careful the next time I buy a train ticket in Venice." The Clerk listened carefully. Adirk interpreted briefly. We said good-bye and she thanked me for staying at the Hotel Beograde. I thanked her for the hospitality, and for the kindness of my friend.

Along the way to the Railroad, Adirk thought I ought to experience a bit of Yugoslavian commercial culture, so we stopped at a bookstore where Adirk again showed generosity by buying me a book. We went on, to a men's clothing store, a souvenir shop, and a pharmacy; we then headed for the Railroad Station. On the way, however, we had a second eat-with-your-fingers helping of the Yugoslavian version of baklava. We found ourselves caught in a gridlock as we neared the Station. I asked Adirk if all trains left Beograd at noon. He hoped not. Many folks were leaving the City for a National holiday, he explained, and it appeared that all the cousins and other close friends had come to bid them "Good bye, and a safe trip." (A common custom in his country, Adirk explained.) He and I bade each other good-bye, and hugged, and I approached the gate. I presented my ticket. The ticket collector asked for my ID. I feared he would be asking for my Passport, and I was ready to say, "You already have it." However, I showed him my Ohio Driver's License. He was satisfied; he thanked me. He let me proceed to my coach. Upon boarding and after I had located my backpack on the wire rack over my head, I opened Adirk's departure gift. It was a small book about Yugoslavia with both script and black and white photography. The title read, <u>FOR THOSE WHO DON'T HAVE TIME TO SEE IT ALL</u>. The author had the same surname as Adirk. I opened another page of the book to discover a photo of the family. I saw Adirk as a teenager, with his father. Yes, father and son and mother. Adirk's father had authored the Book.

I settled into my seat, but not comfortably. I had a wrench in my stomach: where was my Passport? I had been told it would be on the train. I remembered Adirk's admonition of me earlier, to trust that all would be well, and I repeated, "I waited patiently for the Lord; he inclined unto me and heard my cry." (Psalm 40:1.)

The Lord answered my cry more suddenly than I had expected. A man in uniform showed up at my compartment and pushed open the sliding door. I had a quick flinching in my "gut." He fastened his eyes on me. He did not need to ask my name; he had seen my photo on the Passport. He introduced himself and asked to see my ID. I pulled out my Ohio Driver's license. The officer then handed me an unsealed envelope.

I opened it. It contained a beautiful olive-green document: my passport number showed through the cutout on the cover. I flipped it open and discovered a temporary visa stamped in it. The Official said curtly, in acceptable English, "You have thirty minutes yet to go before your legal time has expired." I said, "Thank you, officer. Let's get this train running on it tracks." The man offered no indication of understanding, and left. I wondered if I would ever enter Yugoslavia again. If I did, I wanted to meet more persons like Adirk and his Mother—and the young men who led me to the address that I had shown them. The wrench in my stomach disappeared. (So far, fifty-six years later, I have not yet returned to the split-up Nation.)

The trip through Yugoslavia to Thessaloniki passed easily and drowsily. Every ten minutes when I was awake, I was either chastising myself for not checking my train ticket thoroughly, or turning the pages of Adirk's father's book. Scene after scene of beautiful countryside justified the Author's reward described in the "Foreword." I turned tired. I shut my eyes and started praying:

"Thank you, Lord, for the hitchhiking in Scotland that had culminated in my good fortune of meeting and spending time with Adirk and his Mother. Thank you Lord for my American citizenship. Let me be patient in believing that 'All things (Sic. eventually) work together for good for those who love God, and who are called according to his purpose....' And those who show more diligence in buying train tickets. Thank you Lord for correcting my mistakes with hospitality beyond my imagining or deserving. Thank you, Lord. Thank youuuuuuu zzzzzz."

I had every reason to anticipate a peaceful entrance into, and a solicitous embrace by, Greece. I was to be the guest in Thessaloniki of Mr. Theophilus Thanatopolis (Lover of God, Victor over Death), the spiritual and adoptive father of my friend at New College, Dimitri. He had written his Father about my coming. He had given me his telephone number and address. I would need to contact him immediately upon arriving, since I was a day off my schedule. After I had had a good rest, and with only one interruption by a Greek customs officer who wanted to see my passport and stamp it with an entry visa, I munched on the snack Adirk's mother had given me. Shortly an announcement came over the sound system that we were approaching Thessaloniki; at least, I presumed that information had constituted the message. An English-speaking fellow passenger confirmed my suspicions.

Mr. Thanatopolis appeared among the crowds standing at the station entrance. He was holding a sign reading, "Father Elgin." My first impulse was to greet him with, "Not yet!" In a sense the words would have been only half true: I did not yet have a son, but I did have a pastoral ordination. I decided not to confuse him. He immediately recognized me, and held out his hands to embrace me, and kissed me on both cheeks. He was surprised that I was traveling so luggage-light.

As soon as we were in the taxi that he led me to, Mr. Thanatopolis informed me that I was to sleep on his studio-apartment bed. I decided not to ask where he would be sleeping. I secretly preferred a hotel room, but lest I offend my humble guest, I graciously thanked him. I eventually learned that he would sleep on the couch. I graciously accepted his sacrificial love, anticipating that neither the bed nor the couch would resemble the back-cracker that I had slept on in Dornoch, Scotland.

It became obvious to me in our first hour together, that Dimitri's adopted Father easily fit into my category of holy company; it also became clear that he loved his adopted Son, even though Dimitri was not a native "Thessalonikian;" he had been born and raised in the ancient coastal city of Beroea. (Read about it in Acts 17:10-13.) Both belonged to The (Protestant, Reformed) Evangelical Church that had been organized in 1858. Dimitri had come to know his spiritual father while studying at the University in Thessaloniki, and through his association with the Evangelical Congregation. Mr. Thanatopolis was an elder in the Church. He had no living family. He expressed gratitude for Dimitri connecting us. The elders of his church had requested that I speak personal greetings to the Church on the Lord's Day morning, and preach in the evening—that is, if I made it into the city on time and could stay that long. When Mr. Thanatopolis asked me if I could do both, I consented, adding that I was honored. However, I would have to leave on the 7:30 train Sunday night. My host assured me that that schedule would work out fine.

All did work out fine. My Thessaloniki visit was a most holy interlude in my travels. Both Mr. Thanatopolis and I filled our time together with holy talk and activity. I had neither the time nor the opportunity to hitchhike. I slept comfortably on his bed, and he seemed restful on the couch; at least he snored deeply and constantly—when I was awake! I was warmly and appreciatively received at the Lord's Day morning worship. It was easy, and joyful, to sense the unity and diversity of the Body of Christ. I had had a holy experience, the deeper interpretations of the Holy Spirit transcending our incomprehensibility of the others' languages. The clarification of the tongues turned my Thessaloniki visit into a revived Pentecost. (See Acts 2.)

At the end of the Evangelical Church service, Mr. Thanatopolis took me to the Orthodox Cathedral, where his landladies worshiped. Their Orthodox service lasts two or three hours. The nave and chancel and windows gave me holy esthetic delight. We joined the approximately one-third of the Congregation immediately inside the entrance to the nave who stood for the entire time. Following a refreshing appreciative portion of the service— we did not participate in the Eucharist—we headed back to Mr. Thanatopolis' residence. His landladies eventually arrived, and continued their preparation of a meal.

Each of the events of the day so far offered its distinctively memorable favor, none more than the flavors of the dinner desert. It introduced a treat I had never been served before. After we had enjoyed our bountiful meal of several courses, and the dishes had been cleared away, the younger woman appeared with a large bowl of Greek strawberries; she placed them in the center of the table. She then provided each of us a dessert plate. Next she brought a large bowl of powdered confectioner sugar. She gave each of us a small fork. Finally, in honor of Mr. T's son in Edinburgh, and my acquaintance with him at the New College, she arrived with a large container of premier Scotch Whiskey. The protocol was explained: attach a large strawberry to your fork, dip it into the Scotch, roll it in the sugar, and hold it for a few seconds, then savor the eating of it. (No re-dipping of the same strawberry the Madame warned us! Pouring a portion of whiskey onto our plate was permissible, however.)

I left the table a bit light-headed, but I managed to find my way to a comfortable chair for a rest, and a last-minute review and revision of my evening comments. I shared with Mr. Thanatopolis that I would be speaking about my understanding of John 14, the verses beginning, "Do not let your hearts be troubled. Believe in God, believe also in me..." I was concentrating on one word: "Also." I also planned to allude to Paul's farewell to the Ephesian elders recorded in Acts 20.

My host wanted to share information about his Church. I said, "Please, do." I needed and desired to know more about his Church, and their relations with the established Greek Orthodox Church. He started off by relating that evangelical churches had suffered considerably in the past, ironically because of their break from the "established Church." He believed that because of its oppression and suffering, his congregation and his denomination had become the Church it is today. Though small in numbers of members and of congregations, the Greek Evangelical Church constitutes the largest Protestant Body in Greece. It reaches out in ministry to Albania and Bulgaria. One of its social outreaches in Thessaloniki supports the Philemon Center, a ministry to persons struggling with substance abuse. I expressed to Mr. T. my hope that I could go to the Center Sunday afternoon, if time and transportation allowed. He appreciated my interest, but unfortunately, he informed me, the Center is closed Sundays: too many of its staff attends worship and enjoys a "Sabbath of rest." Maybe on another visit I could have the privilege. (Note: I have returned to Greece at least four more times, but unfortunately, I have never traveled back to Thessaloniki.)

Mt. T. engaged a taxi to take us to the service. A large number of the Church was present. My host gave me an eloquent introduction, and since I was a prophet away from home—and possibly for other reasons—I felt that I was being held in high honor. When in my opening sentences I spoke about Dimitri, the Congregation applauded. I kept my homily to the twenty minutes allotted—that is, ten minutes for proclamation, and ten for interpretation. I challenged the holy people to be—and I had good reason to believe that they already were being—a congregation of whom it could be written in such loving and laudatory terms as Paul had written to the first Thessalonian Christians. The Apostle began his Epistle with: "For the word of the Lord has sounded forth from you not only in Macedonia and Achaia, but in every place your faith in God has become known." (1 Thessalonians 1:8.) I related what I had heard of the testimony and witness of the current Thessalonian church, both the Evangelical and the Orthodox families of the one family of Christ. I closed with prayer. The Congregation offered thankful remarks, most of them in their language; Mr. Thanatopolis interpreted. I felt spiritually intoxicated.

He and two or three elders of the Church walked me to the Train Station. Again as frequently happened with Paul, particularly the last time he visited the Ephesians, several of the Thessaloniki congregation arrived at the station before the Train. Evening worship had been dismissed early to make the farewell gesture larger and more inclusive. When it was almost train arrival time, I suggested that, if it were legal and the group would agree, we mimic the piety Paul had practiced when he was saying farewell to the Ephesian elders who had come down to Miletus to support him at the beginning of his fateful trip to Jerusalem, and thence to Rome. I opened my pocket New Testament and read: "When he had finished speaking, he knelt down with them all and prayed. There was much weeping among them all...." (Acts 20:36-7.)

When the train for Athens arrived, the Thessalonian Evangelical Church members were on their knees, along with their American guest. The love for which Paul had praised the early Thessalonian Christian, also written about in his letters to the Corinthian Church, endured, along with faith and hope and the greatest of these, "love." (1 Corinthians 13:13.) We had tears as I boarded the train. The delegation and I waved good-bye for as long as we could see each other. The train whistle blew, and it left Thessaloniki.

The rest of my first visit to Greece unfolded quite differently from how it had for Paul. The missionary found himself in conflict with the pagan religions. He claimed that their beliefs were no religion at all, at least not the one of the "way and the truth and the life" of Jesus Christ. As I rested comfortably on a night train to Athens, I slipped into the peace—perhaps it should have been disturbance—that I would not enter the cultural and classic city with such a bold accusation. Of course, I need not worry; I would not be meeting a congregation.

I did no hitchhiking while in the Nation. I had neither time, nor the need to. I was housed in Athens—at no cost to me—for the next two days in a hotel owned and operated by Dimitri's girlfriend's Father, Mr. Zizimatos. I ate from the Hotel food menu, and it was complementary. When someone at the Hotel, or Mr. Zizimatos himself, did not take me to iconic sites, I acted as my own tour guide. I anticipated that in future years I needed the practice, because I anticipated that sometime in the future I would be hosting church members on tours of Greece. I would plan for them to have the joy of tramping with me around the Parthenon, seeing where the Elgin Marbles had once stood, and especially—for as many as could do it—climb Mars Hill. On the hill, the "Areopagus," I would turn to Acts 17 and read Paul's words spoken there, as recorded by Luke: "Athenians, I see how extremely religious you are in every way...." On his way into town, he had seen an inscription, "To an unknown God." Paul continued: "What you therefore worship as unknown, this I proclaim to you.... God... will have the world judged in righteousness by a man whom he has appointed, and of this he has given assurance to all by raising him from the dead...." (Acts 17: 22 ff.) Some scholars have attributed the apparent failure of a thriving First Century Athenian Congregation—like the Thessalonians' one—to Paul's failure to name God's Judge, or offer more about the life and teachings of Jesus. Regardless, today the Greek

Orthodox and the Evangelical Churches both preach and minister in the name of Jesus Christ in a City where many of the idols have fallen, or are only respected as ancient art, not Christian icons.

While in Athens, I boarded a bus for a tour to Corinth. (The experience has been alluded to earlier.) The date was June 2, Coronation Day. It was the event for which Queen Elizabeth had spent some time resting when a month earlier, hitchhiking friend Robert and I had received a wave from her as her Rolls Royce had turned into the entrance to Balmoral Castle. (See Chapter II.) The tour bus radio was tuned to the BBC as we were traveling alongside and crossing the Corinthian Canal. Recent Greek wars had caused such massacres that the Canal water flowed red. The tour bus passengers listened to parts of the Coronation. I was not hitchhiking, but I was hearing holy music and Holy Scripture—in English—and my Scottish-Irish blood warmed with surrogate patriotism. The taste I received of the Coronation Ceremony, steeped in Scripture and tradition, transformed the bus ride into a holy sanctuary. It also recalled my acquaintance with the Coronation Souvenir Book that I had purchased before leaving London. I quietly said to myself, "Holy, holy, holy, Lord God Almighty, Sovereign of sovereigns."

Euphoria from both the Thessaloniki and Athens visits were elevating my spirit and energizing my body as I traveled by bus to Piraeus, the port of Athens. My taste of the two iconic sites of early Christianity inspired a pledge to return for a feast. But now it was time to turn my attention to the excitement ahead. I would soon taste the water that Egyptians so desperately depended upon, and about which my missionary friends had prophesied, "Once you drink of the Nile, you will return to drink again."

In Piraeus I boarded a ship sailing to Egypt. By previous arrangement on the part of American missionary friends in Cairo, I would be met at Alexandria by missionary, William Fleming. While in Egypt I would have neither the time nor the need to hitchhike. I needed to travel to several large cities to see my acquaintances and move on. Besides I did not feel safe traveling by thumbing. I had persons all up and down the Nile who would facilitate my itineration of Presbyterian Mission achievements. I would have no fear of being where I shouldn't have been without a visa; my passport would be stamped with a visitor's one while I was still on the boat. I was anticipating walking in the land where Mary and Joseph had traveled with a donkey, and where Jesus had probably taken his first steps. The Holy Family had gone south with their infant son shortly after the visit of the Magi, and the beginning of Herod's genocide of infants two years old and younger. Joseph had been warned in a dream to evacuate Judea in order to escape Herod's wrath: "The Lord appeared to Joseph in a dream and said, 'Get up, take the child and his mother, and flee to Egypt, and remain there until I tell you; for Herod is about to search for the child, to destroy him.'" (Matthew 2:13.) Besides, their journey would fulfill a prophecy by Hosea: "Out of Egypt I called my son." (Ibid. 11:1.)

As in Rome and Athens I had walked in the steps of Paul, I would be privileged to walk not only in the Holy Family's steps, but also in the steps of those heroes of the Exodus, particularly the one who had heard God's voice at the bush which was burning but was not consumed: "So come, I will send you to Pharaoh to bring my people, the Israelites, out of Egypt." (Exodus 3:10.) And Moses obeyed God. His obedience helped me conceive a holy description for my journey: "An Exodus in reverse, from the land plagued to the land promised." Before landing on the soil of the land promised, I would confront results of victories of the Gospel in Egypt. I would encounter spiritual descendants of the holy people whose return to the land of promise following the infliction of the plagues had made possible.

CHAPTER VII
_____

The Land Plagued and the Land Promised

> *"Now the Lord said to Abram, 'Go from your county and your kindred and your father's house to the land that I will show you. I will make of you a great nation, and I will bless you, and make your name great, so that you will be a blessing.'" (Genesis 12:1-2.)*
>
> *"The Lord said to Moses to say to Israel: 'I will free you from the burdens of the Egyptians.... I will bring you into the land that I swore to give to Abraham, Isaac, and Jacob; I will give it to you for a possession. I am the Lord.'.... Moses told this to the Israelites; but they would not listen to Moses, because of their broken spirit and their cruel slavery." (Exodus 6:6-9.)*
>
> *"Jerusalem, Jerusalem, the city that kills the prophets and stones those who are sent to it! How often have I desired to gather your children together as a hen gathers her brood under her wings and you were not willing! See your house is left to you desolate. For I tell you, you will not see me again until you say, 'Blessed is the one who comes in the name of the Lord.'" (Matthew 23:37-9.)*

After critiquing an earlier version of this Chapter, my wife commented, "I wasn't aware that you had hitchhiked in Egypt and Israel." How astute! She was correct. Except for once or twice, and a few miles, along the Sea of Galilee, I hadn't hitchhiked extensively in either Egypt or Israel. However, I had begged rides in the latter, from strategic persons at strategic locations to strategic destinations. During the time I was in the two countries on two different continents, I kept reminding myself that both lands had experienced both promise and plague.

In addition to their importance in Biblical and Church history, I had more personal reasons for going to Egypt and Israel. I felt an affinity with the Apostle Paul's wanting to see Rome after he had preached in Asia Minor and Athens; I had seen Rome and preached in Greece and now I wanted to travel to places where I knew residents personally and to whom letters of introduction to me had already been sent. I claimed missionary friends and acquaintances up and down the Nile, and I knew some other Middle East Church leaders. Besides, I needed to be accountable for the one thousand dollars my Ohio landlady, Loretta, had given me as I was preparing to leave for Scotland. On one of the last days I had spent with her, she had handed me an envelope with the comment, "Here, Pastor Elgin, is a check to help with your costs for a trip to Israel before you return from Scotland." My plans even before I had left the United States for Scotland had included hopes to visit the land that had once endured devastating plagues because of their stubbornness toward the captivity of the chosen children of God, that is, Egypt; and the land promised to the Israelites, and plagued both by conquerors from around them and moral turpitude within.

Both Egypt and Israel have benefited from blessing and suffered from cursing. The affliction of the first resulted from Pharaoh's making repeated promises to release God's chosen people from their slave status so they could return home to Israel, and then not keeping his word. Israel's misfortune of foreign invasions and forfeiture of their land came because, though they had promised to keep faithful covenant with the God YHWH, they lapsed into disobedience. Both Africa and Asia Minor held high priority on my "must-go-there" list.

The holy family's venture to Egypt with their firstborn son romanced my desire to go there. Matthew reported the event: "Then Joseph—(Sic., upon an angel's informing him of King Herod's intent to kill the infant Jesus after learning from the Magi of the birth of the King of the Jews)— got up, took the child and his mother by night and went to Egypt, and remained there until the death of Herod." (Matthew 2:13-14.) (Herod's death is widely accepted as taking place in 4 B. C.) Matthew recorded a further prophetic and theological interpretation to Joseph and Mary's leaving Israel for Egypt: "This was to fulfill what had been spoken by the Lord through the prophet, 'Out of Egypt I have called my son.'" (Hosea 11:1.)

Another attraction to Egypt related to history and mission. The United Presbyterian Church of North America began missionary work along the Nile in the 1850's. I had several missionary friends and acquaintances all up and down the River. As Paul had a drive to see Rome after having seen many other places of wonder in his world, I had a thirst enhanced by the proverb I had heard many missionaries repeat, "One who drinks of the Nile will return to drink again." I had drunk from the Allegheny River in Pennsylvania near my hometown, the Ohio in Ohio after I had moved there, and the Mississippi in the Midwest when ministry called us there. I would later drink the water of the Thames, the Seine, the Danube, the Rhine, the Arne, and, more recently, the Aliakmon in Greece. Having drunk from those waters, and then traveling in Europe, I wanted, upon completion of my excursion in Greece, to head for the Nile and the Jordan.

First, however, I want to return to my emotions about Greece. As a Scot's' blooded Elgin, I had spent time at the location where the Elgin marbles had rested before their extraction and purchase by Lord Elgin. I must admit to some vanity. I had already exercised it in Scotland when I spent considerable time traveling to the city of Elgin, rooting round the ruins of the Cathedral, and purchasing and sending postcards to members of my Elgin family in the U.S. I had also relished in my two viewings of Marbles in the British Museum. I had excellent brochures about them back in Scotland, that is; I was delighted that the Museum had provided free information about the history of their acquisition. I had also made an attempt to contact Lord Elgin while living in Edinburgh in 1952-3. His name had appeared in the Edinburgh newspaper, the *Scottsman. An article reported that Lord Elgin had purchased* a new estate, and it named the area. I immediately wrote a letter to the Lord, and I promptly received a reply: he did not have one ounce of Elgin blood in him. He had bought the Title. I dropped the matter.

More recently, I have become aware of the controversy over the Marbles being shipped back to Greece and placed in a new Museum under construction at the Parthenon, allegedly for their safe storage, preservation, and display. The agitation heralds back to the end of the eighteenth and the beginning of the nineteenth centuries. Lord Elgin held the position of British ambassador in Constantinople to the Ottoman Empire. He had obtained the treasures in 1829 after Greece had regained its independence from Ottoman rule. The Nation of origin now wants their cultural icons returned. Britain has so far ignored the desires. The growing agitation for the possession of the icons has become one of the noisiest voices in the art-world's struggles over confiscated treasures. The completion of the new Museum has buttressed Greece's argument for ownership. The gallery opened in the summer of 2009. Several art critics have expressed trust that Britain may be amenable to a plan that would allow the marbles to be displayed for a period as a centerpiece of the Museum, and then returned to London. Cathleen McGuigan commented in *Newsweek,* June 15, 2009, "The ancient Hellenic culture that produced the marbles seeded all of Western civilization, not just the contemporary nation of Greece. The marbles, really, belong to everyone." (P. 63.)[1] Regardless of how one accepts that statement, no one can deny the esthetic power of culture and history. As a person with Elgin as a surname, I traveled to Egypt with a mild case of cultural euphoria and biographical attraction. It gripped me even more fully as I stood on the deck of the boat sailing out of Piraeus for Africa. I kept my post until the Parthenon and Athens were distant in both my view and my feelings. As the Greek shoreline faded, my thirst changed. The prophecy about drinking of the Nile came to my mind. I began feeling more excited anticipation about the foreign adventures that lay ahead. I left the higher deck of the boat and went below to locate my bedroom for the next two days.

I found my quarters and knocked on the door. I heard a voice inside, but did not understand the words. I opened the door and entered. A tall dark-skinned athletically framed male rose from his bunk and came toward me with his hand outstretched. I offered mine. The gesture began our brief, but intimately spaced, acquaintance. "I am Ahmed," he said as he introduced himself. I offered my name. Ahmed informed me that two of his colleagues occupied the stateroom next to ours. I perceived him as a companionable and honest man, and I determined that he and I would be compatible the next two days. I immediately became curious about his religion. Of course, I decided not to ask. I felt that I did not need to. Aware that the man was from Cairo, and with that name, he must be Muslim. (It took me until the ship was nearing Alexandria to confirm my perception.)

The sail on the Mediterranean gave me needed rest. I read, ate, slept, took in too much sun and drank too much coca cola, made a number of acquaintances, and I also worked on my Journal. Time moved closer to our docking time in Alexandria; it was scheduled for 8:00 a.m. I wanted to be up early on our African arrival, eat a good breakfast, and have my backpack with me when I went to an upper deck to observe the docking. I went to bed early the last night on board.

My roommate roused me at 6:30 a.m. He was already dressed, and he informed me that he had eaten breakfast. I commented on his early rising. His explanation alluded to his religion. The season of Ramadan had arrived, he reminded me. I recalled that during that season Muslims neither eat nor drink anything from the moment the sun rises until it goes down. When Ahmed hesitated, I asked, "Don't Muslims have to obey the religious customs wherever you happen to be during Ramadan?" I knew the answer to my question, but I was interested in his response. I did not need to wait long to receive it. He said, "Yeah, you are supposed to. But I am not a very good Muslim—away from home, that is." I would like to have opened my Bible for a quick instruction in Scripture. I would have turned to 2 Corinthians 6, where in a contrasting life "in the flesh," and after resurrection, Paul concludes: "So, then, whether we are at home or away, we make it our aim to please him (Christ)." (Vs. 9.) I screwed up the courage to offer: "Well, Ahmed, I am sure Allah will be glad to have you home again." He surprised me by saying, " I doubt that it makes a damn bit of difference to him!" The boat sounded a loud horn, and I knew I needed to eat hurriedly, pick up my pack, and head for the upper deck.

I had been informed by friends in Cairo that someone would welcome me and give me a tour of mission work there, probably Missionary William Flemming. At the end of my descent of the gangplank, I faced a Customs agent and handed him my Visa-stamped Passport. I noticed a man not far away waving to me, obviously William. When we officially met for the first time in a few minutes, he informed me that he had identified me from the May "United Presbyterian Magazine," our Seminary Graduation Issue. We greeted each other and headed away from the Port in his car. He gave me a comprehensive look at the major mission stations we Presbyterians supported in the Alexandria area. We stopped for lunch at an Egyptian equivalent of a MacDonald's fast foods venue. I spent the night with the Flemming's.

My itinerary for Egypt followed precisely the plan that missionary friends had suggested. The journey was made easier because all the cities where I was stopping were situated on the Nile. Several of the missionary personnel knew me personally. Others knew me by name or association with other church friends. One crucial stop was the Hospital at Tanta, a few miles up the Nile from Alexandria, approximately halfway to Cairo. Before I had left Ohio, a saintly member of the Congregation, Dr. Anna

Watson, in her eighties, had declared that if I did not stop at Tanta, I could no longer be her pastor! What an option! In 1898 Dr. Anna, one of the first female physicians in Ohio, had gone to Egypt, and with another American medic, the two of them had opened the Clinic that eventually became the well-reputed Tanta Hospital.

A synopsis of my first day or two in Egypt follows:

--The Alexandria stop with visits to a mission school and a Church Camp on the Sea, Sidi Bishr. One of my Seminary Roommates, Kenneth Nolin, had been born in Egypt of Missionary Parents. Until World War II had disrupted their peaceful life in the land of the Pharaohs, Ken, along with his mother and father, Ruth and William, and three siblings, had spent many of his early years in Egypt, including summers at the Camp. I would meet the Senior Nolin's later when I arrived in Assiut, south of Cairo. In the 1960's I would become their Pastor in Washington, Iowa, and would officiate William's funeral.

--The Tanta time; meeting personally a man I had read about in Church mission literature for a long time, Dr. Hutchison, with whom I shared native Pennsylvania distinction. He was the Missionary Administrator of the Hospital. Among other historical displays, and after meeting his wife, I was led to a plaque on one of the walls showing photos and offering narration on Dr. Anna's arrival there in 1898. I knew—or knew of— several of the nurses and other staff. The Doctor was pleased that his newly constructed incinerator—the first at the Hospital, maybe the first in Egypt—had just proved successful in its service of burning hospital refuse. It would prove a boon in protecting stray dogs, humans, and the Nile from infectious waste from the hospital.

--The train to Cairo with its fast speed giving me only brief time to work on my Journal. If I had thought that Tanta was holy—or that any of the mission stations where I would be a guest while in Egypt would be—I had not realized that the "The Holy of Holies" was to be discovered in Cairo. Many highly educated women of Egypt claim alumnae status from the Women's University there. Missionaries contacted in Cairo included:

❖ Seminary Colleague, and ordained U.P. Clergy, The Reverend Jack Lorimer, and his wife, Mary Lu. Jack held a top-staff position at the Evangelical (Presbyterian) Seminary. After fifty years of service to the Coptic Evangelical Church, Jack retired, and he and Mary Lu reside at the Presbyterian Retirement Home. Monte Vista Grove, in Pasadena, CA, (Jack has recently published *The Presbyterian Experience in Egypt*

1950-2000, a comprehensive and absorbing work published by the Outskirts Press.)

❖ The Reverend James Pollock (Brilliant Arabic scholar, later organizer of the Indiana University Arabic Library), and his wife Rachel. Rachel's Mother, Vera Buchanan, a former Egypt Missionary whose husband many years before had lost his sight from an infection he had encountered while on an emergency boat trip up the Nile, was visiting while I was in Cairo. Vera and the Pollocks provided me the unique experience of a breakfast at the Giza Pyramids. We also attended worship at the largest Evangelical Church in the City. (Both Vera and the Pollocks eventually retired at the Church Home in Washington, Iowa. Vera has since died.)

❖ I was also a guest of the Bailey's. Dr. Bailey headed the Audio Visual Department of the Egyptian Evangelical Coptic Church. Their son Kenneth was raised in Egypt, and after graduating from Monmouth College in Illinois, and the Pittsburgh-Xenia Seminary, he returned to the land of his childhood and youth as Doctor Bailey and subsequently lived in Beirut, Lebanon and Cyprus, serving ecumenical Church agencies in the Middle East. He founded and taught at the Near East School of Theology in Beirut, directed the Institute for Middle Eastern New Testament Studies and served on the faculty of The Ecumenical Institute for Theological Research in Jerusalem. Ken has written several popular Scripture Commentaries and Expositions from the perspective of Palestinian and other Middle Eastern village living situations. Many of his lectures have been taped as study cassettes and DVD's. I have known Ken since he was a junior in College, and he has been responsible for a large element of my attraction to the lands plagued and promised that are the subjects of this Chapter.

❖ Missionary Margaret Work became my official sightseeing hostess in Cairo. We traveled to several locations by bus, especially the Women's University (exclusively for women at the time). When Margaret retired and moved to Washington, Iowa, I became her pastor.

❖ The Cairo Museum, full of gold and history, approached across a moat on which papyrus was growing, was dazzling.

The Museum could well be named "A Pot of Gold." I had never seen so much gold in one location—even though the glass display counters from which the icons were viewed were covered with layers of dust. Docents in their nightgown-like garments and turbans told interesting and engaging tales about the treasures turned over to their trust—for a day! The sarcophagi are mystically impressive. The Cairo traffic is carelessly aggressive! I would not mind living there, but I sure would not want to have to drive there! A day and night at the Assiut College and Hospital. Ken Nolin's parents were on the College Staff. His father was the treasurer, and his mother performed hosting, instructional and other duties. The College has provided Egypt with several scholars, teachers and business executives. Ken Nolin's fiancé and future wife, Rosella Hutchison—daughter of the Tanta Missionary Doctor, was a nurse there, as was Ken's sister, Ruth. The nurses threatened me with a Delilah Treatment—cutting off my beard while I was asleep the night of my stay. Note: I remained facially hirsute throughout my touring of Egypt and Israel!

❖ Luxor was the final leg of the visit to Egypt. Its Karnak Temple and Valley of (Tombs of) the Kings required a day to see. I went to several places of antiquity, including the pyramid burial places of Egyptian royalty, especially King Tut. I walked underground in one of the pyramids. Sphinx statues guard the desert with watchful eye.

Christian visitors to Egypt need scarce reminder that they are drinking of a culture whose political system had once been devastated by promised plagues because they would not consent to releasing the Israelites from bondage. The prophet Moses, according to the Bible, finally triumphed with the pronouncement: "Every firstborn in the land of Egypt shall die, from the firstborn of Pharaoh who sits on his throne to the firstborn of the female slave who is behind the handmill, and all the firstborn of the livestock." (Exodus 11:5.) The catastrophe wreaked such havoc on Egypt that Pharaoh recanted, and the people of God left the plagues of Egypt for the promised land of Israel. Jews, Muslims and Christians all share the heroes of these events as ancestors. If you belong to any of the three groups, you perform a holy gesture by taking off your shoes or sandals as you walk the soil of Egypt—at least for a few steps. Christians have the added incentive for holy reverence for Egypt since Jesus' Holy Family was here sometime shortly after his birth, and he probably played in the sand as a toddler. Father, Mother, and son remained in Egypt, "until the death of Herod," after which Joseph took the child and his mother back to Israel. Herod's infanticide had served God's purpose, "to fulfill what had been spoken by the Lord through the prophet, 'Out of Egypt I have called my son.'" (Matthew 2:15.)

As I said earlier, I would have enjoyed going farther up south to Aswan but time was pressing on, and I had not yet set foot in Israel. I was comforted by the comment I heard frequently as I traveled up and down the Nile. The epigram about returning to drink of the Nile whetted my determination for future tastes.

The hours on the "Red Eye Special" down North to Cairo gave me plenty of time, both to rest and to do my journal work on my association renewals in and around impressive missionary work and cultural sites that have endured in Egypt. No saga or scene or site stands more impressively in the land of Ahmed and Allah than the monuments constructed for the sake of the Gospel of Jesus Christ. Mission cemeteries tell starkly tragic tales, both of infant and childhood deaths, and also of missionaries in the prime of their careers. One of them is an acquaintance, a young American United Presbyterian mission physician at Assiut Hospital who perished from the fumes of a faulty heater while taking a bath in his bathtub. His wife and children survived him.

While also observing interesting sights along the Nile—like naked men splashing their water buffalo with the muddy water, and women doing their wash from the banks, and children playing —I inscribed in my journal words from Paul's first sermon in Athens: "The God who made the world and everything in it, he who is Lord of heaven and earth, does not live in shrines made by human hands." (Acts 17:24.) I added a mini-sermon: "Nor does God live in shrines made of sandstone, or bodies, or souls, that either have not yet heard, or have heard and rejected, the Judge that the preacher Paul had spoken of in his sermon on Mars Hill in Athens. God is nevertheless the giver of the marble and the sandstone and the genius to design shrines from them, and also from the sweat labor that stacks the blocks in their appropriate slots." That truth applied equally to the Temple in Jerusalem, the Acropolis in Athens, and the oldest of them all, the Pyramids of Giza.

Arriving back in Cairo, I headed for the Airport. Serendipity greeted me in the waiting area. It started when I began conversing with three unsophisticated, but friendly and wholesome appearing, and perceptibly humble, American women. They had been serving the Lord as Christian Missionary Alliance missionaries somewhere in Asia, and they were taking the long way home for a furlough. Like me, they were using the Air Jordan airport south of Aman; many tourists, residents and businesspersons in 1953 were flying into the facility for their Holy Land excursions or other destinations. I shared my itinerary with them, and since they had none, they quietly asked if we could employ a guide in the West Bank and travel together. I perceived that we could be compatible for a few days, and concurred. Upon arrival in the airport north of Aman, Jordan we took a bus into West Bank Jerusalem. I made enquiries at the Air Terminal Information Desk where we stopped, and I located a guide by the name of Hadam. He was highly recommended by the Tourist Bureau representative at the desk, and of course, he had notebooks of substantiation. He had a Plymouth sedan and seemed amenable to our tentative schedule. He began his service by briefly transporting us to our respective places of residence: the ladies to a CMA Hostel, and me to the American School of Oriental Research.

Before he drove away, Hadam looked over my schedule and recommended some adjustments. The plan was acceptable. We would head out by 7:00 in the morning, stop in Bethlehem, and then head for Gerash, one of the best preserved of the ten cities of the Decapolis. We would aim for Petra in the afternoon. It was a big chunk to take in, he said, but we could do it if we let him do the timing—and driving. None of us quarreled with him about the latter. We would return to the Golan Heights above the Dead Sea for a 9:00 p.m. dinner prepared by one of Hadam's friends. (He warned us that we would hear occasional gunfire there, but it would not be aimed at us.) We would plan to be back in Jerusalem before midnight. We could rest the next morning and then explore West Bank Jerusalem. It sounded like almost too much, but we were committed to it. In the meantime he showed us several places of political and spiritual importance in the West Bank. We returned to our residences by dark.

Hadam was prompt the next morning to take us to Trans Jordan. Our first stop was Gerasa, also known as "Gerash," and sometimes called by the collective name for the ten associated Greek cities on the East side of the Sea of Galilee (Trans-Jordan), "Decapolis." The cities were constructed following the conquests of Alexander the Great. Gerash looks like a mini-Ephesus or Bergamum in Turkey; or Byblos and Balbek in Lebanon. It is one of the best preserved of the ten Decapolisan cities. It dates back to the first century, and parts of it before. After tramping around it, all four of us agreed that Gerash would surely compete for renown and appreciation with some of the other spectacular Holy Land sites we would visit. It listed among us as one of the most spectacular displays of ruins we had ever visited, and we had all been to Athens and Rome. (For me, visits to Ephesus and Asia Minor would come in later years.)

Back in the car and on our way, Hadam listened to our acclamations and interrupted, "Wait until you see Petra!" Fatigue from the dry desert air and sun had drained a larger share of our energy than we had anticipated, but we would come up with more when we needed it. We discovered that we needed it when we arrived at Petra. And we received it. We realized our need even more deeply as we mounted a donkey for the narrow path into the depths of the ancient city.

Also known as "Sela," (like "Petra," translating as "rock," like the Apostle Peter) the city of red and pink stone in many ways topped Gerasa in artistry and serenity, or at least rivaled it. It would turn out to be the most interesting wonder we had encountered yet in the West Bank and Trans Jordan, in some ways surpassing famous sites that I had visited in Rome and Athens. Ruled at one time by King Amaziah of Judah (2 Kings 14:7), it came under Arab influence, then Greek, followed by Nabatean conquest and rule. Finally, Sela fell to Rome in 105 A.D. The rough path to it leads through a gorge, mostly traveled by tourists on donkeys. (I rode down and walked back, but for the exercise and the experience, not because I suspected the donkeys had fleas—which I am convinced they had. The missionaries affirmed my suspicion.) Stunning buildings at Petra have been intricately carved into the red rock, and tell stories in intricate detail. Society seemed to have flourished, had been protected, and had prospered in the metropolis. One of the Nabatean Kings, whose rule extended to Assyria-Syria and trans-Jordan, is mentioned in 2 Corinthians 11:32. Describing an episode at the end of his career of suffering and surviving that related to the Nabatean hegemony, and before his deportation to Rome, Paul wrote: "In Damascus, the governor under King Aretas (Sic., of Sela or Petra) guarded the city of Damascus in order to seize me, but I was let down in a basket through a window in the wall, and escaped his hands." (2 Corinthians 11:32.) The time in Petra had exhausted us, but the red rock artistry, particularly the "Treasury," was worth every ounce of energy we had needed to invest in it. The women rode donkeys back up the rocky narrow path to the parking lot, while, as mentioned earlier, I trekked it on foot.

We headed back from Trans-Jordan about dark, planning to be at Hadam's chef-friend's dining room by 9:00 p.m. The house restaurant was situated at the South End of the Dead Sea. We arrived a half-hour early, and as customary in the area, the meal was only partly ready. The Chef, however, was expecting us. He provided us cold cokes and had pillows on the floor of his waiting room. I did not need to ask Hamad if his friend's meals were by appointment and designer meals; I knew it was "by appointment only." We were the only guests on his list for the evening. Several preparations remained before he would be ready. The ladies were content to relax, maybe snooze briefly.

I was ready for a rest also until Hadam asked if I would like to go down to the Sea for a short swim. Of course, I wanted the treat, but neither of us had a bathing suit. "No problem; it's dark," Hadam said. I was not sure what he had in mind. We told the sleepy ladies that we would see them in an hour, and we headed for the Seashore. We arrived in ten minutes or less. The night was bathed in a full desert moon.

Hadam informed me that I could either swim in my under-shorts, or naked. I chose naked. He gave me ten minutes in the water, and of course, I never dipped my head into the salty liquid; I would have a tour-de-salt if I had tried. The exercise and the wetting renewed me. Hadam told me when ten minutes had passed. I made the mistake and put my face on the water. My eyes burned and my sight—it was a full-moon night—blurred. Hadam said it would pass. "I have a surprise for you," he announced. "You mean a towel?" I asked. "Sorry," he replied, and as I moved into shallower water and prepared to expose myself, Hadam pointed to a five-gallon can of water sitting at the rear of the car. I had forgotten our find of the morning. On the way from Jerusalem to Bethlehem, Hadam had spotted the water can alongside the road. It had apparently fallen off a van or a lorry. He had stopped and picked it up and put it in the trunk of the car.

Hadam directed me to step behind the car. In the meantime he was crawling up on the trunk. He stood up and unscrewed the cap on the water can. He instructed me to come as near to the car as I could. He started pouring the cool water over my head and my body. I flinched at first, but then I began to appreciate it. I asked him to save two cups for my eyes. "Now for the towel," I said, and laughed. I grabbed my under shorts and dried as much of my body as they would absorb, and tossed them into the trunk of his car. My hair felt good, wet and a bit salty. I dressed, shaking the sand off my feet, and as we left, I said to Hadam, "Thanks for my resurrection." He asked me to repeat my platitude of gratitude. I wasn't hitchhiking, but I felt as if I were, and so, on the way to our special dinner, I introduced a few minutes of conversation about resurrection. However, perceiving that Hamad was neither interested nor inquisitive, we chatted about the ladies and his privileges of living among so many Muslims and a few Christians. I asked him if he knew much about the Gospel of Jesus Christ. We were pulling into his friend's parking lot. He responded to my question with another one: "Can we talk about that later?" I assured him that I would be delighted if we did.

In ten minutes after driving into the Chef's parking lot, the ladies and I were sitting at his dining table. I prayed, and we shared one of the best lamb meals I have ever eaten. I failed to identify one or two dishes, and I asked for a revelation. I was sorry I asked, but the food was tasty. The three women proved to be good sports, and we all seemed to agree on the delights of the foreign tastes. Besides roast lamb, the menu consisted of beef tongue, cold slices of something like polish sausage, green jelly for the meat, roasted potatoes and other vegetables, cabbage slaw, a brand of pita bread and, for dessert, a rich fig sauce served warm over a Palestinian pastry capped with a small spoon of ice cream. We topped off the meal with strong coffee. It was intended to keep us awake on the road back to Jerusalem, we decided. (I had invited Hadam to eat at the table with us, but he said his Culture of Tourism did not permit it. I did not pursue his answer, but I am sure he had food in the kitchen.)

I paid the bill. We had to pay extra for the dinner cokes. (I had become the unofficial treasurer of our group. I had been advised by the women not to be stingy, and I wasn't.) We said our "Salaam's" to the cook, and left for Jerusalem. We were very quiet on the return trip, so quiet, in fact, that Hadam put a tape of native music in his player, and a choir accompanied by Palestinian instruments serenaded us. We were back at the ladies' hotel and the American School of Oriental Research—they were not farther apart than a couple of blocks—before Midnight. I had fallen asleep. It must have been the swim. The missionaries never asked for details about our activities while gone from them. When I went to bed, I heard shots from the Golan Heights, but as Hadam advised, the shots were regular occurrences. My last prayers were for the peace of Jerusalem, as Scripture instructs. (Psalm 122:6.)

The second day with Hadam would prove less strenuous than our first. He wanted us to see several of the famous West Bank sites of Jerusalem: the Damascus Gate first, and some of the other gates of the city that he would point out to us from various locations; Temple Square, and the Dome of the Rock (so called because it is asserted that the rock in the center was the one where Abraham was summoned to place his son Isaac, and burn him as a sacrifice, but God intervened with a lamb, just in time.) We spent an hour or two in the Old City Bazaar. Hadam pointed out the "place of the skull," one of the reputed crucifixion sites, the Church of the Holy Sepulcher also reputed as an authentic location, and ironically from there to the Garden Tomb (reputed by many scholars as Christ's true sepulcher, but questioned seriously by those who maintain the burial site was a spot under the Church); and a brief time at the Wailing Wall. "Have your prayer written out," Hadam advised, "so you can insert it in one of the mortar cracks."

The third day, while Hadam took the ladies to other sites, the Reverend Najib Khoury came to collect me at the American School. He had lost his home, library and other collections in Jerusalem in 1948, at the time of the formation of the state of Israel on Palestinian land. Najib's reputation had preceded our first greeting. He had graduated from our Pittsburgh-Xenia Seminary (where my fiancé Marjorie was currently a student.) Najib had retuned to Palestine in the early 1940's and had worked in his local Evangelical Church. When his house was confiscated, he moved with his three children and pregnant wife to Bethlehem. He went to work for UNRA (The United Nations Relief Agency), and also became a finance administrator at the famous St. George's School. The two days I spent with him were an orientation on both the Palestinian "occupation" by Israel and on Biblical history. When I met her the next day, Abla, Najib's wife, allowed me to pat Alfred in her belly. Alfred was born, attended school in Ramalah, took university work, and then came to the U.S.A. He studied at Johns Hopkins University, and he now practices medicine in Columbia, Maryland. His older brother is a pharmacist there. His older sister lives in Long Beach, California, and his younger one married an Englishman and lives in London. Their mother, Abla, is a Beirut University for Women graduate. Najib was well known in the Christian Community of Jerusalem. After spending a day with him, I can understand why. He rented a taxi and took me to the "bowels" of Jerusalem, and from there, to Bethlehem, where he introduced me to several significant ministries of the Evangelical Church, and to some of the Church leaders. On subsequent visits to Israel I have had the privilege of being in Najib's home, and of having him come to the hotel where my tour group was staying. He sincerely and broadly updated us on the conflicts between the Israelis and the Palestinians.

I had negotiated with Hadam to rent a van on the fourth day, our last in the West Bank, so the CMA missionaries and Najib could meet each other; and Hadam could also meet him. Maybe after we Americans had finished our time in Jerusalem, Najib could arrange a visit with Hadam and finish the conversation about Jesus. I am sure the cultural affinities between them would make the conversation more meaningful and more productive. (Note: they never saw each other again.) At the end of the day we all agreed that we had spent eight hours in the presence of a prophet. It had been a holy day. Najib's one prophecy that I puzzled over was, "I give Israel ten more years." Hadam agreed. The last time I visited with Najib, in 1987, he said, "Vernon, I have changed my mind. I have finally accepted that Israel is here to stay, not in fulfillment of the promise of the plagued land, but in anticipation of a plague, the 'Last Days.' Now we will just have to learn to get along in peace." I responded to Najib, "To paraphrase Paul, I think you have the mind of Christ. Both of you, like Jesus, have certainly had your times of weeping over Jerusalem." Following Najib's death, Abla came to Maryland to live near their successful children, and their families.

Each day in Israel introduced holiness upon holiness; in fact, it is not an exaggeration to say that almost every moment did. The following were some of the more reverent experiences in both Israel and the West Bank, some of them shared with the CMA's:

- ❖ At Rachel's Tomb I witnessed an Israeli Soldier giving an elderly lady a rifle butting. She had been picking up sticks from the road and ditch, no doubt to make fire to cook a meal. Her sticks had flown in several directions. She was denied a re-collecting.

- ❖ A quick trip to Abraham's family burial purchase, the cave of Machpelah. Several of his descendants had also been buried in the tomb. (Cf. Genesis 49:29-33.)

- ❖ Wading in the Jordan River with water as high up on my hips as I could take it without getting my pants wet. I administered no baptisms on that occasion, nor would I do "re-baptisms" on any occasion. On subsequent visits to Israel I have occasionally officiated baptismal renewal vows, but never re-baptisms.

- ❖ Praying Christian prayers at the Mosque of Omar.

- ❖ Joining an evangelical group from France, in the midst of a Mass-Sacrament of the Lord's Supper at the Garden Tomb. I accepted the elements from the French Priest. The same experience was repeated on the Galilean hillside above Capernaum—Jesus' home after his rejection by Nazareth—the site reputed to have been where Jesus had miraculously multiplied five loaves of bread and two fish to feed 5,000 men plus women and children. (The French priest said later that if he had known I am a "Presbyterian Priest," he would have included me in the leadership of the service.)

❖ Bargaining loudly for a reduction of souvenir prices in the bazaar. I bought some expensive perfume, and when I arrived home and gave it to my fiancé, I offered to help her dilute it with water. I had failed to remember that oil and water do not mix.

❖ A quick trip north to Tiberias and a short hitchhike to a nearby "Kibbutz" (communal living community), but without time to become a holy talker; spending a brief time with a young Professor from Edinburgh who was the Chaplain at the Tiberias Scottish Hospital; swimming in the Galilean Sea—more like a Lake—and requesting a fisherman to allow me to help him clean his nets. I walked the sands where Jesus had walked, but not on the water! I asked the net man, "Is your name Simon Peter?" He laughed.

❖ An experience or two regrettably missed—though in subsequent trips to Israel I would "do" them—was hiking up the hill, or taking the gondola, at Masada, the ancient fortress alongside and to the west of, the Dead Sea, where almost a thousand Jewish soldiers fought to their finish against the Roman conquerors in the first century A.D. A short distance away is the remarkably well-preserved village of the Qumran Community, and on the hills in the distance are the caves in which the Dead Sea Scrolls were discovered.

The sequences above do not follow a chronological arrangement, but I introduce them to serve as an introduction to my crossing from the West Bank to Israel through the Mandelbaum Gate. The walk is, to say the least, intimidating. As I cautiously and nervously made my way through the wire and mesh, I could sense without sight, guns surrounding me within firing and killing range. My recurring fright was whether one of the guards may drop a weapon, or become entangled with a Palestinian, and his/her weapon would fire by mistake or by design! As I traveled around Israel, then and since, I could not help but conclude: The "promised land," both the West Bank and Israel, is plagued—with fear, hatred and a lack of the love of God. As soon as I had walked the "No Man's Land" stretch, I breathed deeply. My Passport had been momentarily taken from me, and stamped with an Israel visa, and once in Israeli Jerusalem I headed out for the CMA offices. My friends would arrive the next day, but by that time I would probably be somewhere else in Israel.

I had really not planned to go "From Dan to Beersheba" in the two days I had left in Israel. However, when I walked into the CMA offices I observed a man loading the trunk of his car. I introduced myself, and of course, he knew the ladies with whom I had been traveling the past few days. I said, with a bit of a hint in my mind, "You must be going on a trip." He told me that he was heading down to Beersheba for the day. I impertinently asked, "Are you going alone?" He answered, "Yes," he replied. "Would you like to ride along?"

I helped Neal finish packing his car, and we were soon headed south to the ancient "City of Seven (arid) wells," Beersheba, the city that in Biblical times had designated the southern extremity of the land, as in the slogan, "From Dan to Beersheba," (I Kings 4:25 et.al.) Dan is, of course, the name of one of the twelve tribes to whom the land had been doled out upon Israel's claim of it. The phrase first appears in Scripture in connection with appreciation for the emerging character of Samuel: "All Israel from Dan to Beersheba knew that Samuel was a trustworthy prophet of the Lord." (1 Samuel 3:20.) I wasn't even formally hitchhiking, and I was receiving a lesson about a holy prophet.

As we drove south toward Beersheba, Neal pointed out famous Biblical landmarks. He also became political; he spoke of the problems that the American Church faces in doing Christian evangelism among the Jews, and he reminded me that there are no closer allies than Israel and the United States. I told him that I pray regularly for Israel, and just as passionately for the West Bank, and as already alluded to, as Scripture instructs, for the peace of Jerusalem. (Ps. 122:6.) My pious supplications became more frequent and my prayers more fervent after chanting another Holy Land Psalm one day in Morning Prayer:

"If I forget you, O Jerusalem,
    let my right hand wither!
Let my tongue cling to the roof of my mouth,
    if I do not remember you,
if I do not set Jerusalem
    above my highest joy." (Psalm 137:5-6.)

Neal delivered his supplies and messages to the CMA Mission Building. He took me to one or two of the "seven" wells—the Hebrew, "sheba," in the City's name, is the feminine form the Hebrew word for "seven"—that Abraham had dug there. Following his occupation of the land he had given seven ewes to Abimelech, king of Gerar, as a pact that they would live peacefully together. Beersheba had other claims to fame: Jacob started on his hike to Horeb from Beersheba; Samuel's sons performed as prophets there; and Elijah passed through the city on his way to Horeb. (I Kings 19:3.) Our tour of Beersheba and the area ended at dusk. Neal headed the car north. He stopped at a roadside stand for fruit and sandwiches, and we arrived back in Jerusalem before ll:00 p.m. I fared better than if I had hitchhiked to Beersheba, and with a lot more certainty that he and I would return in peace to the Holy Capitol.

Before I left Israel, I experienced another serendipity: I was privileged with another day to be with Najib. We took a taxi to Bethlehem, and Abla and the children and I spent some more time together. On subsequent visits to Israel I would either go to their home—they had moved back to Beit Hanina, a Jerusalem suburb—or Najib would come to our hotel and speak to my group. A frequent remark from persons who went with me on tours of Israel was, "One of the most reverent highlights of my trip was the time that the Reverend Mr. Khoury spent with us." Our eighteen year-old son, Paul, made that comment when he accompanied me on a 1980 tour.

Before closing I want to share another of the holy highlights that not every group has the privilege of experiencing when walking in the land "where Jesus walked." I refer to a walk, which Jesus might never have taken, the trek through "Hezekiah's Tunnel." Because the water flow from the Pool of Siloam to a lower reservoir outside the ancient wall of Jerusalem also provides a drinking water source for many of Jerusalem's residents, the walk has to be taken at night, sometime after 9:00 p.m. and before 4:00 a.m. The trip is pleasant, though part of the time hard on the back; one cannot walk the whole way through standing up straight. Nor dare one walk it without sneakers or canvas shoes. The tunnel is called "Hezekiah's" because it is believed that the King had it dug during his reign, since Jerusalem was under foreign siege and its water supply was threatened. In 1880 an inscription was found at the entrance, written in Hebrew and relating an interesting legend. Some words are missing because of weather and moisture. The inscription relates that workmen started picking at the rock on opposite ends of the tunnel. Finally the time arrived when the dramatic meeting occurred:

> "While yet (the miners were lifting up) the pick one toward another, and while yet there were three cubits to be (cut through, there was heard) the voice of each calling to the other; for there was a split in the rock on the right hand... And on the day of the boring through, the miners struck pick. And the water flowed from the source to the pool (Siloam), 1200 cubits; and 100 cubits was the height of the rock over the head of the mines." (*The Westminster Dictionary of the Bible.*)[2]

Let me give you this personal advice about visiting the tunnel: the next time you visit Israel take an old pair of comfortable shoes along so you can do the walk. If I recall correctly, it takes less than an hour.

Time had come that summer of 1953 to leave Israel, head back to London, pick up my possessions, and travel to Southampton. I had reserved passage on the *S.S. Jerusalem* to Italy. It sailed out of Haifa for Naples. The Ship was making its maiden voyage on the Mediterranean and across the Atlantic. It was not a new boat, but it had been moderately refurbished. Every stateroom had been booked.

While the departure from the Israeli Coast does not offer the spectacular view that sailing from Piraeus does, the scene is nevertheless impressive. You have a panoramic view of Mt. Carmel, where Elijah had staged his victorious wet-bull burning contest, winning favor over the priests of Baal that had been conscripted by the wicked pair, King Ahab and Queen Jezebel. (I Kings 18.) Today you see the gold-domed B'hai Temple. The Mediterranean Sea colors compete with the beauty of God's created Sun reflecting on the Temple dome. The scene offers a sentimental and spiritual farewell to the land which God had promised to the chosen people, and which they had occupied for several generations.

One of the most poignant on-board sights on the *S.S. Jerusalem* was the tattoo on many holy Jewish victims of the Holocaust. They bore and bared them proudly. The long string of numbers on several passengers' arms bespoke of a modern plague: the Adolph Hitler Nazism perpetrated Holocaust. A few of the passengers shared their stories of faith with me. They had not lost faith in God. They were extremely grateful for the nation Israel—and the United States and the United Nations. I was curious—and often disappointed with the results—when I posed the question, "What about justice for the Palestinians?" Survival euphoria overwhelmed the conversation. A land promised continues to trump conversation over a land now plagued by a wall in Jerusalem, encroaching settlements in the West Bank, and an infitada in almost any place at any time.

Mt. Carmel provided appreciative inspiration to the crowds on deck as the *S.S. Jerusalem* had left Israel, and Mt. Vesuvius extended one as the ship sailed into Napoli (Naples), Italy. I set foot again on Italian soil, joyful in the knowledge that soon I would be boarding the *S.S. United States,* and after four days of ocean travel, I would set foot on "the land of the free and the home of the brave." I would hope nostalgically to recall and be grateful that the United States can lay claim to being a promised land to God's European people of Seventeenth Century England and other countries of Europe; and currently, to many people of several lands and nations. The United States has proved, and will hopefully continue to prove, to be a land of opportunity, in spite of our plagues—socially, culturally, economically, politically, and environmentally. America is in many ways the most powerful nation in the world, but it is at the same time troubled and endangered by national hubris, social disparities, and considerable pollution. However, it remains one of the world's most promising democracies. Every time I have been gone from the USA for either a long or a short period of time, upon returning I feel like singing: "God bless the West Bank, God bless Israel, God bless Egypt, God bless Europe, and God bless America."

When you raise a thumb along a highway to beg for a ride, whether on Route 210, 422, 40, or 66, say a holy word of appreciation for your nation. Have hope, and someone may stop and invite you into their car. And you may find an opportunity to talk holy.

1. Cathleen McGuigan, *"Newsweek,"* June 15, 209, p. 3.
2. *WESTMINSTER DICTIONARY OF THE BIBLE,* "Siloam," *p. 565.*

CHAPTER VIII

Gotta' Get Out of Africa, Even If I Gotta' Hitchhike; And I did! Both!

"An angel of the Lord said to Philip, 'Get up and go toward the south.' Now there was an Ethiopian eunuch, a court official of the Candace, queen of the Ethiopians, who had come to Jerusalem to worship and was returning home; seated in his chariot, he was reading…. Then the Spirit said to Phillip, 'Go over to his chariot, and join it.' So Philip ran up to it and heard him reading…and asked him, 'Do you understand what you are reading?' And he replied, 'How can I, unless someone guides me?' Philip began to speak, and starting with this scripture (Sic., Isaiah 53:7 ff.), he proclaimed to him the good news about Jesus…. (And) The eunuch went on his way home (to Ethiopia) rejoicing." (And before they parted from each other, Phillip baptized the unnamed eunuch.) (Cf. Acts 8:26-40, selected.)

My contract as a professor of religious studies with the University of Livingstonia in Malawi, Africa, was ending. Both my visa and my South Africa Air Lines Ticket were also about to expire. When I phoned to confirm my flight schedule to Atlanta, I shockingly discovered that my ticket was no longer valid. I had waited too long to renew. If I wanted to fly out of Africa I would have to buy a new one. The cost was $2600.00. Because of the late date, it was cheaper to buy a two-way fare than a one-way. I did not quarrel long or strong with the Airline. I said to myself,

"Gotta' get out of Africa, even if I have to hitchhike." I ended up having to. When a breakdown of our van occurred two hundred fifty kilometers from Lilongwe, I was forced to take to the road on foot. The unfortunate dilemma happened near a rural village on National Route 1.

Leaving Malawi was not easy. I was enjoying my time of volunteer teaching at the University of Livingstonia in the southern Africa nation. It had not been my first time on the Continent. At four times previously I had conducted tour groups in Egypt, and I had traveled there solo in 1953. An opportunity to return to the Continent developed when I learned that a Washington (State) couple, Dr. Henry Kirk, former President of the Community College of Centralia in Washington State, and his Wife, Jenny, a former Californian with University Administration Experience with a California University, had been traveling to Malawi annually for five years assisting the Synod of Livingstonia of the Church Central Africa Presbyterian (CCAP) to start a new University. Dr. Kirk was the Vice-Chancellor of the University, and Jenny was the Director of Public Relations. Learning of my willingness to volunteer by teaching religious studies in the College of Education, they coordinated plans with the Principal of the College, Eliezar, and the Synod Executive, The Reverend Doctor Matiyah Nkomah, for me to spend a semester with the College. In August of 2005 I flew to Lilongwe and was met at the Airport by Principal Eliezar and his driver, Cheeza. We drove to the Synod Offices in Mzuzu, where I met the Kirk's. After a few days of orientation, we drove up on the famous Gorodie Road to the Rumphi Plateau and the village of Livingstonia. The University was about to begin its third year. My responsibilities would engage me with First Level, (Freshman), students.

The Kirks, The Reverend Nkomah, and the Synod of Livingstonia, with minimal support from both the Synod and the national Ministry of Education, had struggled to open and to keep the institution going without either significant financial or political help from either the Church or the Government. Neither one had the resources to contribute. A Foundation had been set up, and contributions had come from individuals and organizations, both in Malawi and the United States. The University had borrowed facilities from the Primary and Secondary Schools, both of which had opened on the Plateau early in the Twentieth Century. Dr. Robert Laws, a cleric from Scotland, had arrived there in the 1870's and had remained a missionary to Malawi until 1926. Dr. Law's interest in education matched his efforts in improving life in the village of Livingstonia by bringing in electricity, opening a medical clinic, supply pure running water to the village, and constructing the problematic Gorodi Road. Another Scotsman, Lord Overton, had provided the Synod funds for the construction of a substantial native red-brick Church building, with stained-glass windows, and a large sanctuary with an attached sizeable vestry. Missionary David Livingston had visited the Plateau some years previously, and the Church was dedicated to his memory. The institutions and their supporters comprised what was known as a "Mission Station."

The parent ecclesiastical administrative body of the University, the Synod of Livingstonia, extends the northern one-third of Malawi. Its principal city is Mzuzu, with a population in the range of 50,000. The first University Class opened in 2003 and was graduated in 2007, with approximately thirty-five students. (The class lost only one student.) The 2008 and 2009 graduations have averaged the same number. The University currently holds provisional Accreditation status with the Malawian Ministry of Education. Five Colleges comprise the Institution: Theology, Education, Technical Education, Nursing, and Business/Commerce. The Education and Technical Colleges are located in Livingstonia, on the Plateau; the others are situated a three-hour drive away, in Ekwendeni, near Mzuzu.

Malawi, after turbulent years under an autocratic ruler, currently enjoys peace—if not prosperity—under President Bonjou. The University benefits from his strong emotional support. The Nation compares in size with Pennsylvania. It is a "long, skinny country," with Lake Malawi covering a large portion of its eastern border. It is "landlocked" between Tanzania, Mozambique and Zambia. Its population numbers approximately fourteen million, of whom an estimated ten percent has a family HIV-AIDS problem. Its principal export is tea. The official language is English. (A major portion of the instruction in the University is in English, the rest in Chichewa, the official language.) The GDP per capita is $800 (the cost of tuition, including room and meals for a semester at the University). More males than females are literate. Life expectancy is 43.45 years. *

The beginning of mission work at the "Station" of Livingstonia connects with Scotland. The Reverend Doctor Laws was the principal pioneer missionary. The village and the Church respectfully revere his memory. The treacherous rocky and curved Gorodi Road takes off from the major northern-Malawi asphalt tarmac Route One, more than a hundred kilometers north of Mzuzu, and proceeds up fifteen kilometers to the Plateau. More than twenty curves on the route are marked with numbered posts. Arrival at the terminus of the Road requires approximately one hour of travel in a rugged all-terrain vehicle, after two hours on the road from Mzuzu. Dr. Robert Law's home, overlooking Lake Malawi, has become a guesthouse and the center of social and educational activities.

The residents in the villages on and contiguous to the Plateau have to deal with less than efficient and up-to-date communication and transportation facilities and opportunities. Internet services are unreliable, as are media and other communication technologies. The University now has limited Internet communication, a moderately effective telephone service, local radio broadcasting reception, and very moderate television programming. Most Malawians cannot afford television, certainly not computers. My computer was one of four in use in 2005. The Livingstonia Clinic Physician, who came from Ireland in 2005, graciously offered the Kirks occasional use of her phone line. Kirks made weekly trips to Mzuzu to purchase supplies and attend the local Rotary meetings, to do University business, and to take advantage of <u>Internet</u> <u>Cafes</u>. To send or receive ground-posted mail with the United States usually requires two or three weeks. Postage and <u>Internet Café</u> costs tax the resources even of those of us Americans and Europeans residing in Livingstonia.

As in many African nations, Malawians are sincerely and fervently religious, and in comparison with my theology, wholesomely and reasonably conservative. (<u>Note</u>: the statement is meant more complimentarily than pejoratively.) Malawi, like Ethiopia, Kenya and many other African nations, claims a larger Protestant constituency than Roman Catholic. Muslims are a minority. The CCAP is one of the most influential ecclesiastical denominations. Islam is present in Malawi, but in "pockets" of the country. Students are Biblically versed. Vice-Chancellor Kirk informed me in my first visit with him to explore the possibilities of teaching at the University, "Your students will be able to quote more Bible than you." Hank was correct. Malawian children and youth receive religious education at their primary and secondary schools, whether they attend a private or a public one. Several churches also offer Sunday School classes.

If the Apostle Paul were to visit Malawi today, he may very well have the initial perception that the Apostle Paul had as he arrived in Athens—to paraphrase: "Dear citizens of Malawi: I see how extremely religious you are; for as I went through your villages and looked carefully at the buildings you have for worship, I was impressed, and I know that you believe in the living God who will one day judge the world by his son, Jesus Christ," (Paraphrase of Acts 17:22-3, except the Apostle did not name the Judge's name.) If Paul were to attend 7:00 a.m. "Daily Devotions" at the University, he would see enthusiastic and sincere evidence of the young Malawians' faith. Where in the United States would you find ninety-five percent of the students at a church-related institution of higher learning show up for voluntary devotions /worship at 7:00 o'clock in the morning—with about three-fourths of them standing because of a lack of seating? Where in Great Britain would you hear over one hundred students singing the better-known hymns of the Church with approximately twenty hymnbooks to share? Where in Ireland or New Zealand or Australia would you discover over half the student body willing to volunteer to lead morning devotions, deliver a sermonette, offer evangelical prayers, and possibly give an invitation to "accept Jesus Christ as your Lord and Savior?" And where would you hear "Onward Christian Soldiers" sung once a week, all four stanzas from memory?

Most students are church members, some of them even lay-pastors; and they are evangelical, but like the CCAP member congregations, they are also becoming more social-action oriented, especially about HIV-AIDS, too many pregnancies, and protective "safe sex." Condoms are ubiquitous and inexpensive. Boxes of them may be found at the end of checkout counters at the larger grocery stores. One Saturday during the 2005-6 academic year students and staff made a Saturday afternoon presentation on the problem of HIV-AIDS in Africa. The program was well attended. The Secondary School had also been invited.

University students, or youth of university age, and elementary and secondary students present a public persona that could be described as subdued or reserved, at least in public. They study hard and play occasionally. A small group of them may show up at the Principal's office or the Vice-Chancellor's residence, or at other administrative doors or facilities, to protest quietly over dissatisfaction of administrative policy, or housing or financial issues, like increases in tuition costs or monotonous meal menus. Students are liable to eviction from the University if they are caught smoking, drinking or behaving immorally. They receive a moral behavior lecture once or twice during the school term. They seldom, if ever, act violently; their demonstrations are more non-disruptive, non-violent, Martin Luther King Jr. style, as opposed to frequent Black Panther demonstrations, or anti-Iranian government ones.

The most blatant misbehavior that I was privy to happened one weekend when most of the staff was attending a conference in Mzuzu. Saturday was Football (Soccer) day at our playing fields. The College of Education occasionally played the College of Technology—as already noted, the only two of the five colleges of the University on our campus—and the "Techies" often beat us. Our Team occasionally took on the Upper- Level Secondary Students, and infrequently they won.

One Saturday morning about mid-term, three male students came to my door at the University House and asked to speak with me. We sat down. (Two were "jocks," one was a Student Body officer—handsome and athletic; both were good students.) First, they apologized for bothering me on my day off—I actually had three days "off" per week, that is, not in the classroom. I asked them to present their problem. A Football Game had been planned for the afternoon, but the University Dietitian—the only other Staff member on campus that day besides myself, and who the guys had just previously visited—had not been authorized by Principal Eliezar to allow the event. In fact, she might not even have known that it was happening. The game opponent of the College of Education "Edies" was the almost unbeatable Technical College "Techies." The Dietitian sent the students to consult me, the nearest to an official Staff member currently in residence. She told the young men that if they received my permission, they would have hers. I raised a few questions with the students, and finally decided that the non-scheduling was an administrative oversight, a common happening at UNILIA; and since the Principal could not be reached by phone, again a frequent happening over which Eliezar had little control except for perhaps forgetting to charge his battery or pay his phone bill, I decided that the campus would be quieter, and the temptations to be mischievous would be fewer, if the event proceeded. So I said, "Go ahead."

The student emissaries thanked me, jumped up, and took off to pass the word around and dress for play. I immediately walked over to the Student Dining Hall and conversed with Edith. We were both pleased with the decision. Word that the game was on soon spread across our tight-knit, close-quarter community. I detected an elevated spirit. It soon became obvious that student activity and spirit had taken on a peaceful pace. The Football Game would go on. Many of the students would also be studying the lesson notes that they had taken. The library contained few textbooks. I decided that I had better show up at the Football field. If anybody broke the rules and caused trouble on the campus, it would probably be the Technical College students; at least, they would be blamed! My presence might reduce the temptation.

I went to the playing field about 1:30 p.m. when the game was supposed to kick off. The game started well, and on time, with student officials, and no fights. Thank God. At the half, however, a cacophonous noise came wafting over the milling fans and teams. Suddenly from behind the trees a rag-tag band marched onto the field playing crude instruments—more making a noise than sounding a tune. The students seemed to be enjoying the creativity. When the student officials called the teams back for the second half, however, some of the band remained on the field. They were aggressively requested to remove themselves so the game could go on. For the most part, they complied, and stayed away, playing their noise among the (standing) crowd. I knew one of the band members. His name was Mac, the son of a minister. He was acting erratically. On another occasion when I had had a talk with him, his breath reeked of alcohol. He had probably been down to a village. I spoke to Mac, and again I detected drinking. Fortunately, their charade ended before the game, and both team and fans seemed to take the band in good fun. I later reported the event—and Mac—to the Principal of the Technical College, and he assured me that he would handle the matter. For some reason, in spite of the no-drinking policy, Mac was still in school at the end of the Semester. On a later occasion when I commented to him about his addiction, he walked away.

The center of religious activity—apart from the daily early-morning gathering of students for devotions—is the beautiful redbrick Overton Memorial Church, mentioned earlier. The architecture is typically Protestant, and Presbyterian. It has a long nave, a large chancel, no obvious transepts, no organ or piano, a beautiful Table with carvings of angels and saints, and a large pulpit and lectern. The English service convenes at 8:30 a.m., and if it finishes on time, the Chichewan speaking congregation gathers—or waits around outside until the "Englishers" have finished. A children's Sunday School meets in the small chapel at the chancel end of the Church. Sunday mornings when school was in session the services usually drew a full house. Most of the students attended worship, as did many of the village residents and school-connected staff, including myself. Pastor Ted, with liturgical assistance from one of the elders, administered the worship proceedings. I preached three or four times, with Ted interpreting on the first or second occasion, and letting the service be at the mercy of my English—and preparation—the other times. For the first three months I was on the campus, I never heard Ted preach; he enlisted visitors as the preachers of the day. Two or three women's choirs of approximately thirty members each, in beautiful print dresses and wearing headpieces, and sometimes barefooted, sang regularly. Two university choirs made presentations, sometimes on the same day as the women sang. A children's group occasionally offered an anthem. And there were always specials— solos, duets, and quartets. Congregational singing was 'a cappella;' no organ or piano was available. One of the musically gifted students had a keyboard. (The next container brought one that Marjorie and I had donated.) Occasionally the student choir leader played the accompaniment. On special occasions a trained choir director prepared a student group with a "special." Swaying dance movement usually accompanied singing.

My "Presbyterian Order" compliance received a shock my first Lord's Day at worship on the plateau. The Semester was beginning, and the students typically showed up en-mass. The church was well filled. A number of the congregants lived in Livingstonia and nearby villages. (Seating capacity easily amounted to four hundred places, and seating furniture consisted of unpadded wooden chairs or benches.) Upon Pastor Ted's invitation, Jenny Kirk introduced the new Professor from the State of Washington, with his Scottish Ph. D. Degree from the New College of the University of Edinburgh. I responded briefly. The Choir sang and danced. Pastor Ted spoke words of welcome, and as I was returning to my seat he announced: "I am happy to report today that Dr. Elgin will be the Associate Pastor of Overton Memorial Church while he is among us." What an honor! But don't let that secret reach Seattle Presbytery! According to the polity of the Presbyterian Church (U.S.A.), both the Presbytery the congregation belongs to and the Presbytery the clergy belongs to have to approve ministerial calls. Nevertheless, I accepted the assignment humbly and gratefully. I followed a "Don't ask, don't tell" policy. I subsequently carried out my Associate Pastor duties by regularly pronouncing the Benediction, and occasional preaching.

The rest of the Chapter will relate details about my Malawi hitchhiking. I did not frequently stand at the side of the road with my thumb up. Nor did I often see anybody else doing it, except in an emergency. Cars on the road were usually filled to capacity. When the time arrived that I had to get out of Africa, however, I had to finish off my trip to Lilongwe, where the airport was located, by hitchhiking.

My departure from Livingstonia was complicated by a flight ticket faux pas. I blamed it on several disturbing circumstances: a deteriorating hip; a weight loss due to a decline of appetite over a monotonous diet lacking fresh fruit and vegetables, bread, cereals, milk, desserts and other nutritious foods; sleep deprivation due to studying and correcting papers, frustrations and anxiety about my students and their poverty, and other matters. I attributed to these distractions a large share of the blame for my failure to renew my South African Airlines reservation for Atlanta. When I phoned the office in Lilongwe to correct the oversight, I was too late. Fortunately my flight reservation had been held, but my money was lost. And my ticket might as well have been. Because of such a short time left before the date of my departure, it was necessary for me to purchase a two-way ticket. There went the money that I had been skimping to save and planning to donate to the University Foundation, money that our Son had helped solicit for my mission. I found difficulty reconciling myself to the loss.

As the semester came to an end, I became extremely busy: leading my classes in review of the semester lectures; meeting with students concerned about the class lecture notes they had missed recording or had questions about; conferring, with young men particularly, who had no resources in sight to return to school the next semester, and wanting a gift from me, or for me to find American sponsors for them; preparing and administering and correcting final exams; giving away clothes, magazines, books, stationery supplies, school utensils, toiletries, room decorations, and other commodities; tutoring some of the slower students; and other end-of-semester chores.

However, I would go home with great memories and many new friends, like these activities and persons:

--Campus (community) social life on Saturday afternoon "Football (Soccer) Games," and an occasional presentation such as HIV-AIDS AWARENESS Sessions. No parties or dramas; dancing was prohibited. Church life plays a significant role in the students' lives, but Study hours came first.

--Librarian Augustin taking me in his pickup to his "plantation" on a plateau across from ours, to the home on the land he owns, and which also provides residence for his ninety-some year-old Mother. He went weekly to travel down to the river with barrels to collect her water supply. If he could not make the trip, his hired young man (or men) who lugged the barrels down to the stream below her house, filled them, and then struggled back up the hills with them. On the day that I was privileged to accompany Augustin, besides lunch and visiting with his mother and other relatives in a neighboring house, we picked pineapples. The trip provided me one of my most pleasurable Saturdays. (Augustin and his wife had also entertained me at a meal in their home.)

--A Saturday installation in a nearby village of a new Headman. Professor Msista had relatives in the village and he planned to attend. He invited me to accompany him. On the way down the hill in his pickup, he informed me that the Installer had come a day or two early to enjoy the villagers' free hospitality, with lots of bootleg liquor. His leadership gave evidence of his lugubrious indulgence. We sat on the sloped ground around one of the homes, maybe of the new Headman—I do not recall. He and his wife and the Assistant and his wife were led blindfolded to the center of the ground designated for the ceremonies: a log on the red dirt. Music blared from a cassette player. Folk, mostly males, spontaneously stepped out to dance, sing, or perform.

--A three-day safari to Kusungu State Park north of Mzuzu; overnight stays in the Guest House. Elephants stomped through our area one night, but seemed to have left everything as they had found it. Hippos, birds, and smaller native animals bathed and swam in the lake in front of our residences. Both mornings at 6:00 a.m. and afternoons at 4:00 p.m. the Reserve Guide took us on safari drives. On occasion we passengers had to exit his van and help him make a road through the brushes. We saw elephants (much blacker than seen in captivity), zebras, giraffe, deer and other animals, but we saw none of the twelve or so cats reputed to be residents of the park. Drought had driven them elsewhere in Africa. Since it was the end of the dry-hungry season, the trees and bushes gave evidence of a depletion of the animals' food supply and major devastation by the elephants.

--One day a beautiful co-ed came up to my desk at break time and asked if she could run her hand through my (bountiful white) hair. Several girls lined up behind her to take a turn. I looked out at the guys and said, "Now, aren't you envious?" Patience answered ("Patience" really is his name), "Yeah, Professor Elgin, but we don't have to buy permanents!"

--Nearing the end of the Semester as Final Test time neared, I was asked to turn my Final Test Drafts in to the Principal's Office. I had prepared documents that combined objective and subjective sections. The Principal called me into his office the next day and said that my tests did not fit the school's standards: tests have to be totally essay, so the students have to think more creatively. I did not argue with the Overton Memorial Church Elder again; the time was too near to my having to get out of Africa. I did raise the issue with some colleagues about why the students never saw their papers after they had been corrected. I received an answer like, "That's the way it is according to the Ministry of Education." Some of my colleagues related that they had held "rump" sessions with students to go over issues related to the students' answers to the test questions. I was happy for that process, but could not arrange time to do the same before I had to get out of Africa.

The eve of my departure arrived. The University faculty and staff still on the Plateau held a party. Cook Robert prepared a meal with food he had never had the money or supplies to fix the previous five months. Principal Eliezar and Augustin and several others spoke flattering and encouraging words about my time among them. Now if only Henry and Jenny Kirk could have joined us! (Of course, they were back where I would be after New Year's.) The group presented me a gift: a wood carving in mahogany in the shape of a map of Africa. I had admired it in our local gift shop. Now I admire it in our Guest Bedroom. No champagne had been served at the gathering, and no one smoked! I was appreciative of the adulation and the austerity. I felt appreciated and accepted. In spite of our racial and academic differences, I had become one with the staff and the students. In fact, one of my last days as I was shaving and preparing for my shower with the traditional washbasin of water, I looked into the mirror, and I was startled. I said to myself, "Who is that white guy?" Then I laughed.

The morning after the party Glen and I loaded the van, said our goodbyes to Cook Robert, Housekeeper James, and other friends who stopped by, and headed down the plateau for Mzuzu. Our first stop was at a Lake Malawi waterfront Hotel. What luxury to have a good dinner and order a good breakfast! The next day we drove by the historic Bandawe mission and eventually arrived in Zomba. We sought out the nearby mission in Domasi, but we were too late to find any one who had a key to open the Stewart Guest House. Former Stewart parishioners from our Iowa Church had built it. We spent another comfortable night at a hotel on a plateau overlooking the plains of Zomba. We traveled the next day to Blantyre, the largest city in Malawi, named after the Scottish birthplace of Missionary David Livingston. Glen had a "close call" as we drove through throngs of pedestrians. They occupied both the sidewalks and the streets; one could have guessed they were celebrating a holiday. Vehicle horns were blowing. Driving slowly through the milling crowds, we encountered our first airport destination dilemma. Both our front windows were rolled down. Suddenly a commotion erupted. I observed Glen struggling to keep control of the vehicle and trying to shut his window. A young man had reached into the car and grabbed Glen's shirt-pocket leather billfold holding his money and passport. Glenn won; he had apparently inflicted enough pain on the potential thief that he withdrew his hand. No police could be spotted. We stayed that night at the Synod Guest House.

The next morning found us on our way to our final destination, the capitol and international airport city, Lilongwe. The distance covered three-hundred fifty kilometers. It could easily be accomplished in four hours. Glen had stayed at the Baptist Mission before, and he was confident he could find it easily. Our goal was to arrive in the city before 4:00 p.m. in order for me to claim my flight tickets to Atlanta. We could arise by 8:00 a.m. the next morning, and leave for the airport by 9:00.

After a breakfast—another like ones I had not eaten for several months (I, the non-breakfast eater)—we purchased petrol and headed North on Malawi Route 1 for Lilongwe. The street crowds had diminished. We made good time through villages and small towns, past CCAP Churches, food vendors and hawkers of used clothes spread out on the ground along the highway, and coming upon an occasional vehicle breakdown. I silently prayed, "Oh, Lord, please, not us."

The Lord had either not heard my prayer, or had chosen to ignore it. With two hundred fifty kilometers left to travel before we would arrive in Lilongwe, the car lurched, steam poured out from under the hood, and the motor died. Glen steered us onto the narrow shoulder and parked. The van had ruptured something. We both stepped out onto the highway and Glen looked under the hood. He discovered a fan belt in ribbons. The radiator was steaming and emptying its contents on the motor and on the road.

Villagers started gathering; fortunately many of them spoke English. They suggested that Glen head out hitchhiking to the Petrol Station ten or eleven kilometers back in the direction we had just come. (I recalled noticing it as we had passed.) He kept examining the damage, and other villagers and passers-by started gathering and offering their suggestions. Glen made a decision: I would stay and guard the van, protecting my footlocker and luggage, while he hitchhiked back to the Petrol Station. Agreed! Glen moved behind the Van, took a southbound position on the shoulder of the road and stuck up his thumb. In a short time he was given a ride. Meanwhile, I entered into a holy conversation. I began talking to a young man who had just graduated from Secondary School and was looking for a university. He needed to find one his parents could afford for him to attend. I told him about Livingstonia, and he expressed serious interest. I gave him the name of the Registrar at the Malawi offices address. He said he would follow through. (When I checked later with Vice-Chancellor Kirk, the registrar had not heard from the boy. I unfortunately had not written down his name. Too much stress, I guess.) Other sightseers who had gathered wanted to practice speaking English with an American. They had chosen the right person. Of course, they also wanted some American money. They had chosen the wrong person.

After a while, Glen returned with a belt. It didn't fit. He would have to hitchhike back to the Service Station. He took off. In a short time he was in a car heading south. In the meantime I phoned the Airline Office in Lilongwe. Fortunately Elizabeth answered. She said that my tickets could be claimed at the Airport, but if I had time in the morning, I should stop by her office at the National Hotel and pay for them. I told her where we were staying. She knew the location. I was to phone her or be at her office at 8:00 a.m. I told her I hoped to see her then. I re-engaged in my conversation with the considerable group that had gathered. They had all sorts of curious questions about the van and about its occupants... and about America, particularly potential benefactors.

Within an hour after Glen had left, a car came slowly toward the Van; it pulled up behind us. It was encouraging to see Glen emerge from the vehicle with another man, who, I presumed, was a mechanic. I was right. He had a different fan belt. The mechanic tried to insert it, but it wouldn't fit. He had others at his Service Station that he knew would work. Lunch hour was long past. Another momentous decision had to be made: how to put the SAA tickets in Vernon's hands? We talked over our dilemma. The only option we could think of at the moment was: Glen would stay with the van, the mechanic would get another belt and return, and Vernon would pick up his backpack and his cell phone, stand by the side of Route 1 heading north and stick out his thumb. The plan sounded workable. I repeated to myself, "Gotta get out of Africa—even if I have to hitchhike." And I did—both!

Glen stationed himself at the back of the Van while the mechanic headed back to the garage. I located myself at the edge of the highway a few yards in front of our vehicle, and put up my thumb. I had not only re-entered the anxious posture of hitchhiking, I had also re-entered the holy posture of prayer. I had an anxious query: what if darkness comes, and I am still standing here, and we still haven't found a belt that fits our radiator? What if I hitch a ride with kidnappers? What if someone sticks a gun to Glen's chest and demands he open the door of the Van and hand over the contents? A few cars passed, ignoring me. I returned to thinking anxiously rather than praying trustfully. It should surely not take too long either to find or fix a fan belt, or to obtain a ride to Lilongwe. Then

I recalled Henry Kirk's words, "Vern, remember that you are in the third world."

Highway traffic was encouraging. I felt reinforced by a comforting idea: Glen and I could keep in contact via our cell phones—as long as our batteries held out. As soon as the car was repaired, he would be back on the highway and travel fast. He had assured me that as soon as he caught up with the bus, he would flag it down and claim me; and I could then travel into Lilongwe in the Van with him. The plan sounded complicated, but workable. I decided that I had better phone Elizabeth at the Hotel. I had her number in my pocket. I dialed and, in spite of it being lunch hour, she answered. I told her the latest news about our dilemma. She gave me peace with her assurance that the tickets would be OK, but I should stop at her office at the National Hotel. If I did not arrive in Lilongwe before the SAA office closed, I would have to stop in the morning before I left for the airport. I told her that I would try to phone her later, and if not, I would see her in the morning. She sounded OK with that arrangement.

One of the persons who had gathered to observe and offer advice on our situation mentioned that a bus for Lilongwe traveled Highway 1 North—almost daily—sometime after lunch. It was usually crowded, however. Perhaps I could flag it and if it had room, I would arrive in Lilongwe before dark. "Not before 4:00 o'clock?" I asked. The young lad with whom I had talked about the University had a cool answer, "No way!" Depression was building up, but I refused to give in to it. I moved farther away from the group again, stepped out onto the highway, and stuck up my thumb. Glen guarded the Van while the mechanic drove away; he was convinced that the vehicle was operable, at least for the time being, if it could just be fitted with a belt. He was hopeful. I was concentrating on the bus.

Finally I saw a large vehicle coming from the south. The young university prospect ran to me and told me to wave my hands; one thumb would not work. I followed his advice, and I almost cried when a bus slowed down and pulled off the highway. I read the signs over the windshield and at the rear window. They read, "Lilongwe." As I hurried toward it, I lost some hope; the vehicle looked packed, including an overloaded rooftop. An official looking man stepped off and motioned me toward him. Passengers were standing on the inside exit steps and in the aisle. He grabbed my backpack and pulled me in. The bus pulled out. I breathed exultingly: I was on board! I kept moving sideways and forward until I had stable footing. As far as I could see I was the only Caucasian passenger. Possibly because of that distinction, other passengers kept pushing me up the aisle. The Porter yelled out in clear English, "I'll protect your bag." I wondered when he would come for my money. I wanted to reply, "You had better take good care of my bag; my camera and many other valuables are in it." My passport and billfold were in my pockets. (The Porter came by later in the trip to collect the fare.) Glancing around the vehicle, I observed that seats on either side of the aisles were double, but they were not wide; still they offered room for two persons. I also observed the variety of cargo: sacks of produce in the overhead bins, and items resting on passengers' laps, under their seats, even in the aisle; chickens, a lap dog, a sleeping cat, many small children, a sucking baby or two, garden produce, and one white man.

I was stuck in the crowd near a young man sitting with an older one. We had not gone ten minutes on the road before the young fellow stood up and insisted that I take his seat. He must have been a good Christian, or a good Muslim. My hip hurt, so I graciously accepted his offer. I would later find a couple of dollars to tip him. The older man was more sleepy than friendly. The younger one tapped my shoulder, and pointing to the sleepy passenger, said, "My Grandpa." I attempted further conversation. I asked, "How long until the terminal?" He seemed to have understood. He answered, "Three hours." I would not have my U.S.A. plane tickets in my hand this day. But I knew where they would be. Elisabeth knew my situation, so I would not need to call her. I wondered how soon I would hear from Glen.

The bus stopped occasionally, and hands went out the windows to purchase apples and tomatoes and buttered bread and chicken wings and African root beer from the roadside vendors. I decided not to bulge my bladder, though I was hungry and bored. If only I had my backpack! I had reading material in it. But I knew that it would require a formidable chore to retrieve it. I hoped it was still on board. I slept a few snores!

After almost three hours had passed, we began to see clusters of houses, and soon we were in a town or city. Passengers started shuffling around. Glen would have to find me in Lilongwe. Where was he? We pulled into an empty lot with one or two trees, and the ubiquitous red clay. I concluded the Bus Stop in Lilongwe was far from pretentious. My seatmate was coming awake. I sighed, "Ah. Lilongwe at last." I began preparation for leaving the bus and finding a taxi to the National Hotel. The young man leaned down, shook his grandpa by the shoulders and said, "Grandpa and I leave here." The elderly man revived. I asked, "Are we in Lilongwe?" He replied, "No. Not for three more hours." I sank back in my seat. We had obviously not communicated clearly about locations three hours earlier.

Food was being shoved in and out the windows of the bus. At least half the passengers left us. A few boarded, with cabbages, cuddling their chickens, and placing their luggage, some in the pile at the back of the bus. Before the vehicle had filled, I sneaked back and found my bag and retrieved the last "Smithsonian" that I had received, and some cookies. The Porter scaled the ladder to the roof of the bus and began to pass down several boxes and suitcases to the driver, and they exchanged pieces to replace on top. I took another quick look to the rear, and spotted my backpack.

By the time I was about to buy an apple, a pastry, and a bottled drink, the bus driver took his seat and sounded the horn. Several continuing passengers had relocated, and new passengers found places to sit—no one standing, yet; the bus motor started, and we pulled out of the lot back onto Highway 1. The lady opposite me sensed my disappointment, and offered me her bag of chips. I took it, dug into it, thanked her, and offered an American quarter. She smiled. My phone rang. Glen was calling to say that the situation looked hopeful. The Van was repaired, and he hoped to be on the road within half an hour. I turned to two or three persons to find out where we presently were, but received little satisfaction. I finally told Glen that someone had said, "Three hours South of Lilongwe." As my connection was weakening, I said to Glen, "I will see you when I see you. Don't leave Highway 1." He assured me he wouldn't, and added that he hoped to see me before three hours had passed. I assured him that I was OK. He comforted me with the news that he was, also.

Fortunately I had taken a seat by a window and nobody came to sit beside me. They were probably afraid of the white man. I imagined how Rosa Parks must have felt on that Montgomery, Alabama, bus. I moved from one hip to the other, read some, and I finally found enough comfort to fall asleep. I awoke, and the sky was turning dark. I wondered if I had missed a call from Glen. I had. I phoned him, and he related a disturbing tale. He had finally succeeded in getting the correct size fan belt, and he was moving along north. He decided that if I were safe and sound he would stay on Route 1. I should proceed on the bus to Lilongwe, as he would proceed there in the Van. He would be at the bus depot when I arrived, and we would head for the Baptist Mission. The plan sounded pragmatic. At this point, however, I placed more trust in the Bus than in the Van.

Finally, finally, we pulled into a clay courtyard. Surely we had arrived at the end of the line. I picked up my backpack, stepped out, and looked for Glen. My phone rang and it was Glen with another pathetic story: the Van had broken down once again. He phoned the Presbyterian missionary in Lilongwe, and Ken was coming out for him. I should take a taxi to the Mission. We both agreed to the suggestion. But what would happen to my luggage? Ken and he would bring it with them. At this point there were no alternatives. We said good-bye.

As I was surveying the scene for a taxi, two or three young men approached me; they had apparently noticed my limp. They wanted to help me with my luggage. They of course would expect a tip. But I was hurting. "It's on my back," I said. With utterly foolish trust, I eased the burden off and let one of them take it. They led me to a taxi, and I thanked them. I gave a tip of one U.S. dollar to the young man who had carried my bag. I told the driver where I wanted to go. I perceived that he had understood; he indicated that he knew the location.

He turned on the ignition key to start the vehicle. He was encountering trouble. He finally had the motor going. What a sound! If the clunker trade-in economic recovery program incentives that were initiated at the beginning of the U.S. American financial crisis had been effective at this time in Malawi, the driver would have had no difficulty qualifying his taxi. The fatal sound continued throughout the trip. We went through Lilongwe City Centre, past the National Hotel. I commented about having to be there early in the morning. The driver wanted to know if I wanted him to call for me. I told him it was not necessary, as I was meeting a friend who was driving a Van with my luggage in it. They could have arrived at the Baptist Mission by the time we arrived. He was interested. I was becoming increasingly concerned about Glen, but I believed that he was in good hands.

We pulled into a courtyard. A large church came into view, its interior light showing through beautiful stained glass windows. Other buildings stood on the lot. I relaxed when I saw the name "Baptist" on a sign. I was hoping that I was near a bed for the night. Just then the phone rang; it was Glen. He was fine and traveling with Missionary Ken in his van. They were in Lilongwe. I was thankful that I had phoned Elisabeth at SAA. "I hope you have my luggage," I said to Glen. He assured me that he did, and that all was well. They would come to the Mission.

I rejoined the taxi driver, and we went into the lighted building. A choir was rehearsing. We interrupted. I told the group about our search and enquired about the Guest House. One of them spoke up and informed us that we were at the wrong place: we needed the Baptist Mission, but we were at the Baptist Church. He proceeded to explain the location to the taxi driver. He seemed to understand. We thanked the man, I apologized for interrupting the choir rehearsal, and the driver and I returned to his clunker. I hoped it would start. It did. But it sounded as if it would not make it to the Mission, especially when we had to return almost to the point from which we had started, back through the city, past the National Hotel, and into the residential section. The motor made such a rattle that I was certain I would have to switch taxis. I prayed some more. God had not turned off his phone for the night! A miracle occurred: we arrived at the Mission, and the front gate opened. The managers had heard us coming—one advantage of a car about to blow a gasket—and they were happy to see us. Glen had not yet arrived. I asked them if he had called, and they reported, "Some time ago. He had had a breakdown." "Yes," I responded, "two of them." I hoped that Ken's car had proved more reliable the last few kilometers than the Van. Where were they now? I paid the driver, but complained about the cost, which was his fault. He reduced the fare slightly, and I gave him a small tip. He had unloaded my luggage and taken it into my room.

I was relieved when the taxi started, even though its rattle alarmed me. I breathed easier when the driver succeeded in moving it out of the Mission parking lot. The Mission Managers showed me around our unit. It looked clean and smelled fresh. It offered a fresh contrast to the odors that I had had to tolerate the last nine hours. My cell phone rang. It was Glen. He was about to arrive at the Mission with Missionary Ken, and my luggage.

They came shortly. Glen and I had a reunion hug, and Ken and I enjoyed a time of getting acquainted. Another car pulled up to our unit. What a surprise! The visitors were one of my Livingstonia students and his brother. I had recalled that Patience's Father was an employee of the Malawi government—in the Department of Agriculture—and that the family lived in Lilongwe. Patience invited me to come to their house and meet his parents. I made a decision I have since regretted: I was too exhausted to go anywhere, and my hip was in pain. Patience understood. I hugged him and said goodnight. He is a young man, appropriately named, I thought, as they drove off.

Before Ken left, he reviewed the plans he and Glen had made for morning. He would keep my luggage in his van, come by and take us to the National Hotel for breakfast, and I could pay for my SAA tickets after their office opened at 8:00 a.m. I told him that the tickets were to be at the Airport, but I was supposed to stop by the SAA office at the Hotel and pay for them. Glen and Ken would work out a Van repair plan. Glen wanted me to join him for pizza at a nearby place operated by a woman we had met at our hotel stop near the Bandawe mission. I was hungry, but I was more in pain than in danger of famishing. Knowing that I could not walk any farther that night, I declined Glen's offer and said "Good Night." The two men left. I went to bed. I fell asleep shortly, but not before going over in my mind the events of the past few hours. I kept hearing, "Gotta' get out of Africa—even if I gotta' hitchhike. Gotta get out...gotta...."

I did not hear Glen come in, but he was in bed when I awoke in the morning. Ken arrived at the Mission at the agreed upon time and took us to the Hotel. We placed my luggage in charge of the Taxi vendor for the hour before I would leave for the Airport. Following a refreshing breakfast I found the SAA offices and took out my Visa card and reluctantly turned over $2,600. I had to get out of Africa, even if I had to hitchhike. I had done the latter, and was about to accomplish the former. Glen would stay in the area with the missionaries until the Van was repaired.

I collected my luggage and boarded the shuttle for the airport. All went well at the ticket counter, and after the flight to Johannesburg and a last-minute purchase or two, I boarded the plane for Atlanta. I spent the long hours in flight reading, "riting," reporting, reflecting, and resting. Self-pity, mild depression, extreme anticipation, controlled joy, explosive gratitude, and many other disparate emotions were shaking and confusing me, some of them beginning to dissipate, others to exaggerate. The plane landed in Atlanta, and I finally stepped back onto the concrete of my native land. As I had anticipated, culture shock momentarily overwhelmed me. I surveyed the contrast between the poverty and simplicity of Livingstonia and the speed and glitter of Atlanta. I let the emotions rumble. I knew they would stabilize. However, I determined that I would never forget my students or the needs of Africa.

Son Mark and I had arranged via email that he would call me when he and Marjorie were on their way from Birmingham. I deserted my baggage near the Delta Carousel No. 5 while I drank a cup of coffee and devoured a pastry. I had a couple of hours to wait for the family, but that presented no problem. I had a journal to update. I found comfortable seating at the carousel. By this time, I had transferred my luggage to a trolley. I was thankful that everything had gone well through customs. The Airport was busy. It was Sunday morning, when all good Southerners should have been at church, I was repeating to myself, and then I reflected that though not a Southerner, I would have been at Church in Livingstonia; well, no,

I would have been going to bed about this time if I were there. My Lord's Day church experience would have been long over. Well, next Sunday I would be operating according to a Pacific Northwest schedule.

Time by the carousel went fast as I wrote and watched the traffic lanes where cars meeting arriving passengers made pick-ups. Mark phoned about 9:30. He said that they were less than half an hour away. He phoned again at 10:00 and said that they were near the Delta Arrival gates. I kept looking for his gray van. Two limousines pulled to the center island. A lovely blonde Alabama matriarch stepped out of the one and stretched. A young black couple that looked like newlyweds exited the other. Was I back in Africa? I had got out of there, even if I had had to hitchhike. A great accomplishment!

I surveyed the sidewalks and pedestrians and the activity in the traffic lanes. I turned back toward my luggage, and I heard a child yell, "Grandpa!" I looked, and Mark, and Olivia (8) and Curry (4), were approaching. What a beautiful sight! But where was Marjorie? I was disappointed that she had not accompanied them. I had thought she was coming along to the airport. It was probably too much of a walk from the Parking Garage.

Mark and Curry piloted my luggage cart. Curry broke the news that Grandma Marjorie was waiting for us. We moved toward the glass luggage-claim doors. They swung open and we headed out. I presumed we were headed for the Garage. We crossed one busy traffic lane, and the median, and headed toward the two limousines. I looked twice: the beautiful blonde woman who I had conjectured was an Alabama dowager was the Kansas farm girl whom I had married fifty-two years ago. The limousine was for us. Mark had decided that after the deprivations I had encountered the past five months, I deserved to be greeted in style. Besides, the limo had plenty of space for my luggage. Marjorie and I had our reunion while Mark and the children loaded my possessions, and we settled in for a luxury ride to Mountain Brook, Alabama. We arrived at Mark's house shortly after noon, had a mini-family reunion; and in a few days Marjorie and I would go home to Washington State. No hitchhiking!

I would return home from Africa, after having joyfully deposited a significant share of my heart and mind and spirit and body on "the dark Continent." I had also deposited large shares of patience, humility, knowledge, and faith. At the end, I had got out of Africa in time, at an extra charge of $2,600—even though for a few hours I had had to hitchhike.

*　*2009 MISSION YEARBOOK FOR PRAYER AND STUDY,* pp. 44-5.

Post-Text

Afterword

Upon typing in or writing down the last word of the last sentence on the last page of a book, an author must share the ambivalent feelings I am experiencing: relief and regret. I am relieved that after two carpal tunnel surgeries, a mastoidectomy, upgraded hearing aids, aggravated spinal stenosis, irritated arthritic fingers, and chronic vertigo I have written the last page of *HOLY HITCHHIKING FOREIGN HIGHWAYS;* and I have a Publisher. I regret the end of a major intellectual stimulation to my brain, the conclusion of the constant recollection and recording of hitchhiking experiences on domestic but principally foreign highways, and the reliving of roadside and roadway adventures from when I was thirteen years of age, until I turned seventy-nine, three years ago. Relief of a gnawing guilt has now ended, guilt over not responding earlier to family requests and my own desires to record my hitchhiking experiences.

With critical help from my wife—and the late Mary Savella, my first critical reader, who died tragically in the snow in December, 2008—I have tendered a manuscript to a Publisher. I look forward to sharing the published work with family and friends, and acquaintances, many of who have said, "I sure want to read your book." My curt response has been, "Buy the Book." Some have even "gilded the lily" with, "I have never personally known an author before." I assure them that I am still Vernon Elgin who has spent a lot of time at the computer and paid a lot of money to have his word published, but writing and publishing do not necessarily an author make. I must admit, however, that I spend some of my insomnia hours organizing and planning a fourth work, *ESSAYS ON SEVEN MORTAL WRENCHES.*

Maybe after a third book—a fourth, if you add in my Doctor of Philosophy Dissertation—I may come closer to qualifying as an Author. If not, I will have to write a fifth! And if I have to, I warn you, I will.

Breinigsville, PA USA
10 May 2010
237687BV00001B/4/P